SIX GRANADA PLAYS

SIX
GRANADA
PLAYS

FABER AND FABER
24 Russell Square
London

This collection first published in mcmlx
by Faber and Faber Limited
24 Russell Square, London WC1
Printed in Great Britain by
The Pitman Press, Bath

1960

B60 - 18177

CONTENTS

INTRODUCTION

These six television plays, which were all performed in Granada's New Playwrights Series, have been chosen to show something of the scope of television plays and to give an idea of the variety of subject, style and mood which television plays can offer.

These half dozen selected plays have an important factor in common—each one was specially written for television. And four of them are not only first television plays but also the "first-ever" plays by writers who had never attempted dramatic writing before. Here, then, are six new playwrights, writing in a new form, for a medium which has in a few years revolutionized our social life and leisure.

No form of entertainment consumes material at such a tremendously high rate, and television relies upon the writer to supply its basic needs—the ideas, the stories, the characters and the situations which give life and meaning to its daily output. Granada hopes that writers will become increasingly aware of how much television needs them and of the opportunities awaiting them.

For the writer with something to say, television holds out an attractive prospect. He—and she—can reach many millions of people with a single performance, and can write for these huge audiences with an uncompromising seriousness of purpose to a degree which can hardly ever be allowed him in working for the cinema or the theatre. Moreover, the television play is an attractive form in itself, a fascinating exercise in literary craftsmanship without too many tedious restrictions—easily adaptable to other uses.

Of the six plays in this collection five were written as sixty minute plays and one (*The Myth Makers*) to play for an hour and a half. In fact, allowing for breaks, the hour-long television play lasts just under fifty minutes and the one-and-a-half hour play just under eighty. The new television writers write mostly for the shorter length. The script for an hour-long play runs to about twelve thousand words, and is divided into three acts with a clearly marked break in time between each act. These specifications provide scope for a quick flowing and amenable narrative form and for a great variety of scene and story.

Television, for instance, is the ideal form for the "slice of life" observed realistically at close quarters. Television's use of close-up, and the intimacy of effect which can be obtained by projecting large

7

images within a small personal frame, are conditions which a play-wright can use with great subtlety, especially when he has acquired the instinct for realizing when words have done their work and the director's pictures should take over.

Clive Exton's *No Fixed Abode* is a good example of the subject—too still and concentrated for film treatment, too austere to be helped by the more obvious aids-to-illusion of living theatre—but which seems naturally made for television. The deeply felt and very simple situation—a study of four vagrants in a common lodging house—gives the director the barest of dramatic trappings. But a few characters in a single setting provided a rewarding test for the director's ingenuity, and an opportunity for the scrutiny of the cameras to show the stuff of poverty with such granular exactitude that one catches the physical feel of dirt, tiredness and old cheap clothing.

The fact that television can excel at the "close look", and can put the texture of life under a magnifying glass, does not mean that it can do little else. It can also do justice to the cast of twenty, the bustling crowd scene, and swift changes of scene, and still make its points with clarity and liveliness. *The Myth Makers*, William Bast's variation of a theme taken from a contemporary legend, shows how effectively the television play can set the pace for a fast-moving narrative, flowing swiftly from scene to scene.

A Bit of Happiness, Alexander Baron's low-keyed but compassionate exploration of the familiar theme of marital infidelity, derives its freshness from the kind of exact observation of which television can make such powerful use. It is a dramatic story perfectly suited to television's resources, which exploits the effectiveness of the medium with such economy that, far from seeming a first television play, it bears the signs of experienced mastery.

The Queen's Corporal, by Graeme Kent, is a neat example of the play of action, both fierce and confined, which comes off especially well on television. This is the story of a group of forgotten soldiers living in a state of demoralized inactivity in the aftermath of the Korean War.

The Bush and the Tree, by John O'Toole, is altogether more homely, a Lancashire small town comedy which sets a simple kitchen comedy drama against a background of local politics.

Peter Nichols's *Promenade* is a youthful experimental play with youth as its subject. This is a theme which finds a natural ally in television, for television is sympathetic to young ideas. In terms of play-writing Peter Nichols's play is fragmentary in shape and elusive in style. It manages, however, to evoke an instantly recognizable world of adolescent gaiety and disillusion, and contains several portraits which convey a sense of the vulnerability of the very young.

These six plays are not only representative examples of the work of Granada's new playwrights but are also proof that there is nothing mysterious about writing for television. What is required of the writer is simply that he should set out his stories clearly, use his changes of scene to good effect, and see that the dramatic curve of his story will carry him strongly through the three acts. In the scripts as printed detailed camera instructions are omitted. There is seldom need for writers to add notes for the cameras. Occasionally a very experienced television writer may offer suggestions to the director, but usually it is enough if writers give clear indications of changes of scene, exits and entrances, and such stage directions as are needed to clarify the plot.

The advantages which the television camera brings are the power of the close-up, the stereoscopic effect of shooting in depth (which can add such force to a dramatic situation) and the mobility of the camera eye, which can carry a story with speed and smoothness from moment to moment and from place to place. In fact the television writer can enjoy something of the best of both worlds: something of the cinema's intimacy, pace and movement, and something of the theatre's love of rhetoric and the grand manner.

There are of course some things which television plays cannot do well—for example, the leisurely evocation of atmosphere which requires a lingering form of pictorial exploration. A story, for instance, which seeks to convey the magical effects of a holiday in the Normandy countryside is something which a film can do better.

Television is also the wrong medium for the projection of fantasy and artifice. Whimsical plays dealing with such unlikely ideas as people transforming themselves into plants and animals, or young girls communing with ghosts, are likely to go better in the theatre. So does the sort of play where characters step forward to the edge of the stage and address the audience in familiar terms. Television is too realistic a form for this.

Apart from such generalizations as these, a television playwright need not be greatly burdened with a weight of technical requirements. Obviously there are certain limiting physical factors, of which newcomers to television should be aware. But essentially the rules are simple.

Unlike films, which are shot piece-meal in any order that happens to be convenient, television plays are shot during a single continuous studio performance in exactly the sequence in which they are written. A television play should not, therefore, demand elaborate costume and make-up changes which require, say, a leading man to transform himself in a matter of seconds from an unshaven castaway on a desert island to a bemedalled and immaculate figure dancing beneath the chandeliers of a London ballroom. Similarly, characters should not be continuously switched from one very short scene to yet another and another.

It is possible to have parts of a television play filmed and inserted into the studio production, but as a general rule writers should be wary of the use of film. Unless it is used extremely judiciously, a film tends to spoil rather than enhance the effect of a studio production.

Granada is always ready to help any writers who may need advice and especially those who want to ensure that they are writing within the bounds of possible production. But in the end the best way to illustrate the "do's" and "don'ts" of television playwriting is by example. Granada hopes that these six plays will both provide enjoyable reading and serve as practical models.

THE BUSH AND THE TREE

by

`JOHN O'TOOLE

CAST

CLERK TO THE COUNCIL	*John Cazabon*
MOLLY SQUIRES	*Doreen Keogh*
SANDRA SQUIRES	*Lesley Dudley*
1ST MAN	*William Croasdale*
2ND MAN	*Alick Hayes*
ALF LIDDELL	*Milo O'Shea*
TOM CARDWICK	*Peter Collingwood*
CLARICE LIDDELL	*Gabrielle Daye*
COUNCILLOR JEPHSON	*Claude Jones*
COUNCILLOR BELL	*Arthur Seaton*
COUNCILLOR WINSDEAN	*William Wymar*
MR. O'RIORDAN	*Fred Godfrey*
MR. BROWNLOW	*Geoffrey Sutcliffe*
CHAIRMAN	*Arthur Brough*
COUNCILLOR JONES	*Victor Tandy*
COUNCILLOR ANDWELL	*Frank Crawshaw*

DIRECTOR	*James Ormerod*
DESIGNER	*Darrell Lass*

11

DIRECTOR'S NOTE

I have always enjoyed plays which have obviously sprung from the author's experience. This charming play by John O'Toole belongs much in that class.

The background of the play is small-town local politics, and no-one can doubt that it is well observed. In fact it was in the little Yorkshire town, Earby-via-Colne, that the author himself sat as a councillor in the local council chamber.

Apart from the bustle of local public life, the play is concerned with that difficult time in a marriage when the elastic begins to go— when something must happen if mutual attraction is not to give place to boredom, indifference and tired acceptance. The success of this play was due, I think, to the author's unusual ability in making the small change of ordinary life assume a proper and very touching importance.

JAMES ORMEROD.

BIOGRAPHY OF JOHN O'TOOLE

John O'Toole was born in 1920 in Western Ireland and educated at a monastery school by Franciscan monks. He came to England at the age of 16 and was apprenticed to an engineering firm. Since 1945 he has lived in Yorkshire where he has been eight years on the Earby Council and was the youngest Chairman in the town's history. He is married and has an 18-year-old son. He is a prolific spare-time writer and contributes regularly to newspapers and literary magazines, and has had short stories broadcast by the B.B.C., New Zealand Radio and Radio Eire.

ACTION

The action of the play takes place in the following sets:

(1) Outside the schoolhouse
(2) Alf Liddell's kitchen
(3) The hall
(4) Front room
(5) Garden with duck house
(6) Caravan
(7) The Council Chamber
(8) Molly's living room
(9) Councillor Jephson's house.

TIME

The time is the present.

Act One

The scene is outside the local schoolhouse which is being used as the polling booth for the Council Election.

The Clerk to the Council comes out of the schoolhouse door.

CLERK [to *Constable*]. That's the lot. It only remains to count 'em.

> *He goes back inside and the Constable locks the door.*

> *A group have gathered. Molly and Sandra join them. Molly is a warm attractive woman of about 33. Sandra is her daughter, aged 12.*

MOLLY. Excuse me, sir.

> *Molly tries again.*

Excuse me, sir, but when will the results be known?

1ST MAN. Any time now.

MOLLY. Thank you, sir.

MAN. Who's the . . . er . . . ?

2ND MAN. It's—*Her!*

MAN. Oh! Her at . . . er . . . ?

2ND MAN. Aye.

MAN. Oh!

> *The Clerk comes out, followed by the Councillors.*

CLERK [*reading, very quickly*] I, the Undersigned, being the Return ing Officer at the Poll for the election of Urban District Councillor for the North Wards of the Urban District of Pulby, held on the 4th day of April, 1959, do hereby give notice that the number of votes recorded for each candidate at the election is as follows: Andrew Adams—four-one-eight; Alfred Liddell—five-eight-two, and I do hereby declare that the said Alfred Liddell is duly elected Urban District Councillor for the same Ward.

CHEERING [*cries for Alf*] Good old Alf—Speech, Alf—Come on, Alf—Speech, Speech!

> *The Clerk gives way to Alf Liddell, an ordinary looking man of 45. At the moment he is very shy and flustered. He waits for silence and then proceeds to read from a piece of paper.*

ALF. Thank you all very much for voting me in. I'll do the best I can for everyone. I'll always champion the cause of the individual.

Cheering and shouts of "Good old Alf!"

ALF. If I can help anyone I'll be glad to do it.

The crowd claps and cheers and we see Molly standing at the back. Several of the crowd come up to shake hands with Alf. One of them is a large pleasant-looking man, Tom Cardwick, Alf's brother-in-law.

TOM. Good lad, Alf! I said at four o'clock you were in! [*nudging Alf*] Can't beat having your own brother-in-law Party Secretary, huh?

ALF. Thanks, Tom.

TOM. And our Clarice will be pleased. Perhaps she'll pick up a bit now you're on the council.

ALF. [*sadly*] Aye.

At this point Molly and Sandra come up to them.

MOLLY. Mr. Liddell?

ALF. Eh? Aye, that's me.

MOLLY. Can I speak with you?

TOM [*interrupting*] He's busy at the moment. Come on, Alf.

ALF [*to Molly*] What is it?

MOLLY [*hesitates*] It's . . . nothing. Thank you.

She turns and goes with Sandra.

ALF. What did she want?

TOM. Never mind about her. Would you like me to pick you up on Thursday?

ALF. Thursday? What's Thursday?

TOM. Meeting of the Council. Your first one.

ALF. Oh, aye. Thanks very much.

TOM. I'll come around about six.

ALF. Right. Our Clarice'll give you a cup of tea.

Tom goes. Alf stands looking off in the direction taken by Molly. We mix to the Liddells' kitchen the following Thursday. Clarice Liddell is brewing the tea in a bored, disgruntled, sloppy way. She hears a knock and goes to the front door. It is Tom.

CLARICE. It's you!

Tom comes inside.

TOM. You get fatter, our Clarice.

CLARICE. Thanks very much.

TOM. Brotherly love!

CLARICE. I know.

She leads the way back to the kitchen followed by Tom.

TOM. I thought with it being Thursday, I'd cheer him up before the Meeting, like. I was nervous myself at my first Council Meeting.

CLARICE. Aye, so was our Maggie on her wedding night! Shame to throw this away—it's half full—would you like a cup?

TOM. Aye, but make us a fresh cup. Where's Alf?

CLARICE [*pointing through the kitchen window to the caravan*] In the caravan, as usual.

TOM. What—this evening?

CLARICE. Aye. Wood ornaments and ducks. Get out from under me feet!

TOM [*indicating empty vase*] No flowers? I thought you always had flowers.

CLARICE. I've given up. Waste of money.

TOM. You used to like flowers, our Clarice.

CLARICE. Well I've given up liking them.

TOM. It'll be a change for our Alf to get round a bit.

CLARICE. Huh! You'll not change Alf, I'll be bound.

TOM [*thinking*] You two used to be so happy.

CLARICE. There didn't used to be wood ornaments and ducks!

TOM. Well, what's wrong with keeping a few ducks?

CLARICE. Nothing. Ducks are wonderful. They all have Christian names. He comes home from the foundry. He has his tea. I don't see him again till bedtime. It's the ducks.

TOM [*taking his tea*] Ta—well, a man needs a hobby.

CLARICE. Then it's the caravan. Wood ornaments! There's no *go* in him. Just walks around with a moon face!

TOM. He can't help his moon face. He had a moon face when you wed him. He always did have a moon face!

CLARICE. He still has it!

TOM. One time you two used to be a bit on the romantic side.

CLARICE. Don't talk so soft!

TOM. I'll tell you something, our Clarice—Alf's a *little* man; you're big.

CLARICE. Well, I. . . .

TOM. Ah, but that's it. I'll put it in a nutshell, Clarice. You married a bush, but you're not satisfied. You want a tree!

CLARICE. If only he'd do something daft now and again—like other men. Let himself go for once!

TOM. I'll slip out and have a word with him.

CLARICE. Tell him there's a cup of tea.

TOM. Aye—right'o.

Tom goes out by the back door. Clarice takes Alf's mug off the shelf.

17

In the caravan Alf is working at his lathe making a wooden candlestick. He goes on working throughout the scene.

TOM. Now then, Alf.

ALF. Hello, Tom.

TOM. There's only an hour to Meeting, you know.

ALF. Oh! Well, I'll not be long. This is my new lathe.

TOM. Very nice—there's a cup of tea for you in the kitchen.

ALF. Oh, right.

[*Concentrates on tool point*] That's it, I think.

TOM. How do you feel?

ALF. Frightened. Never been to an important Meeting before.

TOM. Nothing in it, lad. Sit still and say nowt.

ALF. Oh, I won't say anything. I've nothing to say.

TOM. That's the drill. Watch how our side votes and just put up your hand. We'll do the gabbing!

TOM. It's a quarter-past!

ALF. Aye. I suppose I'd better shape. Are you coming.

TOM. No, *I'll* go right through. I got to see a chap before the Meeting.

ALF. I'll just look in on the ducks.

TOM. See you later.

ALF. Aye.

Tom goes. Alf looks admiringly at his candlestick. Places it on the bench and goes into the yard. He pauses for a few moments to watch the ducks.

CLARICE [*through the kitchen window*] Alf! It's gone a quarter past.

ALF. I'm coming.

As Alf enters kitchen.

CLARICE. You'd better if you want your tea.

ALF. Black drake's looking sad.

[*Clarice drops mug. It breaks*] Clarice!

CLARICE. I didn't do it on purpose. I don't know what you bought that mug for, anyway.

ALF. I—I like a mug—makes the tea taste better. I always did want a mug. We can get another.

CLARICE. Now don't let's have any bother. Get a move on or you'll be late. [*Drinking tea*] Here's your pink shirt.

ALF. The—pink one?

CLARICE. What's wrong with the pink one?

ALF. It's tight at the neck.

CLARICE. It's size fifteen the same as all your other shirts.

ALF. It always seems tight to me.

There is a knock at the front door.

CLARICE [*crossing to door*] Now who?

ALF. I'm not expecting anyone.

CLARICE. You'd better change your shirt.

Alf starts taking off his shirt. Clarice goes to the hall.

Clarice opens front door to Molly.

MOLLY. Oh. Good evening. Is Mr. Liddell in?

CLARICE. I expect so. What do you want?

MOLLY. I wanted to speak to him. It's . . . it's rather important.

CLARICE. All right. Wait here and I'll see.

She turns back towards kitchen.

Alf is putting on a clean shirt as Clarice enters.

CLARICE. There's someone to see you.

ALF. Who?

CLARICE. *I* don't know *who* she is.

ALF. A woman? Where is she?

CLARICE. At the front door. Where else should she be?

ALF. Ask her to wait in the front room.

CLARICE. In my front room—she can wait in the hall.

ALF. *Put* her in the front room, Clarice.

Clarice goes. Alf is struggling with his collar stud.

Clarice shows Molly into the front room.

CLARICE. He says wait in here.

MOLLY. Thank you.

CLARICE. I dare say he won't be long.

MOLLY. Thank you.

In the kitchen. Alf is in front of the mirror addressing himself archly.

ALF. Yes, madam, I think I can spare you a moment.

Clarice enters.

CLARICE. She's there.

ALF. Aye. [*Putting on jacket*]

He goes and shuts the door after him. Clarice goes to the door and opens it again so she can have a chance of hearing the conversation.

Molly is standing as Alf enters.

ALF. Don't stand, lass. Sit down.

MOLLY. Thank you. I'm Molly Squires.

ALF. Who?

MOLLY. Molly Squires. They call me *Her*.

ALF. I thought it was. You're the Squatter.

MOLLY. Yes.

ALF. And now the Council are putting you out of your place.

MOLLY. I'm desperate, Mr. Liddell. Why have the Council condemned it, Mr. Liddell?

ALF. Well, I'll tell you the truth. *I* don't know. I've only just got on. It's my first Meeting tonight.

MOLLY. I'd better explain. Six months ago Ronnie—he was the—the man . . . he got a job with the Council. He was a lorry driver. They let him stay at Cragg House. I got to know and I came here. I knew him a long time ago. He's Sandra's father.

ALF. Sandra—your little girl?

MOLLY. She's 12. I didn't know where Ronnie was for years. It was only by accident I found out. I thought it was going to be—all right.

ALF. Aye, there's been talk. He's gone?

MOLLY. Yes—Australia.

ALF. He wouldn't marry you? I know. You can't shut out all the talk.

MOLLY. He was married already.

ALF. And you didn't know.

MOLLY. I did. I loved him.

ALF. Aye. I see.

MOLLY. And then—they condemned it. But, Mr. Liddell—I know. It's not the house they're condemning—it's me!

ALF. Yes, but it wouldn't be hard for someone like you to get somewhere. You're a—a—well got-up young woman.

MOLLY. I have a job at the laundry. But it isn't that. I can't *keep* running—not any more. I made one mistake and now I'm—*Her*—well, I've made up my mind. I'm going to *stay*.

ALF. You've pluck—I'll say that.

MOLLY. I'm not going to run any more.

ALF. Well—what can I do?

MOLLY. I saw the other Councillors, but everyone was against me until now.

ALF. Until—now?

MOLLY. Yes.

ALF. How do you mean?

MOLLY. Please, Mr. Liddell, don't let them put me out. Stop them.

ALF [*stricken*] *Stop* them? *Me* stop them? Me stop *them*?

MOLLY. I liked that bit in your speech. The bit about "championing the cause of the individual".

ALF. Oh—that. I didn't write that, you know.

MOLLY. Oh!

ALF. The Party Secretary wrote it and they all voted on it down at the Rooms. . . . Do you know something?

MOLLY. What?

ALF. I like talking to you!

MOLLY. Thank you.

ALF. Do you ever have flowers in the house?

MOLLY. Oh, yes, I love flowers.

ALF. Aye. Makes you think of things that's alive and—*growing*!

MOLLY. Do you think it's *right* for them to put me out?

ALF [*with conviction*] No, I don't. You're as good as they are and maybe better than some of them. [*He rises*]

MOLLY [*rising*] Thank you—oh, thank you. You've given me hope.

ALF [*sighing*] Aye, hope!

MOLLY [*extending hand*] Thank you.

ALF [*shaking hands*] You're welcome, lass.

> *He steers her into the hallway and opens the front door.*

MOLLY. Goodnight and thank you.

ALF. Goodnight.

> *Molly goes. Alf closes the door and returns to the kitchen.*

CLARICE. What did *she* want?

ALF. Well, it was sort of private.

CLARICE. Oh, we're on the Council, are we?

ALF. Well, we're not *both* on. There's been too much talk already—it was Molly Squires.

CLARICE. *Her*?

ALF. Why *do* people have to call 'er *Her*?

CLARICE. Why, she's—she's immoral!

ALF. She's as good as you and me.

CLARICE. Don't start comparing *me* with *Her*.

ALF. If I hadn't wed you, you'd be immoral!

CLARICE. Alf Liddell! Of all the. . . . [*Pause*] What did she want?

ALF. She wants me to stop the Council putting her out.

CLARICE. Stop them! She wants you to stop them?

ALF. Aye. I don't know how I'm going to do it—I don't know, honest. I'll have to try, I suppose, some road.

CLARICE. You don't say you're going to walk into that Council Chamber and tell them all to change their minds?

ALF. What else can I do? Eee, I'm late! Look at the time! [*Makes for door*]

CLARICE. What about ducks?

21

ALF. Ducks—I haven't time to bother with ducks!

Alf runs out of the kitchen.

Mix to the Council Chamber.

CLERK. There's just one other item in correspondence, sir. This is from Mr. Pilton again.

BELL. Eee, that's the sixth letter.

WINSDEAN. No, it's the seventh.

CLERK. It would appear, sir, the lights at the Zebra Crossing continue to annoy him.

CHAIRMAN. Well, he certainly does try! [*Jephson rises*] Yes, Councillor Jephson?

JEPHSON. Mr. Chairman—and—ah—gentlemen. I think it now proper to have Mr. Pilton's letter read.

CLERK. Dear Sir. . . .

Alf enters. All stand.

CHAIRMAN. Welcome, Councillor Liddell.

ALF. Thank you, Mr. Chairman. I'm late. I'm sorry.

CHAIRMAN. That's all right. We've only reached the correspondence.

ALF. Thank you.

He shakes hands with Tom and his party, then sits down.

CHAIRMAN. I'm sure, Gentlemen, you'll all join me in welcoming Councillor Liddell.

ALL. Hear, hear!

CHAIRMAN. May I say, in all sincerity, I hope you'll be happy with us. [*Silence*] As I say, I hope you'll be very happy with us.

ALL. Hear, hear!

ALF. Oh, oh, thank you one and all.

But Alf remains standing.

CHAIRMAN. Now then, where were we? I—did you wish to say something, Councillor Liddell?

WINSDEAN and ANDWELL. Ssh—sit down.

TOM. Keep your mouth shut. [*Pulls him down*]

ALF. I—er—no.

CHAIRMAN. If you have something to say—out with it. We don't stand too much on ceremony.

ALF. I—I don't think it's right to put Molly Squires out. She has nowhere to go.

TOM. Ssh—keep your mouth shut.

ANDWELL. You can't bring that up now.

WINSDEAN. I was going to say. . . .

JEPHSON. Mr. Chairman and—ah—gentlemen. Unless I am gravely

in error the correct item to discuss now is the last item in correspondence—a letter from a *ratepayer*. From Mr. Pilton.

ALF. Then I'm sorry I spoke out of turn. I'll bring it up later.

JEPHSON. Mr. Chairman—and—ah—gentlemen. May I be permitted a word? We have already discussed this ah—lady—to the last full measure of our tolerance and—ah—understanding. The facts and—ah—principles involved have had a full hearing.

CHAIRMAN. Yes, exactly.

ALF. Does that mean it can't be brought up again?

JEPHSON. The decision is irrevocable. Every atom of Christian charity has been exercised. The book is closed.

TOM [*to Alf*] Sit down, sit down.

CHAIRMAN. Can we have Mr. Pilton's letter read again, please.

CLERK. Dear Sir: What about those blinking lights before our house? They blink day and night and neither my wife nor myself can sleep for them. What about it, gentlemen? Yours disgustedly, Thomas Pilton.

ALF [*rising*] I consider Molly Squires more important than Mr. Pilton's blinking lights.

CHAIRMAN. I'm afraid you're out of order.

ALF. But I haven't said anything.

CHAIRMAN. You're out of order. . .

ALF. But can't I say anything at all?

JEPHSON. Mr. Chairman and—ah—gentlemen—whilst acknowledging Councillor Liddell's ignorance of procedure. . . .

ANDWELL. Mr. Chairman, I object to Mr. Jephson's remarks. . . .

ALF. I'm still on my feet, Mr. Chairman. Doesn't anybody else do any talking here except him?

WINSDEAN. I was going to say . . .

JEPHSON. This is an insult!

ALF. You're not being insulted at all . . .

JEPHSON. *MISTER* Chairman!

TOM. Mr. Chairman—I don't think it right for Mr. Jephson to shout at a new member.

ANDWELL. You talk too much, that's your trouble.

WINSDEAN. I was going to say . . .

BELL. What about Mr. Pilton's lights?

CHAIRMAN. Order—Gentlemen—Order. Councillor Liddell, I'm sorry to say that some of your remarks have been unfortunate . . .

ALF. Well—I'm sorry, Mr. Chairman.

CHAIRMAN. Kindly keep personalities out of it.

ALF. It's all right him talking about my ignorance . . .

CHAIRMAN. Well, will you please address yourself strictly to the matter in hand?

ALF. I don't want to insult anyone. I'll say I'm sorry now and be a *man* about it. [*Pause*] Well—I am. Mr. Chairman, if it hadn't been for this case I wouldn't have said anything at all. But she came to me. Even if you *have* said "No", what's wrong with giving it another think? That's all I want to say. When all's said and done we're all individuals. [*Reaction*] Well—I—I thank you Mr. Chairman and Gentlemen.

CHAIRMAN. Thank you Councillor Liddell. Mr Clerk, are we in order in accepting a Notice of Motion so as to discuss the case again at a later Meeting?

CLERK. Well, sir, I suppose it *might* come under section Three of the "Special Provisions" in Standing Orders.

CHAIRMAN [*to Alf*] Do you wish to move a Notice of Motion?

ALF. If that's the way, Mr. Chairman, yes.

JEPHSON. Mr Chairman, as you yourself stated, the house is condemned.

ALF. Oh no it's not—it's the woman who's condemned.

JEPHSON. It is the house that is condemned. It is no part of our—ah—functions to impute a lack of moral excellence to anyone . . .

ALF. Look—why don't you put it in plain English?

JEPHSON. *MISTER* Chairman!

ALF. Well, you get my back up.

TOM. Alf—take it easy.

WINSDEAN. I was going to say . . .

ANDWELL. Won't you shut up, Jephson . . .

BELL. Can't we get on . . .

CHAIRMAN. Order, order, please. The Notice of Motion is accepted. Perhaps the Health Committee would like to appoint a small subcommittee to see Cragg House again.

JEPHSON. This is nonsense. That house is condemned and condemned it will remain.

ALF. Well, if that's all you care about the individual I might as well go home. Isn't Molly Squires an individual?

BELL. You can't just consider the individual in a case like this . . .

TOM. Alf—you've got to take the party line on matters of this kind . . .

WINSDEAN. I was going to say you ought to bring this up at a Party Meeting first . . .

ANDWELL. Mr. Chairman—can't we pass on to the next business? We've already agreed to a proposal.

CHAIRMAN. Order, gentlemen, order. . . .

JEPHSON. Mr. Chairman—I move the removal of Mr. Pilton's blinking lights. . . .

Fade out.

Act Two

In the duckhouse Alf is trying to catch the black drake. Clarice comes into the shot.

CLARICE. 'Ere—What are you doing?

ALF. I'm trying to catch the black drake.

CLARICE. Why?

ALF. I'm going to kill it.

CLARICE. Kill it? Why?

ALF. I've a reason.

CLARICE. Only last Thursday before you went to the Meeting you were saying how sad it looked.

ALF. Aye—well, it's going to look sadder in a minute.

He makes another attempt to catch the drake.

CLARICE. I just don't understand you these days.

ALF. Do you try?

CLARICE. You're not really going on with it, are you?

ALF. With what?

CLARICE. *Her.*

ALF. I've told you, Clarice. That's enough of the "*Her*".

CLARICE. You didn't make much headway at the meeting, did you?

ALF. No, I didn't. But they're going to talk about it again, anyway.

CLARICE. Couldn't—couldn't you give up the Council?

ALF. Give up? I've only just got on.

CLARICE. You were happier with the wood ornaments and ducks.

ALF. I don't know. It's nice to try and do a bit of good now and then . . . I see you haven't got them corsets yet.

CLARICE. What *is* the matter with you?

ALF. Well, I keep asking you. You want to trim yourself up a bit.

CLARICE. *I* don't know, I'm sure. Perhaps you'd like me better if I was like *Her*?

ALF. Well, there'd be more of you in the right places!

25

CLARICE. If you thought anything about me you wouldn't talk like that.

ALF. Happen if you thought anything about me I shouldn't have to.

CLARICE. All right. So you act the way you're doing. What do I care? Show us all up. Have the whole place talking about us. Go on. Choke all the ducks. Set the caravan on fire.

ALF. Clarice—the reason I'm going to choke this drake is because it squawks too much!

Mix to Tom and Clarice alone in the kitchen later that day.

CLARICE. I don't know what's got into him.

TOM. How long ago was it?

CLARICE. It wasn't *five* minutes since.

TOM. He might have sold the drake.

CLARICE. I'm getting worried—he's gone off his chump.

TOM. Not he, not he.

CLARICE. It's the first time he's ever killed one.

TOM. Well, I suppose there's always a first time. He told you about the Meeting?

CLARICE. He didn't. Others did, though.

TOM. The way he stuck up for her—you should have seen him. He must see something in her.

CLARICE. He—I don't suppose he'd. . . .

TOM. What?

CLARICE. Nothing.

TOM. Huh! She is pretty, you know.

CLARICE. Eee, but he couldn't have.

TOM. You said you'd like him to be like other men. Let himself go once in a while!

CLARICE. Oh—you!

TOM. You see—you're not satisfied with him.

CLARICE [*petulantly*] He—he keeps saying his shirts are too tight. The collars—they're size fifteen—they've always been size fifteen.

TOM. You know, our Clarice, women sometimes *drive* men to caravans and ducks. And worse.

CLARICE. Worse?

TOM. Aye, worse. Sympathy and understanding should be found at home. That's where a man first looks for them. If it's not there, well . . . [*Goes to window*] By Gum—it's going to pour down. Shouldn't like to be on the moors in that lot.

We mix to the bravely polished, neat interior of Molly's broken-down cottage on the moor known as Cragg House.

A knock, repeated.

MOLLY. See who it is, Sandra.

Sandra opens the door

SANDRA. It's a man.

MOLLY [*going to door*] Mr. Liddell!

ALF [*coming in*] Aye, it's me.

MOLLY. But—you're drenched!

ALF. Aye. It's throwing it down. [*Handing basket to Sandra*] 'Ere you are, lass.

SANDRA. Mummy—a duck! A duck!

ALF [*to Molly*] The wife sent it . . . I was going to kill it but I hadn't the heart.

MOLLY. How kind . . . Take it in the yard, Sandra.

ALF. Aye, well, she's a bit like that. They make wonderful soup. Is that fire welcome!

MOLLY. But—you're absolutely drenched.

ALF. Nothing that fire won't cure.

MOLLY. Oh, you *can't*. You'll catch your death. If there was only . . . [*Molly looks round and sees an old pair of her own jeans on a chair*] Maybe you could *squeeze* into these. [*Takes up jeans*]

ALF. What's them?

MOLLY. They're old jeans I use.

ALF. Well. . . .

MOLLY. You could put them on a while . . .

ALF. Nay . . .

MOLLY. Oh, please, Mr. Liddell, you couldn't sit about in those. You'll catch cold. Is your shirt wet?

ALF. No. I'll be all right, honestly.

MOLLY. Please—you can change in the bedroom. In there.

ALF. Well—I—I'm not stopping.

MOLLY. I'll dry your things before the fire. It won't take a minute.

ALF. Well, then, if you think . . . [*He takes the jeans and goes into the bedroom*]

SANDRA. My Daddy was bigger than him.

MOLLY. Shsh! You mustn't say that.

SANDRA. Mummy, when is Daddy going to send for us to come to Australia?

MOLLY. Soon.

SANDRA. Less than a month?

MOLLY. Perhaps.

SANDRA. Why has the man brought us the duck?

MOLLY. Because he's very kind.

SANDRA. Is the man going to kill it, Mummy?

MOLLY. No, love.

SANDRA. I don't like soup.

MOLLY. All right, poppet. You can keep it.

SANDRA. The man said it was for duck soup.

MOLLY. Yes, but you can keep it. The gentleman won't mind.

Alf comes in wearing Molly's jeans and carrying his jacket and trousers.

ALF. Now then, then?

Molly takes wet clothes and puts them in front of the fire.

MOLLY. Sit you down. Are those—the jeans—all right?

ALF. Aye. They fit me.

MOLLY. If you move they'll burst. . . .

ALF. Nay, I . . .

MOLLY. And they're half-way up your legs.

ALF. Well, maybe they are a little tight.

MOLLY. A *little!* [*Indicates for Alf to sit*] There! [*Feeling his socks*] You can't sit in these. [*She removes his socks and shoes*] A towel, Sandra.

Sandra fetches towel, Molly dries Alf's feet.

MOLLY. My slippers—the big ones.

SANDRA. You've only got the one pair!

MOLLY. Never mind talking. Where are they?

Sandra brings slippers.

ALF. You know—I feel just like a child.

MOLLY. All *nice* men are like children. The kettle won't be a minute. We'll have tea.

SANDRA. Are you going to let us stay in this house?

MOLLY. Shush child. The questions children ask!

ALF. It's about the Council I've come.

MOLLY. Yes?

ALF. I—I've managed to make 'em hold their horses a bit.

MOLLY. Thank you. Oh, thank you. Does it mean they're going to let us stay?

ALF. It's up again on Thursday . . .

MOLLY. I'm so grateful.

ALF. Nay, it's nothing . . . I always did like flowers on wallpaper. The gold dot sets them off.

MOLLY. Bless you. Oh, my loaf!

Molly crosses to oven.

ALF. Is it a soda cake?

MOLLY. Yes. Do you like soda bread?

ALF. D'ye know, there's nothing I like better.

MOLLY. I'm so glad.

ALF [*sniffing*] Oh, and that smell! H'mm, you know I thought I'd never see a soda cake again.

MOLLY. Bless you!

ALF. Are we all having some?

SANDRA. Of course.

MOLLY. Being so hot mightn't be good for the tummy, though.

ALF. Oh, blow the tummy! Eh, Sandra? You know when I was little —when I was *young*, we sometimes had our tea round the fire. At my mother's. We had mugs in them days. Strong tea, and big chunks of soda bread right out of the oven. Aye, swimming in butter.

MOLLY. Get the butter, Sandra. And the cups . . . oh!

ALF. What's the matter?

MOLLY. I meant to get some cups. They're all broken except two.

ALF. Don't fash yourself. I'll wait.

MOLLY. No, I'll wait.

ALF. No, I'll wait . . .

SANDRA. Can I have mine now, Mummy?

MOLLY. There's a mug. Sandra, get the mug.

ALF. Ah!

MOLLY. I can have the mug.

ALF. No, if you don't mind, I'll have the mug. . . .

SANDRA [*bringing mug*] This is the mug.

ALF. That's a grand 'un. I always did like a mug.

MOLLY. I think a man *should* have a mug. Bring the teapot, love, and tea caddy.

ALF. Aye, it brings back them days right enough. I never liked the straight slices in the middle of a soda cake as well as a chunk of the outside. Like small boats they were the way me mother cut them. Here, give us the tin, love. [*This to Sandra who has fetched the teapot and tea-caddy. To Molly who is cutting the loaf at the table*] Will a fistful be enough?

SANDRA. I should think it'll be—no, put in two fistfuls. Let's have it strong or nothing.

ALF. These clothes'll steam the place out! Tea's up!

MOLLY [*turning the clothes*] They're doing grand. [*Taking the teapot to table*] Won't be long now. Do you mind if we have it by the fire?

ALF. Do you know there's nothing I'd like better than to have it by the fire.

MOLLY. Yes—I think it's more homely. There you are. [*Hands him the bread*] Watch the butter doesn't run off.

ALF. Molly! A boat!

MOLLY. Bless you! [*Handing him the mug*] I'm sorry about all the cracks. It's like a hair-net.

ALF. A cow painted on the side! Do you know—it couldn't be better.
Molly pours out tea into mug held by Alf.
We mix to Councillor Jephson at his telephone.

JEPHSON. Councillor Winsdean? Ah! I think Councillor Andwell should be ready by now . . . No—we'll use my vehicle . . . No—we'll pick him up as we go past . . . No—my mind is made up about Cragg House. To me this visit is purely perfunctory . . . No—it won't take twenty minutes to get there . . . No, that is to say, yes . . . No!
At Cragg House Alf has finished tea. Sandra is absent.

MOLLY. More tea?

ALF. No thank you. The best tea I've had since I don't know.

MOLLY. I'm glad.

ALF. I see it's cleared up grand. Hope it's not too cold for the young 'un.

MOLLY. She loves playing out.

ALF. Aye. Children.

MOLLY. Perhaps you'd come again sometime?

ALF. Well—I—I mean . . .

MOLLY. And bring your wife.

ALF. No, oh no! I mean, she's no hand at visiting.

MOLLY. Yourself, then?

ALF. I'd like to. You—I think you understand me.

MOLLY. Well—there's nothing very complicated.

ALF. Look—would you *understand* if I said something?

MOLLY. Of course.

ALF. It's about the wife. My wife.

MOLLY. Yes?

ALF. She doesn't . . . She doesn't understand, I mean. It's funny I know, but in some ways you remind me of her!

MOLLY. Do I?

ALF. Not as she is now, but the way she was. Did you notice a small wart on her forehead. The left-hand side?

MOLLY. Yes.

ALF. Aye—women would. Well—we aren't just as happy as we might be. Bear in mind I'm odd in ways.

MOLLY. No. You're anything but that.

ALF. It isn't that she's not a good wife but . . .

MOLLY. In what way does *she* disappoint you?

ALF. Well. There's one thing, for instance—will you promise not to laugh?

MOLLY. Of course I won't.

ALF. She doesn't wear corsets!

MOLLY. I'm sorry.

ALF. Aye, well, I suppose it's funny. She used to be so tidy once over.

MOLLY. Yes, I think I see what you mean.

ALF. Now she doesn't care. D'ye know—I'm gassing! Aye, but that wart—it was always a wart, mind you—only I used to see it as a mole!

MOLLY. She doesn't realize how lucky she is.

ALF. I'll have to be shaping. She wouldn't like it if she knew I was here.

MOLLY. But you said she sent the duck.

ALF. It's a drake. No, she didn't send it. She would have done once over. Sometimes I like to do things—the sort of things she'd do if she was like she used to be!

MOLLY. . . . Would you like to know about me?

ALF. No—I have my own picture. . . .

MOLLY. But I *should* . . .

ALF. No. I'll keep the picture.

MOLLY. . . . Is it a nice picture?

ALF. It's a lovely picture. I'll have to go now.

Alf takes his clothes into the bedroom and Molly busies herself tidying up, spending a few seconds straightening the flowers. Sandra runs in.

SANDRA. Mummy, there's a motor-car! Three men!

MOLLY. Here?

SANDRA. Yes, they're here.

Councillors Andwell, Winsdean and Jephson appear in the open doorway.

MOLLY. Oh!

JEPHSON. Good afternoon, Miss Squires. I am Councillor Jephson. Perhaps you, ah, remember me?

MOLLY. G-good-afternoon.

JEPHSON. These gentlemen are my, ah, colleagues. Councillor Winsdean, and, ah, Councillor Andwell.

WINSDEAN & ANDWELL. How-do-you-do?

MOLLY. Good-afternoon.

JEPHSON. We have come to make an inspection of the—ah— property. Ah, with your permission, of course.

MOLLY [*nervous glance towards bedroom*] Well—I'm not properly tidied . . .

ANDWELL. Don't worry, lady, it's more or less informal. Hello, there! [*This last to Sandra*]

ANDWELL. What's this you've got?

SANDRA. It's a duck. Mummy, where is the man?

MOLLY. Be quiet. Don't interrupt the gentlemen.

JEPHSON. Do I take it, Miss, that we have your ah, permission?

MOLLY. Well—would it be all right tomorrow? Or later on today?

JEPHSON. There is no necessity to apologize for the—ah—condition of the premises. The inspection is intended to be perfunctory. [*Pointing to bedroom*] May I?

MOLLY [*at bay: her back to bedroom door*] No!

JEPHSON. Madam, we have driven five miles . . .

MOLLY. Well, you can't!

WINSDEAN. Happen we could call again?

JEPHSON. No! [*To Molly*] Am I to understand that you refuse?

MOLLY. You can't go in there. You can see the other rooms.

JEPHSON. And is there any particular reason why we may not see this?
   The door opens and they see Alf.

ANDWELL. Councillor Liddell!

WINSDEAN. Well!

ALF. I—I were just in there!

MOLLY. How many inspections must we have? First Councillor Liddell comes and looks all over the house, and now you three.

JEPHSON. I see.

ALF. No, you don't. It's right what she said. I've inspected the premises. I have as much right as anyone else to inspect the premises. I can give the Council a full report on the state of the premises! I know what I'm doing.

SANDRA. You've got your clothes on again!
   Fade out.

Act Three

Liddells' kitchen: Clarice is at the fire with tea.

CLARICE. A mug of tea while you're waiting?

ALF. Aye, I might as well break in the new mug!

CLARICE. I got you two new shirts as well.

ALF. What size collar?

CLARICE. Fifteen and a half. You said the others were tight.

ALF. Aye. What colour?

CLARICE. Different shades of blue. You always liked blue.

ALF. It's a nice colour. Did your Tom say how many of our side were coming?

CLARICE. Two—Tom said you were in real trouble.

ALF. Oh, well!

CLARICE. They're putting all sorts of rumours on it in the town.

ALF. About Saturday, you mean?

CLARICE. Yes, and it's only Monday, bear in mind. Give them another few days and they'll have you and her married.

ALF. Aw, Clarice, are you still at it?

CLARICE. It wouldn't have been so bad if I hadn't to hear about it from other folk.

ALF. What's wrong with giving her a drake?

CLARICE. Nothing—not if you'd kept your trousers on!

ALF. Nay, Clarice, you don't think . . .

CLARICE. How do you think I feel?

ALF [*quietly*] I don't know. I know how I feel. There was pleasantness up there. She laughed. Aye, and she has very little to laugh at. I suppose she'll always be a *Her*.

CLARICE. They were talking about it in the shop when I was buying your shirts.

ALF [*grateful*] I read a story once about a man who sold his watch to buy a set of combs for his wife's hair. She had beautiful golden hair. [*Clarice touches her own hair*] And when the man got home his wife had cut all her hair off.

CLARICE. What for?

ALF. She'd sold it.

CLARICE. Sold it?

ALF. Yes. She sold it so's she could buy him a chain for his watch!

CLARICE. Well?

33

ALF. Well, you shouldn't have bought those shirts Clarice—you should have spent that money on yourself.

CLARICE. What do you mean?

ALF. Well, I can't very well buy you a pair of corsets. I can give you the brass though.

CLARICE [*rising*] Are you still on about corsets?

ALF. Well, you waddle around like a—like a . . .

CLARICE. A duck?

ALF. Now, I don't mean it that way.

CLARICE. I must say it's a nice thing. . . . I suppose she doesn't need them. . . .

ALF. Nay, love, I didn't mean it. . . .

Door knock.

That'll be them.

CLARICE. I'll let them in. [*Clarice goes*]

Clarice opens the front door. Tom Cardwick, Winsdean and Andwell enter. There is a murmur of greetings.

Clarice shows them into the front room with Alf and then goes out.

ALF. Now then, sit ye down.

[*He manoeuvres each into a chair and then sits at the head of the table himself*]

I'll be Chairman meself!

CARDWICK [*half in jest*] Well, I don't know if you can be Chairman. Officially it's a Party matter, you know.

ALF. Aye, well, I'll be the Chairman. I've never been Chairman of owt, so I'll be one now. [*Half in jest*]

CARDWICK. Well, I . . .

[*Cardwick looks at Winsdean and Andwell; they shrug acceptance*] I suppose you're right, Alf. I'm sorry it's come like this. Our Clarice'll have told you?

ALF. She said I were going to be on the carpet.

CARDWICK. It was to be in the Party Rooms really . . .

ALF. I'd have come. Only, the Missus thought if I were going to be on any carpet, it might as well be my own.

CARDWICK. Aye, well, nobody likes this. I—can you take it up? [*This to Andwell*]

ANDWELL. The thing is, we'd like you to withdraw your Notice of Motion for next Thursday's Meeting.

ALF. Withdraw it?

ANDWELL. Exactly. It is better left alone.

ALF. But I don't want it left alone. I want something done about it.

ANDWELL. Yes, but—sorry—[*To Winsdean*]

WINSDEAN. I was going to say an issue like this results in a note of discord.

ALF. She came for help, I promised to help.

CARDWICK. Well, you can honestly say that you've kept your promise.

ALF. But it isn't a case of promising. I *want* to help her.

WINSDEAN. I was going to say that the other side will naturally take advantage of this. They will endeavour to discredit us in the Council.

ALF. All I want is to do what's right.

CARDWICK. Look, Gaffer, there's good causes and there's bad causes. This is a bad cause.

ALF. But she is an individual.

CARDWICK. Aye. So I believe.

ALF. Everyone's again' her. What's wrong with someone being for her?

WINSDEAN. I was going to say that we must always be on our guard against—er—behaviour which is inimical to the best interests of the Party. I was going to say you mustn't do us an injustice.

ALF. But this is an injustice.

CARDWICK. Not it.

ALF. You all voted for her to be put out.

ANDWELL. What else could we do?

WINSDEAN. I was going to say that one must uphold the prestige and authority of the Council.

ALF. She has to live somewhere.

CARDWICK. Not where she is now.

ALF. But where can she go?

ANDWELL. That isn't our responsibility.

ALF. What about the little girl? Isn't that something in her favour?
[*Silence*]

ANDWELL. Well—to get back to the point again. If you'll only withdraw the Notice of Motion——

ALF. I'll not.

ANDWELL. Hem—hem. Well, Mr. Liddell—sorry, Councillor Liddell, I—ah—there's another point.

ALF. I know. About Saturday.

WINSDEAN. I was going to say. . . .

ALF. You needn't trouble. You can all think what you like.

ANDWELL. It isn't a case of what we think. It's others. I tell you there's a lot of talk.

ALF. Aye. Someone made a good job of what happened up there.

CARDWICK. You know who that was, Alf.

WINSDEAN. I was going to say Jephson hates you. When he gets his teeth into someone there's no hope.

ALF. I haven't finished with him. Damn and blast it, there's nothing but rottenness everywhere. If this is public life you can have it from me . . . I'm resigning.

ANDWELL, WINSDEAN and CARDWICK [*together*] Resigning from the Council!

ALF. No, from the Party.

CARDWICK. But—nay, Alf, you can't do that. That will make a right split.

ALF. Well, it's what you want.

ANDWELL. Of course it isn't.

ALF. It were all right for you to split with me. Well—I'm splitting first!

ANDWELL. But Councillor Liddell!

CARDWICK. Alf!

WINSDEAN. I was going to say——

ALF. Well, you needn't bother! [*He rises*] I always thought the Party was out to help folk. It isn't at all. Well, I've done. I'm on my own. The only folk that's any good for individuals—is individuals.

The others rise.

CARDWICK. You're just being stupid, Alf. What can all this get you? Nothing!

ANDWELL. Nothing!

WINSDEAN. I was going to say——

ALF. Nothing! All that talk and nowt but a roomful of echoes!

Alf exits to hall. Councillors file out. Cardwick, Winsdean and Andwell go from the room into the hall. They leave. Alf shuts the front door after them. Clarice comes down the stairs.

CLARICE. What were you all shouting about?

ALF. It's what they call politics. They're all against me, Clarice.

CLARICE. You mean you're going to resign?

ALF. On no—I'm not resigning. But I'm not looking forward to the next meeting.

We mix to the Council Chamber. Everyone is present.

CHAIRMAN. All in favour? [*Show of hands*] That is carried. Now to item seven on your Agenda: "Notice of Motion". Councillor Liddell.

ALF [*rising*] Aye, well, I'll be brief. This lady—I don't want her put out. There's a Minute on the books to put her out and I move to have that Minute re-re——

CLERK. Rescinded, sir?

ALF. Aye. Knock 'er off the books. Aye, then we can tackle the job again. I——

JEPHSON [*rising*] Mr. Chairman and—ah—gentlemen. Might I be permitted a word?

Alf regards him with resentment but sits.

CHAIRMAN. Certainly.

JEPHSON. I should merely like to enquire if Councillor Liddell has an interest to declare?

ALF. An interest? Of course I have. I don't want her put out.

JEPHSON. I mean an *interest*, Mr. Chairman.

CHAIRMAN. I think I know what you mean. He means—would you, Mr. Whalley?

CLERK [*speaking quickly*] Well, sir, it is a rule of all publicly elected bodies that a Member must declare any interest he may have in matters under consideration. That is to say, any interest which might bias him for or against a motion and he is required by law to declare if such an interest exists.

CHAIRMAN. Thank you. [*To Alf*] Is that clear?

ALF. Well—I don't rightly know.

BELL. It means having a finger in the pie!

ALF. Well, I haven't.

BELL. How about the duck?

ALF. It were a drake. I don't see what that has to do with it.

CARDWICK. I agree, Mr. Chairman. The remark was quite uncalled for.

WINSDEAN. I was going to say, Mr. Chairman, I agree. Absolutely uncalled for.

ANDWELL. Absolutely. It is easy for Councillor Bell to sit back and jibe.

BELL. Piffle!

CHAIRMAN. Order, Gentlemen. No personalities, please. Private affairs are private affairs. Councillor Liddell?

ALF [*rising*] Some folk'll put lies on anything. If it wasn't for all the gossip in the first place the Council might've been a bit easier on that poor girl.

JEPHSON. Nonsense.

ALF. It's not nonsense at all.

CHAIRMAN. All remarks through the chair, please.

ALF. Aye. Well, I want that Minute re-re—knocked off the books.

JEPHSON [*rising*] Facts, Mr. Chairman, are facts. I regret, Mr. Chairman, that Councillor Liddell's remarkable solicitude for this lady——

ALF. What's remarkable about it?

JEPHSON. Remarkable to the extent that it obscures the facts. [*Drawing attention to a basket on the table in front of him*] Last Saturday, when, with—ah—Colleagues, I visited the good lady, I took the liberty of collecting a few—ah—specimens. [*He takes a glove from his pocket and puts it on his right hand. Then he takes a handful out of the basket*]. This, gentlemen, *grows* in one of the rooms. Fungus. Different kinds of fungi. A basketful. This alone is enough to condemn the property. Here, Mr. Chairman, I am dealing in facts.

CHAIRMAN. We all know the condition of the property. [*To Alf*] Do you formally move the Notice of Motion?

ALF. I formally move it.

CHAIRMAN. Any seconder? [*Silence*] Is there no seconder? [*Silence*] I'm sorry, Councillor Liddell. The case is closed. Anything to say?

ALF. You're all rotten!

CHAIRMAN [*shrugging*] Sorry.

JEPHSON. Mr. Chairman and—ah ladies and gentlemen: before moving progress . . .

ALF. You're all rotten.

JEPHSON. I should like for the benefit of our friends, the Press, to say . . .

ALF. You're all rotten.

JEPHSON. . . . that this Council has, in my judgment, given fair and considerate hearing to this case . . .

ALF. I tell you, you're all rotten . . .

JEPHSON. It has been suggested that this eviction has been based upon lies and rooted in small-town prejudices.

ALF. D'you hear me—you're all rotten . . .

JEPHSON. . . . Completely untrue . . .

ALF. Rotten. Rotten. Rotten. Bloody, stinking rotten. [*Throws fungi everywhere, which produces a general bedlam with all the Councillors talking and shouting*]

    A few days later. We see Clarice opening her front door. Molly is standing there.

MOLLY. I'm sorry to trouble you.

CLARICE. It's no trouble. My husband hasn't come home from work yet.

MOLLY. I'd like to speak with you, if you can spare me a minute.

CLARICE. Come in.

MOLLY. Thank you.

They go into the front room.

CLARICE. Won't you sit down?

MOLLY [*sitting*] Thank you. I just want to say that all those rumours —I mean the way they talked about us—about Mr. Liddell and me, they're all, well, you must know they're all——

CLARICE. Nonsense? Of course I know.

MOLLY. Do you mind if I say something to you?

CLARICE. No.

MOLLY. I think you look very nice.

CLARICE. Thank you.

MOLLY. Your husband made me cry.

CLARICE. Alf?

MOLLY. Oh, not when he was there. On Saturday. After he left.

CLARICE. What did he say to you?

MOLLY. It was the way he talked of you.

CLARICE. What did he say?

MOLLY. That he loved you!

CLARICE. Hey?

MOLLY. It was sort of double talk, like they say. All it all meant was that he loves you.

CLARICE. Aye, well, that's as may be.

MOLLY. He tried so hard to help me.

CLARICE. He tried but they'll still put you out. So it isn't much help after all.

MOLLY. Oh, but he has helped.

CLARICE. How?

MOLLY. He's made me feel that I don't have to run. Oh, I know this talk of running seems old-fashioned but there's more to it than people think. You're either wanted or you aren't. I'm not—at least I never have been before.

CLARICE. What will you do?

MOLLY. Well, that's where he's helped me. I've had several offers of jobs and homes all over the country. And three offers of marriage!

CLARICE. Do you like working in the laundry?

MOLLY. Yes, very much.

CLARICE. Over the hill from Cragg House there's a place where people have caravans.

MOLLY. I know. I tried for one.

CLARICE. You see—I know my husband better than anyone.

MOLLY. I beg your pardon?

CLARICE. Last night, after the Meeting, he stood in there by the kitchen window looking out. And do you know what he was thinking? [*Molly shakes her head*] He was thinking that he'd give his caravan to you.

MOLLY. His—caravan?

CLARICE. Yes. It's his work-shop. It's out the back.

MOLLY. But—*give* me it?

CLARICE. Yes.

MOLLY. Bless him.

CLARICE. I want you to have it.

MOLLY. But—why?

CLARICE. I could say to help you. If it will help you then I'm glad. I *hate* that caravan. I can't explain, but I hate it.

MOLLY. But you said it was his work-shop.

CLARICE. Yes. Wood ornaments and ducks. Out there all the time. I just can't explain.

MOLLY. I think I understand.

CLARICE. Will you stay and have some tea?

MOLLY. Thank you, but I'd rather not. Sandra is at home. I promised I wouldn't be long.

CLARICE. He'll be here in a few minutes. I've got his hotpot in the oven.

MOLLY [*rising*] Please thank him for me. Tell him—tell him I'm so happy.

Clarice opens door.

CLARICE. He'll come and see you then. I know him. I always did know him, but—I forgot. Sometimes you *do* forget.

MOLLY. I know.

CLARICE. Oh, and—Molly?

MOLLY. Yes?

CLARICE [*as they face each other*] *Thank* you.

MOLLY. Me?

CLARICE. Yes.

MOLLY. But why?

CLARICE. Just—thank you.

Molly goes and Clarice shuts the front door.

40

Duck house. Alf home from work, looks at them. Then he stares for a moment at the caravan before moving to the house.

Clarice is putting a hotpot on the table beside a vase of flowers.

ALF. Clarice—there's flowers!

CLARICE. What's wrong with flowers?

ALF. There's nothing wrong with flowers. I like flowers. Clarice, I've got it. I'm going to give her that old caravan.

CLARICE. Whatever you say, love.

ALF. Now it's no use arguing. I've made up my mind.

CLARICE. Just as you say.

ALF. Now, I've told you. Clarice!

CLARICE. There you go, you see.

ALF. You *don't* mind?

CLARICE. It's a poor do if you can't do what you like with your own property.

ALF. Clarice!

Alf sits.

CLARICE. Busy at the foundry today?

ALF. Aye. Reporters everywhere.

CLARICE. What did you say?

ALF. Nowt. I've had enough.

CLARICE. It's been warm today.

ALF. Aye . . . I'll finish my year on the Council and then I'll give up. [*A pause while he looks at her*] You know, Clarice, you seem different!

CLARICE. Well, thank you very much!

ALF. Aye, but I don't mean outside. It's inside, Clarice. It's inside.

CLARICE [*about the dress*] Do you like it?

ALF. Aye. Olive green. I always did like olive green. It's a soft, warm colour. Your hair, too. You used to have it that way.

CLARICE. What's wrong with it this way?

ALF. There's nothing wrong with it that way. I always did like it that way. And do you know something?

CLARICE. What?

ALF. Don't bother about getting any corsets!

CLARICE. Hey?

ALF. The way you look now you don't *need* corsets.

Clarice smiles.

Fade out.

41

PROMENADE

by

PETER NICHOLS

CAST

TRICIA BLAKE	*Susannah York*
NICKY BLAKE	*William Young*
ANDREW TURTLE	*Tom Bell*
MAURICE GOODMAN	*Trader Faulkner*
RHONDA HOLLOWAY	*Pauline Yates*
CY WHELAN	*Peter McEnery*
LOTTE	*Sydonie Platt*
JIM	*Louis Haslar*
GUITARIST	*Mark Brackenbury*
CUSTOMER IN BAR	*Ronald Masters*

DIRECTOR	*Julian Amyes*
DESIGNER	*Darrell Lass*

DIRECTOR'S NOTE

My own personal preference for television plays is for that kind of mood play in which the plot may be indiscernible and structure invisible. *Promenade*, by Peter Nichols, is very much a play of this kind, possessing those qualities of mood and atmosphere in abundance.

It has also, to my mind, the special merit of neither belonging to, nor imitating any particular school of television play-writing. It is constructed with deceptive casualness and is always unassertive. Indeed, its theme—as has been said of it—is very far from being rammed down the audience's throat. On the contrary, it lingers like an afterthought so that at the end of the play one's impressions become stronger and continue to expand in the imagination, enriching the meaning of what has gone before.

JULIAN AMYES.

A BIOGRAPHY OF PETER NICHOLS

Peter Nichols was born in 1928. He went to school in Bristol and later studied acting at the Bristol Old Vic Theatre School. For five years he worked as an actor in repertory and television. Afterwards he tried various odd jobs, working for short spells as a cinema commissionaire, a barman and a park-keeper, and finally as a teacher at several London primary schools. After the success of *Promenade* he gave up teaching to become a full time writer. He is married and lives in Devon.

ACTION

The action of the play takes place in the following sets:

(1) Nicky's room
(2) Rhonda's room
(3) Inside Maurice's car
(4) Saloon Bar, "The Grapes"
(5) The beach
(6) Station platform
(7) Interior of railway carriage.

TIME

The time is the present.

Act One

A typical South Coast seaside resort. We see the beach, the pier, the promenade. We mix to interior of a room. The room is a smart contemporary clutter. There is a chic divan in the centre with a fireplace behind it. The bookshelves are partly filled and on one of them stands a sculptured head. In one corner we see a bamboo cocktail bar. Near this is an antique full-length looking glass, standing on its own. On the wall is a contemporary print. There is a frosted glass door through which we see the dim shape of a man and hear the sounds of a shower.

TRICIA [*voice off*] Nicky!

> *Sounds of the shower cease. The door opens and Nicky Blake emerges. He is a good-looking boy of 24, slow of speech and movement—partly genuine, partly a pose to defend himself. Tricia, his sister, comes into the room. She is like him in appearance and is dressed in expensive casual clothes.*
>
> *As Tricia stands beside the painting on the wall, we see the likeness between them.*

TRICIA. Nicky—you here?

NICKY. Yes. Come in and get me a Scotch, will you?

TRICIA. Don't panic—you're as beautiful as ever.

NICKY. He's lovely . . .

TRICIA. He's successful . . .

NICKY. He uses "Evergreen" . . .

> *Nicky stands before the mirror, naked to the waist. We still see Tricia in the background. Nicky continues dressing.*

NICKY. Where've you been?

TRICIA. With Daddy. Where've you?

NICKY. With Mother. Talking about marriage.

TRICIA. Snap!

NICKY. Don't use those dreary schoolgirl expressions the whole time, Trish. You're nineteen now.

TRICIA [*bringing his drink*] What did she say? About marriage?

NICKY [*shrugging*] You know Mother. "Follow your star, my dear, in work and love and everything else." "But, Mother, there may be complications." "Complications, Nicky, are for inferiors. Wait till the day you see the stars dancing."

TRICIA. Poor Mummy—obsessed by stars. I suppose it's having nearly been one.

NICKY. Come here. [*Now wearing his shirt*] Perhaps we should have gone on the stage too.

He seizes her and turns her to the mirror. They stand looking at their reflections.

TRICIA. Not me. All the actors I've met have bored me stiff. But I can see the attraction for you—that blissful half-hour before the looking-glass every night.

NICKY. I might yet, if I can summon up the energy.

TRICIA. Did you tell Mummy it was you you meant?

NICKY. No. I said it was someone in the Crowd.

TRICIA. Snap! I mean, so did I.

NICKY. They're not fools. They guessed we meant ourselves.

TRICIA. You know, it'll be marvellous when you marry Rhonda. My best friend and sister-in-law as well. And you'll have a gorgeous flat and we'll come and visit you . . .

NICKY. Who's "we"?

TRICIA. Andrew and I, of course. What I like is we'll both be marrying someone in the Crowd—not outsiders or anything.

NICKY. Trish, you've got years before you think about marriage.

TRICIA. Thank you very much. What am I supposed to do until then?

NICKY. Meet a few more men, learn about them—never give them a thing.

TRICIA. How can you learn if you don't give anything?

NICKY. People will hurt you if you let them.

TRICIA. I've been out with plenty of men and no-one's hurt me. They've never had a chance with you watching me.

NICKY. And why do I do that, do you think?

TRICIA. Because you fancy yourself as a big brother?

NICKY. Because you're very attractive and one day you'll have money like me. It's a special trap.

TRICIA. I want to be married. So do you.

NICKY. I did think about it—for a time. [*Car horn outside*] There's Maurice.

Nicky moves to look through the window and Tricia turns to face him.

TRICIA. But—Rhonda—aren't you going to marry her?

NICKY [*at the window*] It wouldn't work. Andrew's with him. [*Shouting through the window*] Come on up! [*In normal voice*] I don't suppose the old man wanted you to marry Andrew? I can guess. He said it's something to do with class. An archaic word, but he has a point, I think. Let's face it, we don't know a thing about Andrew's parents. He works as a labourer and they make plenty these days. Even so, there can't be very much left when you think what he spends on clothes and going around with us. Never been to his *house*, have you? [*Pause*] There'd always be the suspicion he was after your money. No, if Father said anything . . .

Andrew comes in by the door beside the bar. He is the same age as Nicky; although his clothes are not as good he is obviously imitating his rich friend.

TRICIA. Shut up, Nicky!

NICKY. Like that about Andrew . . .

TRICIA. Hullo, mate. [*She kisses Andrew*]

NICKY. He was right.

ANDREW. What's this with me?

NICKY. She's been talking to the Major about you . . .

TRICIA. Drop it, Nicky . . .

NICKY. And marriage and everything . . .

TRICIA. Your hair's sticking up at the back!

This stops him for a moment and he twists before the looking-glass.

ANDREW. No, it isn't. What did your old man say?

TRICIA. Why ask him? He wasn't even there.

NICKY. He's told me before. He thinks she's far too good for you and you're the complete rubbish person.

ANDREW. I agree with him.

NICKY. I knew you would.

ANDREW. Real gent, the Major. No side with him either, that's what I like. This the new shirt?

NICKY. Thought you'd seen it?

ANDREW. No, some of the Crowd were talking about it in "The Grapes" last night. The collar's really very good, isn't it? Like Maurice's in shape, but this sea-island seems to fall better than poplin.

NICKY. Maurice still outside?

ANDREW. Yeah, polishing his car.

NICKY. I'll see him on the way out. Going to pick up Rhonda. Be around "The Grapes" later?

ANDREW. Saturday, isn't it?

NICKY. See you.

ANDREW. Ciao!

NICKY. 'Bye, Trish!

TRICIA. Go on——!

Nicky kisses her and goes.

ANDREW [*at once taking Nicky's place before the glass and tidying his costume*] So your old man doesn't dig me as a son-in-law?

Tricia comes up behind him and puts her arms round him.

TRICIA. Are you going to kiss me before Maurice comes?

ANDREW [*wipes hands in handkerchief, goes to table which has powders and bottles, takes powder and sprinkles in hands*] The obsessive fear of the manual labourer, body-odour and bad skin. You should see my lotions . . .

TRICIA. Have you been to work to-day, then?

ANDREW. Yeah. Last day on the airport. The Queen or somebody's coming down to open it next week . . . "God bless her and all who sail in her . . ." They're laying off the men now. Practically nothing to do.

TRICIA. Andrew—you're on holiday!

ANDREW. Unemployed.

TRICIA. Then let's go—now!

ANDREW. Go—where?

TRICIA. And get married!

ANDREW. Do me a favour, Trish.

TRICIA. You don't love me?

ANDREW. Oh, I can't say that. I'm very fond of you, you know *that*. I like you a lot. But we've only been going around together for a few weeks. Anyway, you're being finished at the Art School for some suave international geyser with handmade shoes. Face the facts, dear, I'm a casual labourer. Come next week, I'm even on the dole. The Major's right.

TRICIA. Andrew, what d'you think Daddy is?

ANDREW. I don't know. I've not had very much to do with him, have I?

TRICIA. All right, let's go and talk to him now.

ANDREW. No.

TRICIA. Anyway, what about your people? None of us has even met them.

ANDREW. No? My old man's from the army too.

TRICIA. Oh. Is he retired or . . .

ANDREW. Let's drop the parents, shall we?

TRICIA. It was you who brought them up.

ANDREW. And now I'm dropping them.

Pause.

TRICIA. Andrew——

ANDREW. Yes?

TRICIA. Kiss me.

ANDREW. Sure Nicky's not watching?

TRICIA. Sure!

ANDREW. Incredible!

They kiss. Maurice enters and it is as though he's sprung from a trapdoor.

Maurice Goodman is the same age as the others, bearded and spectacled, with a Roman hair-do and rings on his fingers. His costumes are more dashing than the others', his gadgets more outrageous. He speaks quickly with his voice sometimes rising to a triumphant howl when he has scored off someone.

MAURICE. That's all you people ever think about—bed! Nicky told me he feared this might happen and hinted I should come up here as soon as possible and put a stop to it before all was lost . . .

ANDREW. Thanks, Dad.

MAURICE. All included in the cover-charge. Not that your brother is any improvement in this respect, Tricia. [*He makes straight for the looking-glass and strikes a few attitudes, seizing a hand-mirror and looking at himself from various angles*] A man with money, looks, talent, opportunity and money, wasting it all on small-town chicks when he might be making a name for himself if only he'd stick to composing the music for this show I've written. But no! he's got to see Rhonda, couldn't even spare ten minutes to run through a lyric . . .

ANDREW. Drinks, Trish.

TRICIA. What do you want?

ANDREW. Gin and French.

TRICIA. Maurice?

MAURICE. No, thank you, bad for the breath. I'm sticking to peppermints. [*Takes a bag from his pocket and eats one*]
But can't Nicky see how he's wasted here?

TRICIA. You forget, Maurice, we've already lived in London. It's too big for Nicky.

MAURICE. I don't believe this small-pond stuff.

ANDREW. He's *lazy*, why not face it?

MAURICE. What about those scathing tunes he wrote for that avant-garde revue at Oxford? Sort of Kurt Weill with a dash of Brubeck.

51

ANDREW. What about the girl who sang them? It wasn't her *voice* he was interested in . . .

TRICIA. You're always saying that about Nicky . . .

ANDREW. Trish, you're being naive again. Anyway, Dad, I don't think you'll ever make the same appeal to him.

MAURICE. Not even if I shave off my beard? . . . You know this is going to be an expensive summer. I've lost two pairs of sunglasses already. Not around here, by any chance?

[*Tricia is at the bar pouring drinks, Andrew lying on the divan, Maurice searching for his glasses*]

I must have these glasses before to-morrow. If this weather keeps, parade on the Esplanade ten-hundred hours with the full complement of lotions, pomades, sun-shields, Italian canvas windbreakers and blancoed webbing.

ANDREW. Maurice, I forgot to tell you, I picked up six straw boaters in a junk-shop yesterday for half-a-crown.

MAURICE. Oh, that's classical! Remember to ask Cy to bring the camera for Victorian family group series—in and out of the water.

ANDREW. Ever known him come without it?

TRICIA. Your drink, Andrew.

ANDREW. Do you mind.

MAURICE. Goodness gracious, I'm attractive to-day, you can't get away from it, can you, Trish? And I shall certainly be one of the most eligible bachelors at this party to-night, especially when a few dances have put a little colour into this gaslit complexion.

ANDREW. You dance like a praying mantis.

MAURICE. What else is there to do at these places? Certainly never an intelligent conversation. And I'm too old for smooching about in corners.

TRICIA. What party are we talking about?

MAURICE. Whichever we manage to gate-crash. So far I've heard of three to-night. Or perhaps you'd rather not go.

ANDREW. What else is there but hang around "The Grapes"?

MAURICE. Exactly. [*Moving round the room he comes up against the bust of Nicky on the bookcase*] It's the complete Kafka—Wherever I go, I find these terrible heads of Rhonda Holloway's staring at me. I've finished with that coffee-bar on the front since they let her decorate it. A whole row of these things against a wall of melted milk chocolate.

TRICIA. It's terra-cotta. And the heads are only old life-class remnants she thought might come in useful. Look what it was like *before*—fishing-nets and a horrible mural of Clovelly.

MAURICE. I liked it.

TRICIA. Rhonda's easily the most talented of all the girls at Art School. Isn't she, Andrew?

ANDREW. God bless Rhonda and all who sail in *her*.

MAURICE [*Singing*] Art School, Art School—good old wonderful Art School. . . .

[*Maurice picks up photograph of Rhonda*]

I simply fail to see why Nicky could be attracted to that fat girl.

ANDREW. You missed your vocation, Maurice. You should have been a woman.

MAURICE. All right, but what would all the chicks around here do with their evenings?

ANDREW. From what I've seen, I can't think it would have made much difference.

MAURICE. Then it's time you got your facts straight, friend! But Rhonda Holloway. It honestly astounds me. I mean—she's fat— and growing fatter!

We mix to Rhonda Holloway, 24, sensual in appearance and nature. Attractive, though rather heavily built. She dresses in a style that seems to need bracelets and ear-rings.

Rhonda's room. It is small and unattractive but Rhonda has done her best to improve its appearance by hanging reproductions of good modern paintings. A single bed, a bedside table, books upon it, a curtain across the corner to make a wardrobe partition, a dressing-table. We begin on her face as she sits at the table. She is wearing glasses and leaning down to take a tissue from a drawer. It sticks when she tries to close it afterwards and she shows the state she is in by kicking at it angrily. There is the sound of a car-horn. She takes off the glasses, stands up and looks through the window beyond the dressing-table.

RHONDA. Come on up! The key's on the string.

NICKY [*from below*] Roger!

Rhonda dabs at her eyes, tired from crying, and attempts a quick restoration. She puts on some heavy bracelets. Nicky comes in. There are only two places to sit—the dressing-stool and the bed.

NICKY. Aren't they in?

RHONDA. No, Mum's shopping and he's at the football.

NICKY. And your sister?

RHONDA. With Ron, as usual, on the scooter.

NICKY. Well, then . . .

He puts his arm around her, but she evades the kiss.

53

RHONDA. No. [*She stares into the mirror at him*]

NICKY. All right. [*He throws himself on the bed*] Shall we go to meet the Crowd straight away?

RHONDA. No.

NICKY. Where then?

RHONDA. Anywhere away from here. They'll be back soon.

NICKY. The old man being his usual charming self?

RHONDA. Worse.

NICKY [*suddenly alarmed*] You haven't told them?

RHONDA. No. I'd steeled myself to, but when I saw him playing up again, I thought better of it. . . .

NICKY [*relieved, lounges back again*] What *was* it about then?

RHONDA. Same as ever. He asked me what your intentions are.

NICKY. What did you say?

RHONDA. I said I didn't know you'd ever had any. We're just going around together—was that right?

NICKY. What did he say then?

RHONDA. Oh, he made a list of the people I'd been "just going around with" before you and it isn't good enough and he hates the sight of you all and you're a lot of pansies and why don't I get engaged, like my sister?

NICKY. H'mm. [*She turns to look at him*]

RHONDA. Well, what's the answer? Why don't I get engaged?

NICKY. I don't know. *Why* don't you?

RHONDA. You were going to speak to your mother?

NICKY. Listen, Rhonda, you know Mother. She's so happily married and all that jazz. It must be true love and the stars dancing for her, otherwise it isn't real.

RHONDA [*tensely*] And what about this situation—is that real enough?

NICKY. I just *know* how she'd feel about it!

RHONDA. Anyone would think it was her who was having the baby.

NICKY. Don't be disgusting.

RHONDA. Disgusting! Are you disgusted? It's me who's having it—in seven months—and you're disgusted?

NICKY. Not at you. At your saying that about Mother. I told you, she married for love.

RHONDA. Well I love you.

NICKY. Yes, but Mother was luckier in the man she chose. I told you in the beginning, I've never felt anything like that for a woman.

I always say that in the beginning. We've all got some kind of disability, I suppose—mine's not being able to fall in love.

RHONDA. I know you told me that. But you seemed to change afterwards.

NICKY. Yes, I seemed to. I always seem to. Otherwise it'd make things pretty dull, wouldn't it? But honestly, Rhonda, I'm as cold as ice. If this hadn't happened, we'd have finished the usual way and soon have forgotten all about it.

RHONDA. But I'm not cold. Don't speak for me. I don't easily forget. [*She turns away from him. Pause*] I love you.

NICKY. I envy you, believe me. I'd like to know how it feels. Perhaps one day I shall be hit for six—that'll be when the stars dance. So far they always keep their places.

RHONDA. Then what shall I do?

NICKY. Now if I did what people call "The Right Thing By You", it would be the wrongest thing ever, right?

RHONDA. No.

NICKY. If I don't love you?

RHONDA. What *you* want is the wrongest thing.

NICKY. D'you honestly think it's more right to make that kind of marriage than make sure the kid's never born at all?

RHONDA. It's a kind of killing.

NICKY. You can't kill something that isn't born.

RHONDA. I bear him. He's alive.

NICKY. You see how different we are. I don't begin to understand.

RHONDA. I don't believe you spoke to her.

NICKY. Who?

RHONDA. Your mother.

NICKY. I didn't tell her about it, any more than you've told yours. I said someone in the Crowd thought he had a good reason . . .

RHONDA. I'll go and see her.

NICKY. She'll ask me how I feel about you and then she'll do what I've done—offer to pay.

RHONDA. Your father then? You've always said he's kind.

NICKY. Yes, but sensible too.

RHONDA. Sensible means letting the money take care of everything?

NICKY. When it can.

RHONDA. It can't—not everything.

NICKY. Most. Why else does everybody want it?

RHONDA. You talk as though it would be as easy as—paying for a licence.

NICKY. It won't be easy for you, I know that.

RHONDA. It will for you. Just find a doctor and sign a cheque.
    A door slams off camera.

NICKY [*shrugging*] That's the way it is. Men are luckier. [*Girl's voice off*] Rhonda, you in?

RHONDA. No! [*She is quiet. Long pause*]

NICKY. I didn't force you, or anything.

RHONDA [*hardly audible*] No.

NICKY. And it's not as though I was the first.

RHONDA. No. [*Pause*] It's all right, Nicky. You and I couldn't make a marriage.

NICKY. That's what I've been telling you.

RHONDA. I've heard at last. Forget I ever suggested it.
    Nicky comes to her, bends down and kisses her cheek. She stares ahead.

NICKY. Shall I speak to this doctor, then?

RHONDA. No. I spoke to mine this morning.

NICKY. But yours says . . .

RHONDA. Mine says—we're safe. It was a scare, but it's over and there's nothing.

NICKY. No danger?

RHONDA. Nothing.

NICKY. Is it certain?

RHONDA. Yes.

NICKY. And you knew, but you let me go on thinking . . .

RHONDA. I wanted to know for sure if there was any hope with you. Don't worry. I could never have carried it through . . .

NICKY. And don't you worry either, dear. I'd never marry on a scare.

RHONDA. I know that now.

NICKY. Thank God. I don't mind telling you, I worried like hell about it. Things wouldn't have been the same afterwards. . . . But as it is, everything's the same as it *was*.

RHONDA. The same as it was, you said?

NICKY. Yes, back where we were before . . . aren't we?

RHONDA [*laughing*] Oh, Nicky! Let's go and meet the Crowd, shall we? Then you'll be happy. . . . [*Rhonda exits*]

NICKY [*half to himself*] What's the matter. . . .

Act Two

Later in the evening. Lights, cars, people. Maurice's car, small and Continental.

Inside Maurice's car, Maurice is driving, Tricia sitting beside him, Andrew behind them, centre. The car radio is playing jazz and for a moment they all sing with it.

MAURICE. Let's crawl along the inside and scratch the paint on that complacent Daimler. [*He turns the wheel and manoeuvres the car, making sound-effects to himself all the time. Suddenly he stops the car with a jolt, leans out of the window and talks to the people in the car alongside*] Call yourself a driver? You couldn't drive a bargain. Madam, you deserve a medal to sit there with him. Jump out quick while we're waiting for these lights. A woman of your age, he ought to be ashamed! Very well, if that's your attitude, pass me my briefcase, Tricia, will you? We'll soon take the wind from their sails. [*Tricia does, he takes out a toy revolver and points it at them*] Now perhaps you'll change your tune? No? Very well, bang, bang! [*He and Andrew make gun-noises. Maurice throws the gun to Tricia*] We must get some caps for this thing. [*He starts the car*]

ANDREW. What incredibly pompous people!

TRICIA. Not a muscle moved!

MAURICE. I might as well not have been wearing this beard and glasses at all. I don't think they even recognized me—and when you consider their appearance and mine, that takes some gall!

ANDREW. D'you know them then?

MAURICE. Know them! He's the potato-crisp manufacturer who tried to get my licence suspended for travelling over thirty in a built-up area.

ANDREW. On the pavement, too, wasn't it?

MAURICE. Admittedly. . . .

TRICIA. Was the woman his wife?

MAURICE. From time to time. Before he picked her up, I believe she slept under the pier in a copy of the Financial Times.

ANDREW. At this moment, he's probably just remembering you.

MAURICE. It comes of living here. Everything's so slow it's hours before they realize anything's happened. I've had enough of it, I can tell you. Look at this for a Saturday.

[*Maurice sees someone on the pavement, and leans across Tricia to yell through the window*]

MAURICE. Zoe, leave that man alone, you never know where he's been.

[*Maurice leans back to look through the back window at her reaction*]

MAURICE [*continuing*] One of my earlier things. . . . What were we saying?

ANDREW. About Saturday night . . .

MAURICE. Oh yeah, Saturday night, and the regulation pint at "The Grapes".

ANDREW. Cy Whelan going?

MAURICE. Yes.

TRICIA. Poor Cy.

ANDREW. He's a loser.

MAURICE. You know what he said to me yesterday?

ANDREW. No.

MAURICE. I don't want to be a sick joke.

ANDREW. No!

MAURICE. Yes. . . . Always "The Grapes" on a Saturday night—ye Gods! The monotony!

Inside "The Grapes". Our view is from behind the bar-counter. A number of young people drinking, someone playing a piano— modern jazz again. We see Cy Whelan and Lotte, seated at the bar. Cy is 22 and a parody of the others, his voice a mixture of tin-pan-alley, Maurice and the South Coast natural to him. Lotte is 19— blonde, pretty, greedy, excitable.

CY. I thought you might just like to say hello . . . this is where we usually meet, you see.

LOTTE. I can't stay too long. I have to meet these people from this International Friends Society.

CY. For the barbecue, yeah. Well, you don't mind if I come along with you, do you? You said you didn't mind.

LOTTE. No, I don't mind.

CY. But I shouldn't mention it to the Crowd. Saturday night, they're sure to ask you if you know of anything.

LOTTE. No, that's okay, I don't want this kind of people along.

ANDREW. Remind me to tell you—I heard a good sick joke yesterday.

TRICIA. Andrew . . .

LOTTE. Darling, buy me another Scotch, h'm?

CY. Sure. Er—Jim!

58

LOTTE [*her hand on his*] You're sweet to me.

CY. Another whisky here.

MAURICE [*off camera*] Make that four more whiskies, Jim.

We move along to take him in, beside Cy, with Tricia and Andrew.

CY. No! One whisky and three beers!

MAURICE. Two beers! It's bad for the breath. Make mine tomato-juice.

CY. One Scotch, two beers, tomato-juice.

MAURICE. Terrible service in this place.

CY. Well, Dad, how've you been?

MAURICE. Not bad, man, not bad. Who's your friend?

CY [*proud but confused*] Oh, this is Lotte—Maurice Goodman, Tricia Blake, Andrew Turtle—Lotte's over from Germany looking after my baby sister.

They mutter hellos while Maurice moves between Cy and Lotte.

MAURICE. And who's looking after you, may I ask?

LOTTE. I can look after myself.

MAURICE. Too bad.

LOTTE [*receiving her drink*] Cheers, Cy!

MAURICE. But this man who buys you whisky—what d'you know about him, have you had him screened?

LOTTE [*ogling Cy*] He is a very nice boy.

MAURICE. Nice! He's educationally sub-normal.

CY [*delighted, putting up his hand*] Sir's telling tales!

MAURICE. Put your hand down, back to your place, you brat! This boy's one claim to fame is two years on Salisbury Plain, during which he was mentioned in despatches for being the only man on his whole unit who could find Stonehenge on an Ordnance Map. Yes, he came back a hero—[*Cy sings "Land of Hope and Glory" as background*] but the world, the world was disillusioned, heroes were ten-a-penny. His white-haired Dad—

CY. Ginger!

MAURICE. His auburn-haired Father gave him a partnership in his timber business . . .

CY. But was I lumbered?

MAURICE. No! He had a vocation—he became a street photographer. And now you can see him any day on the Promenade, a lonely figure with a wistful smile . . .

CY. "Picture, lady, take your picture?"

MAURICE. And that's the way it is with heroes . . .

We move along to Andrew and Tricia as Nicky and Rhonda arrive.

59

NICKY. This place seems dead tonight.

ANDREW. Cy and Maurice are doing that bloody awful turn again.

NICKY. God! Two beers, please.

TRICIA. Rhonda, hullo, darling!

NICKY. Trish, I've told you not to be so gushing. Anyone would think you hadn't met for years.

RHONDA. Hullo, dear. Wotcher, mate.

ANDREW. Hullo.

RHONDA. Looking very brown.

ANDREW. Open air work, finishing the airport.

RHONDA. Freddie told me it was nearly ready. You know Freddie Gardner, Trish, he was in my first year at Art-School. Doing very well now—big car, tuppence to talk to him.

ANDREW. Yeah, I've seen him around up there, bit of a creep, I thought.

TRICIA. Oh, no, he was terribly handsome . . .

RHONDA. He's got fat.

TRICIA. What a shame.

ANDREW. 'Course, he never comes to take tea with us lads in the shack. Not that I blame him—it's horrible.

RHONDA. I know, Trish, what I meant to tell you. It's pretty certain you'll be the Arts Queen this year.

TRICIA. Oh, Rhonda, is it definite? [*Nicky makes a mocking expression at her enthusiasm*] I know it's nothing really. The whole carnival's utterly pathetic, but what else is there.

NICKY. Horrible Dutchmen and pirates and sweaty men in women's underwear.

ANDREW. And most of them paralytic on half-a-pint at the Arts Ball.

RHONDA. Yes, and you two paying fifteen bob for tickets.

ANDREW. For the kicks, let's face it, only the kicks.

RHONDA. Well, I was Queen last year and it's marvellous.

ANDREW. You couldn't see yourself on that horrible float—what was it meant to be?

RHONDA. Cleopatra's barge . . . [*she is laughing too*]

NICKY. The eunuchs were certainly convincing.

TRICIA. Anyway, this year that won't apply, because Rhonda's designing it.

RHONDA. I'll probably have to turn it in, dear . . . there are so many other things to think about.

We close on Nicky, who is looking along the bar. We follow his glance—moving towards Lotte.

MAURICE. And you're quite sure you've heard of no parties tonight?

LOTTE. Quite sure . . . thank you.

MAURICE. Well, I must go to work. [*To Cy, quietly*] Do you want to be a sick joke? What did you bring her here for, to prove something?

CY. What d'you mean?

MAURICE. You'll never learn, will you?

He moves off. Cy looks after him nervously, then closes up to Lotte.

CY. D'you feel like going now?

LOTTE. In a minute—have you got another cigarette?

CY. Sure. Maurice is a character, don't you think?

LOTTE. Not really. He is like one boy who doesn't want to grow up. I meet a lot of them in England. We don't have them any more in Germany.

CY. Maurice is incredibly sophisticated!

LOTTE. What does he do for a living?

CY. Nothing. His old man supports him.

LOTTE. Why?

CY. He's one of the old-type Liberals. You wouldn't know about them. He drove an ambulance in the Spanish War or something and married an Austrian refugee. He believes in democracy and all that jazz.

LOTTE. Doesn't Maurice like him, then?

CY. Too much. That's the trouble—it's inhibiting. Maurice should be a top lyric-writer by now, but his old man's always there.

LOTTE. He's a spoilt boy.

NICKY [*moving between them*] Who's this?

CY. Maurice. She says . . .

NICKY. She's right. I'm Nicky, hello.

LOTTE. I'm Lotte.

CY. She's from Germany, looking after my sister.

NICKY. I was there in '48 with my Mother—she was playing in musical-comedy in Berlin.

LOTTE. I'm from Berlin. Is your Mother an actress?

NICKY. She was.

CY. I guess it's time we were going, Lotte.

LOTTE. Just a minute. Why don't you buy me another drink?

NICKY. I'll do it. Jim, a Scotch here. Anything, Cy?

CY. No. We've got to be going.

NICKY. Where, in such a hurry?

CY. Nowhere special.

LOTTE. A barbecue on the beach. These International Friends and all that sort of thing. It isn't charged for coming in, you know . . .

CY. Hey, Lotte!

NICKY. Actually I'm with Rhonda.

LOTTE. Why don't you all come?

MAURICE [*arriving back*] It's no go the Yogi man, no go Blavatski.

CY. Who said that—Aldous Huxley?

MAURICE. Aldous Huxley! The only author he's ever heard of!

CY. False, utterly false!

MAURICE. Well, friends, the outlook is very bleak. These chicks are insufferable! "We don't want your Crowd along," they tell me, "you kill every party." "Girls, do me a favour," I said, "these parties are dead before we get there."

NICKY. Maurice, I've got news for you. We're invited to a bonfire— a beach barbecue.

MAURICE. A bonfire?

NICKY. Of International Friends.

MAURICE. That's marvellous! That's great! I can smell the sacrificial flesh already. The only summer resort with its own auto-da-fé! Hey, Dads, it's Frying Tonight!

Moves off.

NICKY [*following him*] See you later.

LOTTE. 'Bye.

CY. You said you wouldn't mention it. I don't always want to be with them. I suppose an evening alone with me was not . . .

LOTTE. Don't be mean to me, Cy, darling, or I shan't like you. I'm so silly sometimes. Try to be kind to me, I don't know what I'm doing.

As she caresses him carelessly, we mix to a section of the beach. People are sitting round a bonfire and far off someone is singing to a guitar.

Rhonda is seated, a coat around her shoulders, light flickering on her face. Sounds of people talking, laughing, speaking and singing in various languages continue through this scene. Andrew arrives and sits beside her. He shows her two sausages.

ANDREW. Banger?

RHONDA. No, thanks, Andrew.

ANDREW. I love 'em. Two meals I never tire of—sausages and fish-and-chips. Thank God there's no spaghetti or anything here.

RHONDA. You being the Average British Workman again?

ANDREW. D'you blame me honestly—in this international atmosphere?

RHONDA. You used to like international atmospheres.

ANDREW. Yeah, not any more.

RHONDA. What about the Italian suits?

ANDREW. I can't help it if they make good clothes. Everyone has a way with something. The Germans, for instance, with sausages.

RHONDA. All right, you've convinced me. I'll try one.

ANDREW. There you are.

We see Lotte joking with Nicky in the background.

LOTTE. Darling . . . I never said that.

ANDREW. Mostly Germans here tonight, you notice. Bit too hearty for the Latins.

RHONDA. Yes, the Germans are doing all right.

ANDREW. She's no good.

RHONDA. No good for what?

ANDREW. Nicky for a start.

RHONDA. I wonder who is.

ANDREW. We had to come on to him in the end, didn't we?

RHONDA. And Tricia.

ANDREW. Yeah, her too.

RHONDA. She likes you.

ANDREW. Mad about me.

RHONDA. She wants to marry you. [*He looks at her quickly*] She told me.

ANDREW. Oh.

RHONDA. We used to tell each other everything.

ANDREW. Still do, by the sound of it.

RHONDA. No, it's not the same as it was.

ANDREW. She asked her old man this afternoon and he said he doesn't agree with people marrying outside their class—that's the okay jargon for people without much lolly. But even she won't see sense. She wants me to run away with her and marry her in Dorset or somewhere, like those American films, you know, with the J.P. in a nightshirt.

RHONDA. Don't make fun of her.

ANDREW. I can't help it tonight. Nicky makes me sick the way he's behaving, he should be over that kind of thing by now. You and I must have been mad to fall for a set-up like that.

RHONDA. I didn't fall for any set-up. I fell for him.

ANDREW. Are you trying to tell me the glamorous Mother and military Father and the Jaguar meant nothing? And Nicky being his rich uncle's favourite nephew?

RHONDA. Trish will come in for some of it. Is that all you wanted from her?

ANDREW. No, I'm fond of her, you know that, but she's a part of it, you can't separate her, that's unrealistic. When I first met them it was the nearest thing I'd ever known to High Class—except the days I'd paid my half-crown admission to a Stately Home. Remember the one we went to in Hampshire? Yes. Remember the peacocks showing off their feathers on the terrace, and you said how beautiful they looked and I agreed with you. I meant it, too, but even as I said it, I'd gladly have broken their beautiful necks. And if you'd asked me why, I couldn't have told you, until one night at Nicky's his mother was leading off about some party she'd been to when she was a girl.

All about the carriages and the arriving and the people who were there—opera-singers and prize-fighters, princesses and comedians. And the electric lighting laid on for the week-end to illuminate the lake and the fireworks that fell in showers over the Japanese garden and the procession of flunkeys bringing baskets full of fish to feed the decorative birds that lived there. Trouble was, I kept thinking Mum and Dad were kids about the same time and how much food did their families live on? D'you know Mum's old man hit her when she told him she was going to join the Salvation Army? So she ran away and married Dad and they went up North. And the first thing the sailors did when Dad started preaching was throw him in the harbour. They wouldn't let him climb out either, till the police came. He still coughs all through the winter. So I suppose that's why I could have strangled those bloody peacocks.

RHONDA. But your mother told me they were happier then—there was something to fight for.

ANDREW. Oh, yes, no one throws them in the water *now* when they sing their hymns on a Sunday. Nobody even listens. They didn't even blame me when I was fourteen and told them I wasn't going to beat their drum any more. 'Course, their lives are still better than ours, for all that. Better, but so damned unattractive!

RHONDA. Have you told Tricia what your parents do?

ANDREW. *You* haven't?

RHONDA [*laughing*] No.

ANDREW. No one knows but you. I mean, it would be such an easy joke. You know, I've always dreaded that coming out.

RHONDA. You are funny.

ANDREW. You going to mother me?

RHONDA. I can't help liking you.

ANDREW. That's good. I reckon we made a mistake falling for that set-up, you and me.

RHONDA. I didn't fall for any set-up. I fell for him. But it's finished now.

ANDREW. Yeah?

RHONDA. We broke it off this afternoon.

ANDREW. D'you mean it?

RHONDA. I'm going away, that's best. I want a change, but he doesn't care, why should he?

ANDREW. When you going?

RHONDA. Tomorrow. Things at home have been worse than ever. I only waited to see if he had what my Dad calls intentions. Now there's nothing to keep me. Home's unbearable, my sister's more of an example than ever, she looks older than Mum already—and you ought to see her bottom drawer!

ANDREW. No, thanks very much just the same.

RHONDA. And the old man's a Foreman now.

ANDREW. That was only a matter of time, wasn't it? Remember the night he threw me out when I laughed at the General or whatever he was on telly?

RHONDA. He put me straight about modern art yesterday.

ANDREW. Yes. I don't blame you for going. I ought to go as well. Trouble is, I *like* my parents.

RHONDA. I know.

ANDREW. It's inhibiting. What time train?

RHONDA. Eleven-ten in the morning. And when I get to London, I'll stay in a hostel and get taken on as a supply teacher for a few months. Till I learn the ropes.

ANDREW. Sounds great.

RHONDA. I can't help how it sounds.

ANDREW. Got a cigarette?

And we move along the group, from face to face, the young men and women, talking, eating, one playing a guitar, then Cy Whelan singing a blues. A few more people, then Nicky and Lotte. She is drunk, he is looking towards Rhonda.

65

LOTTE. Why don't we go for a ride in your car?

NICKY [*shaking his head*] Wouldn't be fair to Rhonda. [*Lotte puts her hand on his shoulder and moves her face closer to his*] Anyway, I have to keep an eye on my sister.

LOTTE [*impatiently*] Sister!

NICKY. Isn't there anyone who keeps an eye on you?

LOTTE [*shrugging*] The boy my parents wanted me to marry. That's why I came to England—to study. [*She giggles*]

NICKY [*he sighs*] Listen, whatever happens between us, let me tell you that I never fall in love.

LOTTE. You're crazy, darling, I never mentioned it.

NICKY. Don't then. Don't try to trap me, that's all. Then everything will be fine. I hate to be involved with people . . . [*Maurice throws a stone*]

ANDREW. Hey watch it!

Again we move along, this time to Tricia and Maurice. She, too, is looking towards the others.

MAURICE. So these fellows are teeing up, when an adjutant rushes up with "Pardon me, would you mind letting the President play straight through? War has just been declared." How's that?

She is still looking away, but now turns round.

MAURICE. Must have been the way I told it.

TRICIA. Sorry, Maurice, I wasn't listening.

MAURICE. What *do* you see in him? He's quite attractive, I know that, but you should aim for something higher. I know I'm slightly grotesque to look at, but that's all part of the plan—a plan—a plan that so far seems to appeal to no one but myself. Can you tell me why?

TRICIA. Why what?

MAURICE. I'm unsuccessful. I'm clever, energetic and well-dressed, but nowhere. Can you tell me why? It's ruining my health, of course. Honestly, between you and me, I reckon it won't be many months before I have an ulcer. [*Takes sweets from pocket*] Peppermint? [*She ignores it, he takes one and puts the rest back*] It's amazing just how long you can hold on, waiting, waiting for someone to pay attention, dwelling on your obsession, nursing it, feeding it, changing its water.

TRICIA. Perhaps you haven't any talent?

MAURICE. I've thought of that. Another terrible thing is you can't surprise me any more. I've thought of everything before it happens. Of course I have the talent. What do *you* think?

TRICIA. I don't know anything. Why ask me? [*She is almost crying*]
Only this afternoon, I thought everything was fine. And now look
at it! What's wrong? Is it the Crowd, the idea of being a gang?

MAURICE. Could be.

TRICIA. Why don't we break away? Kenny broke away to marry
Rosemary, remember?

MAURICE. Such a plain girl!

TRICIA. They're very happy, aren't they? You're not, neither are
the others. Staying with the Crowd is just a way of not growing up,
that's all it is.

MAURICE. It's you that haven't grown up, dear—that's the last
thing Nicky wants—you're his better half, his innocence, he
protects your honour as though it's his.

TRICIA. I'm not his innocence. I can look after myself.

MAURICE. I've waited months to hear you say that. I've always
longed to see you stand up for yourself. Trish, I know you think
I'm always kidding you . . .

TRICIA [*putting her hand on his*] Don't!

MAURICE. That calls for another peppermint. [*He eats*]

TRICIA. Maurice—

MAURICE. Yes?

TRICIA. Take me home, then.

    Fade out.

Act Three

*A window of Nicky's room from the street. Nicky steps into the
sunshine, wearing shirt and trousers, holding a scotch in one hand.*

*Inside the room. The divan, centre, is unmade, newspapers are
strewn about, some breakfast things on a tray on the floor. Tricia
enters, wearing shirt and slacks. She folds a paper and puts it on a
chair.*

NICKY [*turning into the room*] Morning, Trish . . .

TRICIA. I've seen you before. I brought your breakfast in. Where's
the tray?

NICKY. On the floor by the bed. What's the matter?

TRICIA. I'm washing up.

NICKY. I heard you—it was deafening. What's the bad mood
about?

TRICIA. Bad mood?

NICKY. You're being naive again. When you're in a mood, you always throw this big domestic number.

TRICIA [*collecting tray, etc.*] Mother has mal di testa, it's Sunday, so Sally's away. Someone has to do it.

NICKY [*moving across, quicker than usual*] I'll help.

TRICIA. Finish the treatment. The fräulein will be here before you're ready.

NICKY. You don't like her?

TRICIA. She's cheap.

She goes, letting the door slam behind her. Nicky stops, finishes his drink, continues on across the room, puts the empty glass on the bar counter. He crosses back to the divan, picking up newspapers. He puts them on the bookshelf and takes a cigarette. Lighting it, he sees the sculptured head. We move to a close-up of his cold disappointed face.

Mix to Rhonda's room. She is packing slowly, reluctantly. Her suitcase on the bed is full, but she takes a few metal clothes-hangers from the curtained partition. The room, lacking her additions, looks bleak. She takes from the bed a picture of Nicky, looks at it, puts it in the drawer, which sticks when she tries to close it. The church-clock chimes half-past and she looks at her watch. She stares again into the sheet, is about to close her suitcase, when she thinks again of the photograph, takes it, packs it, closes the case and goes to the door.

Nicky's room. We see Cy, at the record-player, closing the lid as a jazz tune begins.

CY. Have you seen the new featherweight tone-arms they're producing nowadays? Man, they're absolutely the most! And the latest stereophonic tests have proved conclusively . . .

TRICIA [*coming in*] Hullo, Cy.

CY. Hullo. Proved conclusively that . . .

TRICIA. Help me tidy this room a little, will you?

CY. You're talking to the man with the tidiest billet on Salisbury Plain. Week after week we won our thirty-sixes . . .

As they begin to make the bed, we move away to find Nicky in the window-seat with Lotte.

LOTTE. . . . No, he didn't say a thing. I have only to say I'm a silly girl and give him a kiss, he forgets all that's been happening, you know. He even asked me up to his room this morning to see his photographic equipment. Have you seen his room?

NICKY. No.

LOTTE. Full of drums and masks and this kind of thing . . . and one day when I came in without knocking, he was in front of the glass with a chest-expander. [*Nicky turns his head away. She looks towards the others*] Shall I help you with the room?

TRICIA. We can manage.

LOTTE [*to Nicky*] Your sister doesn't like me, does she?

NICKY. No.

Maurice comes in wearing dark glasses.

MAURICE. You people should be ashamed of yourselves. It's the first chance of the year to wear the full tropical equipment.

CY. The new purple glasses are great, Dad.

MAURICE. Do they make me look mysterious enough, that's the point.

CY. They're the complete Mephistopheles!

MAURICE. Only snag is—I can't see a thing! Is that a bed you're making? No, don't tell me, not ten minutes ago, The South Coast's most continually potential song-writer was perspiring in a pre-historic sleep.

NICKY. Maurice, there's a cleaning tag on the back of your jacket!

MAURICE. What? [*Whipping his jacket off immediately, he searches for it*] A filthy lie!

LOTTE [*laughing*] And you believed it.

MAURICE. Who was it said the Germans have no sense of humour? Guten Tag—Fräulein—Burnt any good books lately?

Tricia laughs.

TRICIA. Hello. . . .

MAURICE. Hello. How's the chill today? You were shivering in the car last night!

TRICIA. Haven't had time to think about it. Mother's not too good, I'm running the house.

MAURICE. Have a peppermint—peculiarly strong—do you a world of good.

TRICIA. No.

MAURICE. Half then. Share one with me. [*Tricia takes half, goes. Maurice eats the other*]

NICKY. Did you take her home last night?

MAURICE. Yes, didn't you notice? And if it isn't indelicate, what happened to that bonfire after we left last night?

CY. The tide came in and put it out. After that, Lotte and I went home, but Andrew and Rhonda were still there, and some of those

Nordic people stripped to their bathing suits and waded in. It was raining slightly.

MAURICE. Thanks for that incredibly boring speech.

CY. Well, you asked me.

MAURICE. You needn't have answered. And may I ask where you met up with those funny trousers you're wearing?

CY. Nothing funny, Dad. Just a three-year-old pair of trousers tapered recently to the new width.

MAURICE. A Government job, by the look of it.

LOTTE. Well, anyhow, how can you talk—with that stupid little beard?

NICKY. Don't bother, Lotte. It'll do no good.

LOTTE. Why not? I can't stand seeing anyone made a fool of like that—by a . . .

NICKY. It'll be embarrassing, that's all.

MAURICE. No, let her finish, Nicky. I'm interested. Made a fool of like that by a—what?

NICKY. Drop it, Maurice!

MAURICE. By a non-Aryan, non-working type layabout?

LOTTE [loud] You wouldn't last ten minutes in Germany—you know that?

MAURICE [triumphant] Then give the little lady a Swastika! And I'd like to move a vote of thanks for this timely reminder of the virtues of racial purity! Mumble, mumble . . .

CY. Rhubarb, rhubarb! [They clap]

    Andrew enters.

MAURICE. And here's another member for the rally! Come along, · there, mate, this is better than the barbecue!

ANDREW. I hope so.

MAURICE. You didn't enjoy it? You surprise me. As a matter of fact, you surprise me coming at all to-day.

ANDREW. Why?

MAURICE. Oh, I don't know. I didn't feel you were exactly "with us" last night.

ANDREW. Anyhow, I'm with you to-day, as long as you're going on the beach. I dropped my bag in your car as I passed.

CY. I've brought the camera.

ANDREW. Great! Tricia here?

NICKY. Helping Mother.

ANDREW. Did you see me coming?

NICKY. Yes.

ANDREW. And warned her to go?

NICKY. Do you think she does what I tell her?

ANDREW. Not if she's got any sense—after last night——

NICKY [*moving*] Who's talking about last night?

MAURICE. Andrew, did you bring the straw hats?

ANDREW. What?

MAURICE. Doesn't matter. There's a load of wonderful junk in the back of my car.

We have come in now for a close-up of Andrew. He is tense, upset by his quarrel with Nicky but frustrated by not bringing it to a climax. Maurice goes on talking, while we remain on Andrew.

MAURICE. Listen! I meant to tell you, this wonderful pair of old dears on the prom this morning. One said "Did you see the play on telly, dear, last night"? "No—was it nice"? "Very nice—all about injections". [*Outside, a church clock strikes the quarter*] "H'mm—was there a Chinaman in it?" "Not that I can remember." "Pity! I do like a play with a Chinaman."

NICKY. Maurice, every now and then you tell a joke, and it's terrible, believe me.

Enter Tricia.

ANDREW. Hullo.

TRICIA. Oh. Hullo.

ANDREW. You coming on the beach to-day?

TRICIA. No, Mummy's in one of her states, I'm afraid. She's run out of Scotch. Isn't there a bottle under the counter, Nicky?

ANDREW. What happened to you last night? First I knew, you were tramping up the beach with Maurice.

TRICIA. Why not? I'd spent the evening with him.

ANDREW. I meant to say I was sorry.

The jazz record has finished. There has been a minute or so without music. Now outside in the street. A small Salvation Army band begins to play a hymn.

You see, what happened . . .

[*He pauses, hearing the music*]

TRICIA. What happened was pretty obvious, I should have thought.

MAURICE. Yessir, you behaved like a cad.

TRICIA. I'd rather you didn't try any explanations.

The band plays louder.

CY. What about another record? Got one of those Brandenburg Concertos, Nicky? That Bach is really cool . . .

ANDREW [*suddenly*] Yes, put on another record, Cy, that's right.

MAURICE. Just a minute! God, this is really an English Sunday!

We see them at the window from the street. Nicky and Lotte in front, Maurice moving over to join them.

MAURICE. Not only church bells and a guilty taste in the mouth and the smell of a thousand roasts, but a mission band on the street corner. Look at them! Who d'you think they hope to save in such a bourgeois district?

CY. Men, they're traditional!

MAURICE. With the maestro himself on the old cornet.

LOTTE. You shouldn't laugh at them.

CY. My trombone's in the car. I've a mind to go and sit in for a chorus.

NICKY. Frankly, Cy, I've always felt the Salvation Army was about your level.

They are now grouped in the window, from left to right, Nicky, Lotte, Maurice, Cy, Tricia, Andrew. Andrew has come more slowly.

MAURICE. Be quiet, will you? The horn player's announcing the next number. Hey, let's shout requests.

CY. Dad, play "Didn't He Ramble"?

We close in on Andrew's face as he looks out at the street scene. Then we move along the row of faces away from him.

MAURICE. Professor, what about a few of the old Vocal Gems from Tannhäuser?

CY. He's turning round.

TRICIA. What's the point, that sort of person, the more you persecute him, the more he likes it.

NICKY. Yes, a martyrdom.

CY. The old girl with the concertina's telling him to take no notice.

MAURICE. That's the wife, you can see that. Leave him alone—he's doing all right. Yes sir, good morning, sir, top of the morning. Nice old boy really.

NICKY. God, they're all so nice! It's sad about nice people. I can't bear to look at them.

LOTTE. Well, at least you must admit they've got enthusiasm.

NICKY. I hate enthusiasm. There's far too much of it—even now. What's needed is a lot more apathy. That's what's wrong with you Germans—you bother too much.

MAURICE. Look, now he's giving them the commercial. Friends, I know what it's like to be a slave of drink.

CY. Marvellous!

MAURICE. That's about it. Come on, I'm bored with this.

CY. Hey, where's Andrew?

TRICIA. He's gone, I think.

MAURICE [*shrugging*] One of those funny moods, you know what he's like.

TRICIA. He brushed my arm as he went by. I wanted to stop him, but I didn't even turn my head.

NICKY. Tricia, that's the way, be proud! [*He comes to her and talks to her as she faces away*] Make him feel it the way you did last night when he was with her. I know it hurt, I know all about you. But I was glad he did that, because now you can see he's not for you. Believe me, in a week or two, you'll come to me and tell me I was right.

TRICIA [*turning on him fiercely*] You were never right, you were never right!

  She goes out. Pause.

CY. What's the fuss about anyway? Can't he even leave the room? He'll be back in a minute!

MAURICE. To hell with him! We've had this sort of thing before. He never brings it off—it's part of his good openfaced Charlie act. He'll turn up later on the beach. And we're missing all the best of the sun, I tell you, cooped up here. Trains from town are arriving all the time and if there are going to be any Sunday chicks, we must be there very soon.

CY. Are you coming in my car, Lotte?

  Maurice laughs despairingly.

LOTTE. I don't think I'm coming at all, Cy, I have one or two girl friends to see. Meet you on the beach later.

CY. You, Nicky?

NICKY. Not now. The beach—later.

CY. [*awkwardly*] See you on the beach, then.

MAURICE [*grinning*] Yes, later.

LOTTE. Auf Wiedersehen.

MAURICE. My God, that's all it needed.

  Cy and Maurice go. We close on Nicky, who has not moved since Tricia's exit. Now Lotte comes up behind him and puts her arms round him.

LOTTE. Nicky——

NICKY. Uh?

LOTTE. Nicky—forget it, darling.

NICKY. Help me then.

73

He turns to embrace her as we mix to the railway station, still bright sunshine. A train is waiting to leave the platform, another has arrived.

A close-up picture of the promenade and pier. We pull back to see that it is a photographic view in an empty carriage compartment. Rhonda slides open the door and puts her case on the rack. She looks eagerly through the window and checks the time again. We hear an unintelligible station announcement. Rhonda steps out of the carriage door and looks up the platform. Suddenly she climbs back into the carriage and hides just inside the door. We see Maurice and Cy by the barrier moving alongside the train.

MAURICE. The eleven-five's just in. I'm sure that's the one the revue company will be arriving on. It's absolutely vital to impress them—nothing amateur, you follow me, very smooth and confident. We'll make our contact first with the showgirls, which will be diverting in itself, then through them, make contact with the producer. There's no telling where this could lead. And then to Hell with Nicky!

CY. That's the way I feel, too—to Hell with Nicky!

MAURICE. Please, no broken-hearted clown performances. And Cy do me a favour, don't say a word or you'll ruin everything. Got your cigarettes?

CY. Yeah.

MAURICE. That's fine—just offer those round. Plenty of film in your camera?

CY. Yeah.

MAURICE. Great.

Another unintelligible station announcement. Maurice mimics.

MAURICE. And here's another announcement—will the vicar please go to the refreshment hut—

CY. Where his wife is lying dangerously drunk?

MAURICE [*looking at him in surprise*] Not bad, not bad. Look, there they are. Let's go!

And they do.

Inside the compartment. Rhonda is seated, huddled into herself, obviously doing her best to control her feelings till the last possible moment. The whistle blows and the train is heard to move. She looks hopelessly through the window. She is almost in tears, we hear the door slide open, she controls herself again.

ANDREW. I nearly missed it.

He throws himself down beside her, exhausted.

74

RHONDA. Andrew!

ANDREW. I came straight from Nicky's . . .

RHONDA. I looked for you.

ANDREW. It was all very sudden, you know.

[*Shadows of things the train passes cross their faces*] One moment I was going on the beach, the next I was belting for the train. Only got this—no other clothes. [*He shows the grip*] Only hope there's a heatwave in London . . . otherwise . . .

RHONDA. Maurice and Cy were on the platform.

ANDREW. I know.

RHONDA. When I saw them without you, I thought you must've decided . . .

ANDREW. I jumped in the first carriage to avoid them, just took the risk you hadn't changed your mind, came down through the corridors . . . Any cigarettes?

RHONDA. No.

ANDREW. How about money?

RHONDA. All I've saved.

ANDREW. I'm pretty flush, but it's all at home. I'll send for it. My clothes too. I'm glad I came, though . . . [*He is talking nervously, she is silent because she is restraining tears*] I could see another Sunday starting, another week, another season, another good intention biting the dust.

[*The train enters a tunnel with a scream. Darkness. He switches on the light above them, sees Rhonda sobbing, pulls her towards him. He breaks a cigarette in half and gives her half*] Rhonda—you still thinking about him?

RHONDA. Everything. I'm sorry, I've been saving all this up. I still love him.

ANDREW. That's all right.

RHONDA. This isn't going to be a picnic.

ANDREW. Well—picnics—you know—they're all right for a time.

We mix to Nicky's room. Nicky is in the shower, behind glass.

Lotte is under the sheets in Nicky's divan, which is untidy again. She is smoking.

A window. Tricia sitting at it, very still.

Crowd on the beach with Maurice and Cy in funny hats, Cy is taking a photograph, they move to other groups taking photographs. We see the beach, the pier, the sea, the shot we began with.

The jazz stops. We hear only the sea, then nothing.

Fade out.

75

THE QUEEN'S CORPORAL

by

GRAEME KENT

CAST

SERGEANT MILLIGAN	*Warren Mitchell*
SERGEANT TAYLOR	*Stuart Saunders*
SERGEANT VALE	*Daniel Moynihan*
STAFF SERGEANT WATSON	*Sam Kydd*
SERGEANT CLARKE	*David Andrews*
SERGEANT O'MALLY	*Rory MacDermot*
STAFF SERGEANT BELL	*Peter Welch*
REGIMENTAL SERGEANT MAJOR DRUMMOND	*John Barrie*
COMPANY SERGEANT MAJOR STRAW	*Russell Waters*

DIRECTOR	*James Ormerod*
DESIGNER	*Darrell Lass*

DIRECTOR'S NOTE

Working on this play by Graeme Kent was a stimulating experience, and not least because of the formidable number of aspects which presented themselves the more one considered the right approach to it.

It was a story of army life in the sergeants' mess, and it was also a study of boredom and frustration. It was a story of good and evil; and it was a morality play and a mystery play; it was a crime play, and—in the last scene with the court-martial—it ended by becoming a gripping trial play.

The question was how to condense and highlight these various facets and also do justice to the brooding sullen atmosphere of idleness and boredom at the end of a war in a foreign country which the play so powerfully summoned. The reason, in fact, why I enjoyed doing this play so much was because of the challenge it offered if one was to get across its full flavour.

JAMES ORMEROD.

A BIOGRAPHY OF GRAEME KENT

Graeme Kent was born in 1933 and was educated at Portsmouth Grammar School and Westminster College. *The Queen's Corporal* is his first play, the rough draft of which was written while serving as a National Service sergeant in Korea. It was not until he was demobilized and had begun teaching in various schools in the provinces that he finally completed it. He has now written his first novel.

ACTION

The action of the play takes place in the following sets:

(1) The Mess
(2) The Verandah
(3) R.S.M.'s office
(4) The Garden.

TIME

The time is the present.

Act One

The scene is an undamaged Korean dwelling house which has been taken over by the Army as the Sergeants' Mess. The main living room has been converted into a recreation room and bar. The interior is a mixture of the original structure in Korean style and newly erected hardboard partitioning. The windows are typically Korean with no glass and covered in ornate lattice work. In the room we see Milligan, Taylor, and Watson. Milligan is a dried-up little man who bolsters up his precarious position as mess buffoon with a lot of hard drinking. Taylor is tubby and cheerful and the kind of man who always looks for the easiest way out. Watson is a staff sergeant, bitter and disappointed and somewhat better educated than his colleagues. They are all gathered round a piano in the corner singing raucously.

For he's my brother Sylveste (and what's he got?)
He's got a row of forty medals on his chest (big chest)
He fought forty niggers in the West
He takes no rest.
Bigger de man, strong as a bull, aye, aye, don't push, just shove, plenty room for you and me.
He's got an arm like a leg and a punch that would sink a battleship (big ship)
It takes all the army and the navy to put the wind up Sylveste.

MILLIGAN. All together now. [*And they all sing*]

For he's my brother Sylveste (and what's he got?)
He's got a row of forty medals on his chest (big chest)
He fought forty niggers in the West
He takes no rest.
Bigger de man, strong as a bull, aye, aye . . .

Milligan and Taylor get up and dance, and the song peters out.
MILLIGAN. Buy us a drink, Jim.
TAYLOR. You'll be lucky.
WATSON. What do you do with your money, Milly?
MILLIGAN. Two cow-dung sandwiches, please; one with mustard.
WATSON. I've got a young daughter at home with more sense than you.

81

MILLIGAN [*A flash of interest*] How old?

WATSON. Who?

MILLIGAN. Your daughter.

WATSON. Seventeen; why?

MILLIGAN. How do you fancy me as a son-in-law?

WATSON. That'll be the day.

MILLIGAN. Buy us a drink, Jim; go on, be a pal.

TAYLOR. You'll get sweet Fanny Adams; you're half cut already.

MILLIGAN. Didn't you know, I'm recovering from the war.

TAYLOR. Stop swinging it.

MILLIGAN. No, straight up. The war's over, mate, and I've got the medal to prove it. And there ain't going to be no more fighting, I got it from the C.O. when he brought me cup of tea this morning. "Sergeant Milligan", he says, "the chinkies aren't going to bother us ever again for the simple reason that they've forgot we're here. Everybody has forgot it, that's why we ain't gone home." I believe him too. We're just going to rot here, straight up for the rest of our born days. "Milligan", says my pal, the C.O., "the infantry went home with drums beating six months ago, the sappers have packed up, even the chinkies have had it away; but you and me", he says, "you and me and one or two more like that skiving git Jim Taylor, we're going to stay on for ever and ever amen."

WATSON. You should worry; my tour of duty was up six months ago.

MILLIGAN. Mean to say you didn't volunteer for this? I thought we all stayed on here 'cause we didn't want to stop fighting, even when we'd only got each other to fight.

TAYLOR. Shut up, Milly. We said we weren't going to talk about it.

MILLIGAN. There's only us here——

WATSON. Aw, shut up.

   Watson and Taylor glare at Milligan when the door opens and Tom Vale comes in. He is an intelligent, pleasant young man of twenty. He lowers his kit bag and looks round uncertainly. The others regard him coldly.

WATSON. Is there something we can do for you?

VALE. Well, I was looking for the R.S.M. actually.

MILLIGAN. Oh, actually.

WATSON. He's not here.

VALE. My name's Vale, Tom Vale. I've been posted in.

   This news obviously affects them all considerably.

TAYLOR. Are you sure you've come to the right camp, chum?

VALE. Yes. Number Three Supply and Repair Unit.

WATSON. Have you got a movement order?

VALE. Yes, Staff. [*Hands it to Watson*]

TAYLOR. We weren't expecting anybody.

WATSON [*looks up*] This is pukka. This bloke's a replacement for Reed.

TAYLOR. They haven't wasted much time.

VALE [*he has been watching them, rather puzzled*] They told me at Div Rear I was a replacement. They said someone had had an accident up here.

WATSON. Is that what they said?

VALE. Why, what happened to him, this chap?

WATSON. He had an accident.

VALE. What sort of an accident?

MILLIGAN. A nasty sort.

TAYLOR. All right Milly. [*He sees that Watson wants to be left alone with Vale*] If we're going to have a shufti at those concert party women we'd better be on our way over.

MILLIGAN. You going bonkers or something? We'd never get near 'em.

TAYLOR. 'Course we'll get near them; stands to reason.

WATSON. You never know your luck, Milly.

MILLIGAN. What, with that ruddy mob?

TAYLOR. Come on, you waste half my life you do. See you then, chum.

Taylor and Milligan go on to the verandah.

MILLIGAN. Here, what was all that for? We never said we was going anywhere.

TAYLOR. Couldn't you see Watson wanted to get him on his own?

MILLIGAN. Oh . . . oh.

TAYLOR. Milligan; you act gormless, you talk gormless, and stop me lately if you haven't begun to look gormless.

In the Mess Watson is chatting cautiously to Vale.

WATSON. We're not usually as quiet as this but most of the lads are over at a show in the entertainments tent. They should be back any minute.

VALE. A concert party, eh? Not many of those about now.

WATSON. No, not for us peace-time wallahs. By the way, you don't want to pay too much attention to Milligan. He's a bit of a nut case, paddy field-happy, you know. It's a wonder we haven't all

gone round the bend, the way things are in this set up. It's the
country, it gets you in the end, no doubt about that. Eighteen
months I've been here and there's some who've done even longer.
. . . This your first time in a small outfit?

VALE. Yes, I'm not even sure what you do here.

WATSON. Running repairs, anything too small and too messy for a
base repair job. It's a tricky position. You see, a small camp is
either very good or very bad; and to be blunt I couldn't say that
this was very good.

VALE. What's wrong with it, the officers?

WATSON. Officers? Since when have they had anything to do with it?
It's the senior N.C.O.'s who run any unit. How long have you been
a sergeant?

VALE. Two days.

WATSON. Still a nig-nog. Better wash the dust down. What will it
be? [*Goes to bar*]

VALE. Thanks, I'll have a light ale. But can't I buy you——?

WATSON. Mess etiquette, you know. Officially you're not a member
of the mess until the R.S.M. has welcomed you. And he can't do
that until he comes back from the concert. [*Watson has passed a
bottle to Vale, who pours it*] First time in a small unit, eh? You
won't like it.

VALE. Why not Staff? Cheers.

WATSON. Cheers . . . We're isolated here, up in the hills . . . pretty
well cut off in fact. A hundred men, three officers and nine of us,
not what you'd call a large establishment. Mostly old Regulars.
You a Regular?

VALE. No, I'm a National Serviceman.

WATSON. Oil and water, they don't mix.

VALE. You don't think so?

WATSON. We've got one of your sort here already, name of Clarke . . .
queer lad. Not very happy. Look, I've been thinking. With a bit
of luck I can swing it to get you sent back. We are over strength
as it happens, and if we box clever——

VALE. Hang on a bit, I don't want to go back.

WATSON. If you take my advice you won't want to stay here a day
longer than you can help, believe you me.

VALE. But what's wrong with it?

WATSON. It's a bad camp. [*Vale is silent*] All right then, don't give a
damn. . . . The trouble with your sort is that you should have gone
in for a commission but you were too idle. If you'd done that they

would have made you a buckshee one-pipper and you could have trotted round for your two years having the time of your life and not getting into people's hair. But no, you had to stay in the ranks and get made up on account of your accent and a school certificate. And from then on you're a pain in the neck.

VALE. I'm sorry you feel like that about it.

WATSON. Well, why shouldn't I. I've seen it happen too often; you lads aren't soldiers, you're just civilians in uniform.

Enter Taylor and Milligan, disconsolately.

MILLIGAN.
"Dear Mother, sell the pig and buy me out."
"Dear Son, stay in the army, the pig's dead."
Roll on death, demob's too far away.

WATSON. No luck?

MILLIGAN. What do you think? Show was over already.

WATSON. Where are the others?

TAYLOR. They'll not be long.

WATSON. Well, we'd better get you fixed up with a bed somewhere. Reed, that's the bloke who's gone, used to share my tent. You can have his bunk if you like.

VALE [*surprised*] Thanks very much.

WATSON. Better go across and dump your kit now, then you can come back and meet the others. It's not far.

VALE. Right. [*Rises*] By the way, you didn't tell me. What did happen to Reed?

WATSON [*curtly*] He got drunk, fell in a bren gun pit and cracked his skull open.

VALE. Badly?

WATSON. He's still in hospital. Ready?

VALE. Right with you.

WATSON [*pauses at door*] Watch your step, it's dark outside.

VALE. I will, we don't want another accident, do we?

WATSON [*turns, looks at others*] No, we don't.

Exeunt Watson and Vale. Milligan goes behind the bar.

MILLIGAN. Nosey, ain't he?

TAYLOR. Wouldn't you be, if you walked into this set up?

The door opens and Clarke comes in. He is a nervous, highly-strung youth of twenty.

TAYLOR. Aye aye, Schoolie; enjoy the show?

CLARKE. Not quite up to West End standards.

TAYLOR. I wouldn't know about that.

MILLIGAN. Nor would I, I'm only a dirty common sergeant. [*He goes to get another crate of beer*]

TAYLOR. Look, son, why don't you use your loaf and stay away from the mess for a bit.

CLARKE. Why should I? I pay my mess dues like everyone else.

TAYLOR. Because with things as they are now Bell and O'Mally have got it in for you and I don't blame them either. Coming in here you're just asking for trouble.

CLARKE. If I want to come in here, I shall.

TAYLOR. We've had one accident in here already, you know.

Watson and Vale come back in.

WATSON. That's you fixed up then.

VALE. Yes; thank you, Staff.

Watson and Vale approach bar.

WATSON. Oh, this is Schoolie Clarke—Tom Vale, just posted in.

CLARKE [*warily*] How do you do.

VALE. Pleased to meet you.

Milligan takes his place behind the bar.

WATSON [*moving to table*] Cards up, chips down. . . . Come on Vale, let's see the colour of your money. [*Taylor and Watson sit and begin laying out cards and chips*]

VALE. What are you playing?

WATSON. Rummy. [*Pause*] [*Vale joins them*] R.S.M. will have to see him before he becomes a member of the mess.

TAYLOR. Aye. We'll have to let Drummond see you first.

VALE. Drummond; did you say Drummond?

TAYLOR. That's right, the R.S.M.

VALE. Not *the* Drummond; the V.C.

Watson and Taylor exchange grimaces.

WATSON. You've heard of him.

VALE. Heard of him. Everybody in the Corps knows that name. The only V.C. the Corps ever had.

TAYLOR [*dealing*] That's him, Ted Drummond V.C.

VALE. They make it a part of the history course in basic training— how he won it, I mean.

WATSON. Do they.

VALE. Trapped in a depot outside—where was it——

WATSON. Tripoli. [*Singing heard outside*]

VALE. Tripoli. Picked up a bren gun and carried it firing from the hip and drove back an entire German patrol.

WATSON. Yes, it's quite a story.

VALE. What's he like?

WATSON. He's got two arms and two legs like most other people.

Sounds of singing and shouting become louder.

TAYLOR. Here come the rebels.

The door bursts open and we see Bell and O'Mally. Bell is a hard tough man who knows the limits of his intelligence and uses his strength to dominate the mess. O'Mally is a cheerful Irish boaster, who makes Bell laugh and never strays from his side.

O'MALLY. For the love of mike. Did you see those legs she had on her?

BELL. I saw them.

O'MALLY. Did you ever see such pins, did you, did you honestly now?

TAYLOR. You're a dirty old man you are, Paddy.

O'MALLY. Aw, shut up.

BELL. Hey, Milly, set 'em up.

MILLIGAN. Cor blimey, where's the fire?

BELL. Get your finger out then. [*He notices Clarke*] Well, if it isn't the twelve week wonder. Sitting at the bar like a man an' all. Tell me, Schoolie, did you enjoy the entertainment provided?

CLARKE. Yes thank you.

O'MALLY. Enjoy it. His eyes popped out of his head when that blonde came on.

BELL. I see you're not honouring the mess by drinking with us this evening.

CLARKE. I don't drink, you know that, Dinger.

BELL. Dinger! Who the hell are you calling Dinger? Since when have I been Dinger to you?

CLARKE. I'm sorry.

BELL. That's better. [*Sees Vale*] Who's this?

WATSON. Name of Vale; posted in.

BELL. Regular?

VALE. No.

BELL. Oh, blimey, another student prince. Tell me, sergeant, is it Oxford or Cambridge you're going to when you've finally discharged your beastly National Service obligations?

VALE. Neither.

BELL. Don't give me that. I can tell them a mile off. The look on their faces like they was slumming——You know it really grieves me to see you not drinking, Schoolie. Shall I get Milligan to fetch you a glass of milk?

MILLIGAN. Nark it—R.S.M.

Enter R.S.M. Drummond, he is forty-five, a large powerful wreck of a man. His manner is rather vague and distrait.

BELL [*under breath*] Oh, shove off.

DRUMMOND. Is Bob back from Tokio yet?

MILLIGAN. Not yet, sir.

DRUMMOND. When he comes in tell him I want to see him, I'll be over in the officers' mess.

MILLIGAN. Right.

WATSON. Oh, Ted, a new man posted in.

DRUMMOND. What? Oh . . . oh, pleased to meet you, son. What's your name?

VALE. Vale, sir.

DRUMMOND. Vale eh? Have a drink.

VALE. Thank you sir, I'll have a light ale.

DRUMMOND. Milligan, light ale. Well, you'll excuse me not staying to have one with you but I'm a bit pressed. Hope you settle in all right. [*He wants to get it over with*]

VALE. Thank you, sir.

DRUMMOND. That's right. We'll be seeing something of each other in due course I expect. Don't forget that message, Milligan.

MILLIGAN. No, sir.

Exit Drummond. Vale sits.

WATSON. Not quite what you expected, eh?

VALE. No.

WATSON. It's fifteen years since he won the V.C. That's a long time.

O'MALLY. This place is like a flamin' mortuary. Look at them, the miserable bunch of teetotallers. Come on, let's be having a booze-up. Schoolie, give us a song. Come on you long drink of water, on your feet with you.

CLARKE. Leave me alone.

O'MALLY. Sure and it's just a song I'm wanting.

CLARKE. Well, you're not getting one.

O'MALLY. Will you listen to the Mother's darlin'. Have they changed your nappies tonight?

CLARKE. I told you. Leave me alone.

O'MALLY. Oh—so it's tellin' me you are. About what?

TAYLOR. Leave him alone, Paddy.

O'MALLY. Shut your trap. [*To Clarke*] I said about what?

CLARKE. All right then. [*Produces a book*] Have you ever seen one of these before, Paddy?

O'MALLY. Is it a fairy story you're going to read us now?

CLARKE. Yes, yes, in a way that's just what it is. Tell me, Sergeant, when was it you said you won the Army light-weight boxing championship?

O'MALLY. I've told you, 1933.

CLARKE. Oh, yes, 1933. Well, Sergeant, I came across this little book the other day; it's a handbook of sport in the army. You know, Rugger, Tennis, Boxing. Here's a list of all the boxing champions, but they seem to have forgotten you—they don't mention you . . . they've forgotten to honour the peat-bog-diggers' hero, Sergeant knock-out O'Mally. [*He raises O'Mally's arm like a referee indicating the winner*]

O'MALLY. Let you put the book away.

CLARKE [*delighted*] But it's for you. A little present.

O'MALLY. I said put it away. [*He knocks the book out of Clarke's hand*]

BELL [*contemptuously*] You Irish liar, O'Mally, so you was shooting it all the time. You big mick.

O'MALLY. I could have won the title, if only I could have landed that punch.

BELL. Yeah! You couldn't punch your way out of a paper bag.

O'MALLY. I'm tellin' you . . .

BELL. Aw, shove off, you make me tired.

O'Mally looks around: everyone avoids his gaze.

O'MALLY. I'll have that title yet. I can still . . . I'll show you . . . I'll show the lot of you. [*He exits*]

CLARKE [*who has wandered over to the card-table*] Well, that showed him up.

BELL. Aw, shut up.

CLARKE. That's taken friend O'Mally down a peg or two I fancy.

They are intent on their cards.

WATSON. Has it?

CLARKE. I think so, we won't have so much of his bragging in future.

WATSON. You sound pleased with yourself.

CLARKE. Why shouldn't I be? Anyway, you can't blame me.

TAYLOR. Is that a fact? Now, I wouldn't have said that. Looked more to me like you went to some trouble to find all that out.

BELL. Schoolie! Come here.

CLARKE [*approaches apprehensively*] What for, what do you want?

BELL. I said come here.

CLARKE. What do you want?

BELL. I want to talk to you; have a drink.

CLARKE. I don't drink, Serg . . .

BELL. Milligan; a drink for my friend.

MILLIGAN. For your friend . . . [*laughs*]

BELL. Sure that's right. Well well, so we've got a little Sherlock Holmes in the mess, have we?

CLARKE. What do you mean, a little Sherlock Holmes?

Milligan brings drink round. Everyone watches rigidly.

BELL. You've always got to stir it up. You can never leave things alone, can you? First it's Reed; now it's O'Mally. Well, we'll just make sure it's the last time, shall we?

Bell empties the glass in Clarke's face: he staggers back blindly, then goes for Bell who grabs his wrist and throws him off.

BELL. If you want the other half you've only to say the word.

CLARKE. You bully . . . you bloody bully.

Clarke staggers to door and exits.

VALE. Staff . . . did you see that?

WATSON. I'm not blind.

VALE. But you're the senior rank.

WATSON. If you want my crown you're welcome to it. Well, what did I tell you? [*Long pause: Vale looks at the others, then rises and exits*]

Bell crosses to take Vale's place at table.

BELL. Well, that's the end of that lot.

TAYLOR. Easy on, Bell, we don't want another accident. Your deal, Dan.

Watson and Taylor look unhappily at one another and Milligan, at the bar, slowly cleans the same glass over and over again.

Fade out.

Act Two

The Verandah. Clarke is huddled in one of the chairs, the lamps are lit. Vale is with him.

VALE. Cigarette?

CLARKE. No.

VALE. Funny country this; dirty, smelly, corrupt and yet, oh I don't know, there's something about it. . . . I suppose the truth is you can get used to most things.

CLARKE. Can you?

VALE. I think so.

CLARKE. There are some things you can never get used to; not if you've got any sensitivity at all.

VALE. Sensitivity; you can forget all about that when you're in this outfit.

CLARKE. Together with ethics, morals and any sense of decency.

VALE. Bell is only one man out of a dozen, you know.

CLARKE. They're all the same here; you've only just arrived, you don't know what it's like.

VALE. Look, it's none of my business, but don't you think you're only making it hard for yourself?

CLARKE. *I'm* making it hard! I didn't ask to come here. Is it my fault if I have a different background, a different life to these people?

VALE. There is the other side, though. Here are we, a couple of conscripts with three stripes after a twelve-week course. It took most of them as many years. This is their whole life—to us it's just a temporary inconvenience.

CLARKE. Inconvenience!

VALE. You've been unlucky, that's all.

CLARKE. You really make me puke.

He exits.

VALE [*after him*] Look, if there's anything I can do. . . .

Clarke moves off.

Reluctantly Vale goes back into the mess.

BELL. Been holding his hand?

VALE. Look, Bell.

BELL. Look what?

WATSON. Now, turn it up, will you.

TAYLOR. Come on, let's get on with the game.

VALE. I'm trying to tell you——

BELL. So you're trying to tell me now, are you.

Bell faces up to Vale. The tension is suddenly broken when Bob Straw comes in carrying a kitbag. He is a fat genial man—considerably older than the others and respected by everyone for his shrewdness and length of service.

STRAW. Get to your feet, you great hairy-armed men. The last of the warriors is here.

Milligan, Taylor and Watson crowd round him while Bell and Vale slowly relax in the background.

91

MILLIGAN. Look who it isn't.

STRAW. Come on, let's have a drink.

TAYLOR. Bob, you old devil.

WATSON. What the devil have you been up to? You've lost weight old man.

TAYLOR. Come on, let's 'ave 'em. Intimate confessions, you old sinner.

MILLIGAN. Details, details.

TAYLOR. Look at him. Rest and recuperation leave they call it. Just about fit for the grave I'd say.

WATSON. Overtime for the geisha girls. How many Tokio nightspots did you smash up?

STRAW. Jealousy will get you nowhere. You sex-starved band of monks. [*Milligan hands him a glass*] Aaaah! Milligan, you're a gentleman.

MILLIGAN. That's what my Dad used to say.

STRAW. Where's Ted?

BELL. Saying his prayers, I expect. [*Drummond has entered: conversation dies down*]

DRUMMOND. Hallo Bob. Had a good leave?

STRAW. Oh, pretty quiet, you know; pretty quiet. Nice to be back amongst old friends. [*Silence*] How's my old pal, Joe Reed? The driver tells me he's in hospital.

BELL. Yeh, had a bit of a fall. Too much booze.

STRAW [*to Drummond jokingly*] Sounds like things have been getting out of hand in my absence.

BELL. Ted wouldn't know, would you, Ted? [*Laughter*]

DRUMMOND [*stung by the truth of it*] Were you saying something, Bell?

BELL. All right, all right. No need to get shirty. Only having my little joke. [*Milligan laughs drunkenly: the sound fades away. A pause*]

WATSON [*changing the subject*] Hear anything over there about this redundancy business?

STRAW. No, old man. Not a word.

BELL. If you ask me we're all bloomin'well redundant.

DRUMMOND. No, they've plenty of use for us yet.

BELL. Some of us. [*Laughter*]

DRUMMOND [*with the utmost restraint*] Don't let me keep you from your work. Have you a got a minute, Bob?

Straw follows Drummond thoughtfully outside into the garden. They walk slowly, silently. Eventually Drummond speaks.

DRUMMOND. That was a damn-fool thing to say.

STRAW. What's wrong?

DRUMMOND. You know very well what's wrong. "Looks like things have been getting out of hand in my absence". In *your* absence! What does that make me? Lance-Jack Drummond?

STRAW. Can't you take a joke?

DRUMMOND. Take a joke—some joke. [*Long pause*] It's happened before—you've seen it yourself. You don't know how it happens; you just lose it . . . command, respect, the lot. . . . It just sort of slips through your fingers. Ah, well, it's almost over for me now. I'm leaving next week. That's what I wanted to tell you.

STRAW. Posting?

DRUMMOND. It's all yours, Bob. You'll be taking over until the replacement comes. I'm finished. A soldier can't live on his reputation for ever. All I want is a last quiet week in this Godforsaken hole.

STRAW. Running away?

DRUMMOND. What do you mean?

STRAW. You'd better tell me about Reed.

DRUMMOND [*too sharply*] Reed? Oh, oh, that. I'd kipped down—they had to wake me up to tell me. Got drunk, apparently. Wandered outside, fell into a bren-gun pit and fractured his skull. Nasty accident.

STRAW. Accident?

DRUMMOND. Mmmmm.

STRAW. How is he?

DRUMMOND. Still unconscious—on the critical list.

STRAW. Poor devil. Accident—and that lot let it happen. What were the Staff Sergeants doing?

DRUMMOND. You can't blame them. Watson's been a busy man while you've been away.

STRAW. And Bell?

DRUMMOND. Bell? [*Off balance*] Oh, Bell's all right.

We mix to the mess and see Vale sitting alone at a table. The others are all round the bar.

BELL. It doesn't matter a gnat's gear box to me. All this talk about redundancy's a lot of bull as far as I'm concerned. They'll always need a bleedin' army. Straw doesn't know what he's talkin' about.

TAYLOR [*phlegmatically*] I wouldn't be too sure about that. He's no fool, Bob Straw. [*Looks over his shoulder to see who is listening. Continues more quietly*] You'd better watch your step now that he's back.

O'MALLY. Are you gettin' cold feet or something?

WATSON. He's right, you know, Dinger. Too flippin' curious, old Bob. Don't forget he got on well with Reed. He'll be asking all the right questions, you can bet your life.

BELL. You give me a pain in the backside you lot, you really do. Look, Reed's still unconscious, so he can't say much. There's a rumour Drummond is getting a posting, so all we've got to do is keep our mouths shut.

Clarke enters and goes over to join Vale at table.

MILLIGAN. Hallo! Here comes Laughing Boy himself. I don't give a ship's richard what happens to you lot—I'm all right. Buy us a drink, Jim.

WATSON. Well, it looks as if you two are the only ones here with a future outside the dole queue.

BELL. Oh sure, that sort could fall into a cess pit and come up smelling of violets.

CLARKE. I shouldn't sneer at cess pits, you might be digging them soon.

VALE. Shut up, Schoolie.

He is too late. Bell swings round to face them, an expression of revulsion on his face.

BELL. So you had to put your oar in. I might have guessed.

WATSON. Dinger!

BELL. Keep your nose out. Come on. Come on.

CLARKE. That's right, go ahead, hit me. It's all you're fit for, isn't it? Hitting people——You won't know what the word means, Staff Sergeant, but you're an anachronism. You all are, you're out of date, all of you. You couldn't earn a decent living as civilians and now even the Army doesn't want you. You've had your day and you know it.

VALE. Shut up, Schoolie! Leave him alone, Bell.

BELL. You keep your nose out of this.

VALE [*steps between Bell and Clarke*] I said leave him alone.

BELL. What's your trouble? Want to be a comic paper hero as well? Flip this for a game of toy soldiers.

He snatches a bottle from the bar and breaks it. Quickly Vale seizes a chair. Attracted by the noise Drummond and Straw appear in the doorway. Drummond hesitates but Straw sizes up the situation and snaps into action.

STRAW. Bell! Cut it out.

[*Bell and Vale hesitate then lower their weapons*]

94

Go into the office, both of you. Go on, look sharp. [*Bell and Vale go out into the C.S.M.'s office*] Watson, you're the senior rank, what were you doing, picking your nose? Right, close the mess. [*Drummond enters*] Milligan, lock the bar. Clear out, the lot of you [*Slowly Watson, Taylor and Clarke leave the room. Milligan, practically in a drunken stupor, begins to clear the bar*] Well, Ted, looks as if you've lost your quiet last week.

DRUMMOND. I don't know . . . Why did they have to start now?

STRAW. Want me to deal with it?

DRUMMOND. No, it's my job.

STRAW. Well, all I can say is the best of British luck.

    Drummond's office. Bell and Vale stand waiting. Enter Drummond and Straw.

STRAW. What's this then, market day in the Gorbals? Stand to attention both of you. What do you think you're on?

    Drummond sits wearily.

DRUMMOND. Come on then, what was it all about?

VALE. Private matter, sir.

DRUMMOND [*tries to storm but his voice lacks conviction*] What do you think you are, soldiers or tearaways? Vale, you've made a bad start. As for you . . . Sergeant Major Straw, take Vale outside until I send for him.

STRAW. Sir.

    Exit Straw and Vale.

DRUMMOND. Close the door, Bell. Well?

BELL. Well, what?

DRUMMOND. What have you got to say for yourself?

BELL. We had a barney and you stopped us settling it, that's all.

DRUMMOND. I don't get it. I know you've got a temper, but . . .

BELL. Too true I've got a temper! And if there's one thing I don't like it's a snotty-nosed kid trying to take a rise out of me. [*Nastily*] Somebody's got to handle 'em, you know. So if you're thinking of making an example out of me, you'd better think again! It's a bit too late for examples in this place!

    There is a long pause.

DRUMMOND. Get out of my sight. Get out!

BELL. Suits me, I'll be here, I ain't going anywhere [*Exit*]

DRUMMOND. Sergeant Major.

STRAW [*enters*] Sir.

DRUMMOND. Close the door, Bob.

STRAW. Get anything out of him?

DRUMMOND. Typical mess squabble on the face of it.

STRAW. With a broken bottle and a chair?

DRUMMOND. I'll give Vale a rocket and Bell some extra duties and that's an end to it . . . Well, say something . . . if you don't agree say so. Don't just stand there.

STRAW. If you think that's all that's needed, there's nothing more to say.

DRUMMOND. Send Sergeant Vale in.

Straw goes out and comes back with Vale.

DRUMMOND. Come on, son, what's the sense in beating about the bush. What was it all about?

VALE. I'm sorry, sir.

DRUMMOND. So it's like that is it. A personal matter, something between gentlemen no doubt. No business of an ignorant soldier like me.

VALE. I didn't mean it that way——

DRUMMOND. Not much you didn't. Personal matter.

STRAW. Was Bell pushing you around?

VALE. No. I went for him first.

DRUMMOND. You weren't getting mixed up in another man's quarrel or anything like that, were you?

VALE. I, well, I know you'll do what's right, sir.

DRUMMOND. Do you now. And what makes you so sure of that?

VALE. Well . . . Your reputation, sir.

DRUMMOND. You mean this bit of ribbon? I wouldn't let that fool you. You realize I ought to get you stripped.

VALE. Yes, sir.

DRUMMOND. Yes sir. Stripped. The trouble with you is you think you're still in the Fourth Form of Saint Fannies, or wherever it was. Why should I worry about you—— All right Vale. We'll leave it there for the moment. Go back to your tent. You'll hear more about this.

VALE. Very good, sir. [*Exit*]

STRAW. You seem well thought of in that quarter.

DRUMMOND. It must be very nice to be a young sergeant.

STRAW. Come on, let's call it a day.

DRUMMOND. A damn depressing one and all.

STRAW. I'll get Milligan to lock up. Milligan . . . Milligan!

They walk through into the mess. Milligan staggers up completely drunk.

DRUMMOND. That's all we needed.

STRAW. Situation normal. We put Milligan to bed and lock up ourselves. [*Grinning foolishly Milligan sags down the wall to the floor*] Give us a hand with him. [*Between them they pull him to his feet and start supporting him to the door*] Come on Milly, beddy byes. You've had a skinful to-night. [*The telephone rings, Drummond goes back to answer it*]

DRUMMOND. Sergeants' mess, Sergeant Major Drummond. Oh, yes, sir. Yes. What? Yes, yes I will; goodnight. [*He hangs up and stands immobile*]

STRAW. What is it? What's up then?

DRUMMOND. That was the C.O. He's just heard from the base hospital. Reed died an hour ago.

Milligan shudders and pulls away from Straw.

MILLIGAN. Reed . . . Reed . . . Reed. For God's sake, Bell, stop it, man. Stop it, do you hear? Bell, you bloody fool . . . you've killed him.

He leans sobbing against the wall as Drummond and Straw regard him with horror.

We mix to the garden. It is fifteen minutes later and we see Vale, Watson, Taylor, O'Mally, and Clarke on their way to the mess.

O'MALLY. What's it all in aid of, that's what I want to know? Nothin' to do with me. I was already kipped down.

TAYLOR. My heart bleeds for you.

O'MALLY. What's the matter then, too good to talk to me now?

WATSON. Pack it in, both of you. We'll soon hear all about it.

TAYLOR. What do you reckon it is, Dan? Might be some night exercise or something.

WATSON. Do me a favour.

They enter the mess and lapse into silence.

STRAW. All right, now listen Staff Sergeant Watson, you are responsible for seeing that every member of this mess appears here properly dressed, in one hour's time. Is that clear?

WATSON. Yes, sir. What for sir?

STRAW. You'll be told when it's good for you. Staff Sergeant Bell is under open arrest. That might mean something to you. I don't know. Does it? Well, does it? [*An uneasy silence*] All right then: one hour's time.

Exeunt Watson, Taylor, O'Mally and Clarke. Straw goes into the office.

Cut to office.

DRUMMOND. Well?

STRAW. They know something they're not telling. It doesn't smell right to me.

DRUMMOND. Reed's dead; we can't alter that.

STRAW. No.

DRUMMOND. So if we can't alter it, why don't we forget it? One thing is certain: we'll never get that evidence out of Milligan when he's sober. So what do we do?

STRAW. They'll throw the book at you: you know that don't you? You know what they'd say at a court martial if it ever came to that? "Mr. Drummond, are you trying to tell the court that you weren't aware of what was going on under your very nose? Couldn't you recognize bullying, insobriety and chaos in the Unit under your command?" And what are you going to tell them? "Please, sir, I was bored and time expired. I didn't like the country. I didn't care much for the sort of army I was in; so I let things slide."

DRUMMOND. I couldn't cope.

STRAW. Couldn't cope. Ten years ago—ten months ago you know what you would have said? You'd have said: "What does it matter what they say? If a lad's been killed I'll get to the bottom of it, if it's the last thing I do."

DRUMMOND. Drummond V.C. [*He turns the Victoria Cross idly in his hand*] What about a medal for Sergeant Reed? "Sergeant Reed dies in hospital as a result of a drunken brawl, in the absence of any effective control on the part of Regimental Sergeant Major Drummond". It doesn't matter how he died; whichever way you look at it, it's my fault. That's the simple truth.

STRAW. It's not the whole truth—nobody can go on being a hero, not after this kind of war. I don't know what it is that's got into these fellows. Take 'em apart and they're decent enough, but together, in this place, it's as if something evil's got into them; like a stench you can't get rid of. You're no more responsible for that than I am for the atom bomb. But the fact that it stinks doesn't mean you can stop breathing—V.C. or no V.C. Trouble is you've let that flippin' gong make you into a martyr. You've got to get off your bloomin' pedestal, and sort this lot out. I'm not going to see you give in to Bell or any of them. [*There is a long pause: Drummond puts the medal away. Straw watches him intently*]

DRUMMOND. You're a bastard; you know that don't you?

STRAW [*affected by the warmth of the remark*] I used to think I'd never get through to you. I've been called a number of things in my time, but coming from you that's almost a compliment. You're not leaving this Unit without the respect of every man in this mess. [*Drummond is silent*] Well, sir?

DRUMMOND. Order a mess court-martial.

STRAW. To-night?

DRUMMOND. To-night. You and I will sit on the board. Staff Sergeant Bell is charged with manslaughter. The rest, except the newcomer Vale, will swear it was an accident. Bell will be cleared. And that'll be the end of my career.

STRAW. I'll admit there's not much chance.

DRUMMOND. Not much? Don't be a fool, man; there isn't any. [*A pause*] I can't prove it, but I know it wasn't an accident. The only evidence is Milligan's drunken admission, and that won't stand up for one minute. All the same, I would like to try.

STRAW. Any ideas for prosecutor?

DRUMMOND. It'll have to be Vale. Poor devil. He'll wonder what hit him. You'd better send him in. [*Straw moves to the door*] By the way, you'd better stay around and explain the drill [*He puts V.C. away*] Come in. [*After a moment Vale enters*] Sit down lad. Cigarette?

VALE. Thanks.

DRUMMOND. Look, here, Vale, a little while ago something came up that suggested that whatever happened to Reed it wasn't an accident.

VALE. Oh.

DRUMMOND. That's not all. Reed died this evening in hospital.

VALE. My God!

DRUMMOND. That's how I feel. Well, the long and the short of it is that I've placed Bell under arrest and I'm holding a mess court-martial on him to try and clear things up. Ever heard of a mess court-martial?

VALE. No, sir.

DRUMMOND. What do they teach you in basic training these days? Well, they're much the same as an ordinary court-martial, only strictly unofficial. I'm bringing Bell to face a charge of manslaughter. And that's where you come in. I want you to act as prosecuting N.C.O.

VALE. You're joking.

DRUMMOND. Sure, I'm wearing a funny hat and all.

VALE. But I don't know anything about court-martial procedure.

DRUMMOND. You're an educated lad, you've had advantages the rest of us haven't. You'll have to pick it up.

VALE. I couldn't do it, sir . . . it's absurd, I just couldn't.

DRUMMOND. Now look here Vale, I'm asking you to help me arrive at the truth; and that's something not every man has a chance to do.

VALE. Not every man wants the chance, sir.

DRUMMOND. All right, I'm not asking you any longer. I'm giving you an order. I am detailing you to act as prosecuting N.C.O. Understand what I'm saying?

VALE [after a pause] Yes sir.

DRUMMOND. Right, that's it. Better have a word with Straw.

VALE. Yes, sir.

He leaves and we follow him to the verandah where he meets Straw.

STRAW. Got yourself a job?

VALE. I didn't volunteer for it—I was ordered. I haven't a clue. I haven't a clue.

STRAW. All right, so you were ordered. It's tough on you, Vale, landing right in on this mix-up. There's a lot at stake—a good deal more than you think.

VALE. You mean for Drummond?

STRAW. Why do you say that?

VALE. The Mess is against him over this. And now that Reed is dead—well, he's responsible—I don't see what chance he's got—I mean, what do you expect me to do?

STRAW. What would you say really happened to Reed?

VALE. I couldn't prove it, but I'd say he got into a fight with Bell.

STRAW. Sergeant Milligan dropped that same information in a drunken outburst less than half an hour ago. That's your only evidence—and he'll deny it. The rest will stick together. Somehow you've got to break through. [*Vale says nothing: inwardly he is sick and scared*] Ever heard of the Queen's Corporal?

VALE. Queen's Corporal? No.

STRAW. It's an old soldier's tale. No truth in it as far as I know. But it was told to me and I've told it around and it'll go on being told. The story goes that if ever a British mob fight a battle and after it's over there's only one survivor on our side, then if that bloke's a private he's automatically promoted full corporal. He's known as the Queen's Corporal, because he survived when nobody else did.

VALE. No, I've never heard that.

STRAW. That isn't a bed-time story, son. This court-martial could be Drummond's last battle. The trouble is he can't fight it himself. You've got to fight it for him. I hope to God you win.

Fade out.

Act Three

One hour later.
The scene is the Sergeants' Mess, roughly prepared for a trial.
Drummond, Straw and Vale enter.

WATSON. Mess—shun!

DRUMMOND. Is everybody here?

WATSON. Yes, sir.

DRUMMOND. Right. Sit down. Before we start I want to make sure everybody understands what a mess court-martial is all about. If a member of a sergeants' mess has acted in such a way as to bring disrepute on his rank, the senior N.C.O., in this case myself, can order such a member to appear before a mess court-martial. Now, I want you to understand this; a mess court-martial is entirely unofficial. This means that if a man is found guilty in a court like this we do not have the power to sentence him. What happens is this: a written account of his trial is taken to the Commanding Officer; the rest is up to him. He may decide to prefer charges and order an official court-martial.

TAYLOR. It's a certainty, mate.

O'MALLY. Shut your trap.

DRUMMOND. If, on the other hand, a man is found not guilty, that is the end of the matter, and the whole thing is forgotten. Now, the way it's run. Sergeant Major Straw and myself act as the board. Sergeant Vale will be acting as prosecuting N.C.O. He has read the official reports of Sergeant Reed's death. Have you chosen a defending N.C.O. Bell?

WATSON. He has, sir. I shall be acting as prisoner's friend.

DRUMMOND. Thank you, Staff Watson. Sergeant Major Straw will be making notes of the case as we go along. Will you read out the charge?

STRAW. 3253391 Staff Sergeant George Joseph Bell?

BELL. Sir.

STRAW. You are charged under Section 41 of the Army Act, that is to say: When on active service committing a civil offence, namely manslaughter in that you at Pyontaek on the night of the tenth of August, 1953, were responsible for the death of No. 7842610 Sergeant Joseph Reed. Do you plead guilty or not guilty?

BELL. Not guilty, sir.

DRUMMOND [*writing*] Not . . . guilty . . . All right, Sergeant Vale: you open the case.

VALE. Sir. I want to say that I know nothing about correct procedure——

STRAW. You let us worry about that.

VALE. Yes, sir. [*Sips water*] I'm going to start by outlining the facts of the case, as given in the Orderly Sergeant's report book for the night of the tenth of August. At 23 hundred hours an ambulance from seventh field hospital came to this unit to pick up Sergeant Reed in response to a telephone message. The M.O. discovered that he was suffering from a fractured skull and was unconscious. Ten days later, that's tonight, at 23.53 hours, Sergeant Reed died without recovering consciousness.

MILLIGAN [*now sober*] Tell us something we don't know.

VALE. According to evidence given at the Court of Enquiry, Reed had fallen into a bren gun pit in the dark and the Court gave the cause of his injury as an accident. That verdict was accepted as correct, until tonight. An hour or so ago evidence came to light.

WATSON. What evidence? We don't know whether it was evidence yet.

VALE. Sergeant Milligan made a statement——

WATSON. He now denies that statement.

DRUMMOND. All right, Staff Watson, you can have your say in a minute. Get on with it Vale. Call your witnesses.

VALE. Sergeant Taylor.

DRUMMOND. Sergeant Taylor.

Taylor sits in witness chair.

STRAW. Do you swear that the evidence you shall give will be the truth, the whole truth and nothing but the truth?

TAYLOR. I do. 476937 Sergeant Taylor J.

VALE. Now, Sergeant Taylor. Were you in the mess on the night of the tenth of August?

TAYLOR. I was.

VALE. How long were you there?

TAYLOR. Most of the evening . . . from seven until ten.

VALE. What sort of evening was it?

TAYLOR. It was just an ordinary evening. Until—you know.

VALE. Who else was there?

TAYLOR. In the mess? Well there was Milligan and Watson and Bell . . . oh yes and Clarke.

VALE. Anyone else?

TAYLOR. Yes, of course, and Reed.

VALE. Six of you. You'd say it was an ordinary evening—you all had your usual amount to drink?

TAYLOR. That's right.

VALE. How was Reed behaving that evening?

TAYLOR. He was drunk if that's what you mean.

VALE. Was he the only one?

TAYLOR. Yes.

VALE. But you just said you'd all had the usual amount to drink. Why should Reed be drunk while the rest of you were sober?

TAYLOR. Simple, he got drunk quicker than we did.

VALE. Did Reed quarrel with anyone in the mess that night?

TAYLOR. No, not as far as I know.

VALE. He was a quiet peaceful drunk?

TAYLOR. I suppose so.

VALE. He peacefully walked out of the mess, and quietly cracked his skull open?

TAYLOR. I dare say.

VALE. What does that mean?

TAYLOR. It means I didn't see him crack his skull open; nobody did.

VALE. You were the one who discovered him, weren't you?

TAYLOR. I was.

VALE. How exactly?

TAYLOR. Reed left the mess early, about half past nine, he was pretty well sloshed already. I left half an hour later. I got about half way across to my tent when I heard him groaning. I thought he was just having a spew so I went across to see if I could help him. Then I saw him lying in the pit.

VALE. You heard him groaning; but I thought he was unconscious?

TAYLOR. He was just about conscious until we got him back to the mess; then he flaked out.

VALE. I see. So you are saying Sergeant Reed left this mess alone, and you found him lying in a gunpit with his head split open?

TAYLOR. Yes.

VALE. You're quite sure that's the truth?

TAYLOR. I took the oath didn't I?

VALE. All right, that's all.

DRUMMOND. Staff Watson?

WATSON. No questions, sir.

DRUMMOND. Thank you, Sergeant Taylor. Who do you want next, Vale?

VALE. Sergeant O'Mally, sir.

DRUMMOND. Sergeant O'Mally.

O'MALLY [*forestalls Straw by taking the Bible, and reciting glibly*] I swear that the evidence I shall give will be the truth, the whole truth and nothing but the truth. 397623 Sergeant O'Mally K.

VALE. Sergeant O'Mally, were you in the mess on the night of the tenth August?

O'MALLY. No, I was not. I was Orderly Sergeant and I spent the night on rounds or in the guard tent.

VALE. Don't you know anything about what happened?

O'MALLY. Not until I was sent for, then I had to phone for the ambulance.

VALE. When you saw Reed, did it appear to you to be an accident?

O'MALLY. What else could it have been if a fellow's picked up in a pit at that time o' night stinking like a brewery?

VALE. All right, that's all.

DRUMMOND. Staff Watson?

WATSON. No questions.

VALE. Sergeant Milligan.

DRUMMOND. Sergeant Milligan.

STRAW. Do you swear that the evidence you shall give will be the truth, the whole truth and nothing but the truth?

MILLIGAN. I do. 398723 Sergeant Milligan L.

VALE. I'm not going to ask you anything about the night of August the tenth for the moment. Instead I want you to try to remember something you said to Mr. Drummond earlier this evening.

MILLIGAN. I don't remember saying nothing.

VALE. Well, let me remind you. Didn't you accuse Staff Sergeant Bell of killing Sergeant Reed?

MILLIGAN. I don't remember anything about it.

VALE. Are you saying that Mr. Drummond——

MILLIGAN [*interrupting*] I'm saying I don't remember, I was drunk: I'm still half-cut. I don't remember things I say when I'm drunk.

VALE. But you did say it. Mr. Drummond and Sergeant Major Straw heard you.

MILLIGAN. All right, sonny boy, so I said it.

VALE. Then why did you make that accusation?

MILLIGAN. Oh, how many more times. I was drunk. I must have been barmy. It wasn't me talking, it was the beer.

VALE. You were telling the truth when you said——

MILLIGAN. I'm telling the truth now. I was in the mess all evening. I swear that Bell didn't touch Reed.

    Vale sits.

DRUMMOND. Staff Watson.

WATSON. Sergeant Milligan, how many times have you been drunk in your life? [*Laughter*]

MILLIGAN. More times than you've 'ad 'ot dinners. [*Further laughter*]

WATSON. Has it ever happened before that when drunk you said something which wasn't true, and when you were sober you knew it wasn't true?

MILLIGAN. Eh?

WATSON. When you're drunk you usually say things that are not true?

MILLIGAN. That's right. I don't know what comes over me.

WATSON. Thank you. That's all.

VALE. Sergeant Clarke.

DRUMMOND. Clarke, let's have you.

STRAW. Do you swear that the evidence you shall give will be the truth, the whole truth and nothing but the truth?

CLARKE. I do. 22715440 Sergeant Clarke P.

VALE. Sergeant Clarke, you were in the mess on the night of the tenth of August. I want you to tell us your version of what happened.

CLARKE. It's the same as everybody else's.

VALE. I'd like to hear it if you don't mind.

CLARKE. I was in the mess with Watson, Taylor, Milligan, Bell and Reed. Reed spent the evening by himself at the bar. He was drinking heavily. He left the mess about nine-thirty and the next thing I knew was Taylor running in saying Reed was lying in the gunpit.

VALE. Why were you in the mess that night? You don't drink, and you don't seem to get on with anybody, do you? Well, do you?

CLARKE. I pay my mess dues. I've as much right to use the mess as anyone else.

VALE. How would you say you were treated in the mess? Isn't it true you were always being pushed around and bullied?

CLARKE. Bullied. That's an exaggeration. They take the micky a bit.

VALE. What about Bell this evening? Would you call that micky-taking?

CLARKE. Oh, that.

VALE. You're not going to tell me that was just an isolated case, are you?

STRAW. Hang on a minute, Vale. May I say something, sir?

DRUMMOND. Of course.

STRAW. I don't know where you get this bullying idea from, Vale. I'm a member of this mess, too, you know. If you think I'd allow bullying in the mess you can think again.

VALE [*beginning to see the light*] But I saw. . . . Tell me, sir, when did you go on leave?

STRAW. Fortnight ago; sixth of August. What's that got to do with it?

VALE. It seems odd, to say the least, that Clarke gets into trouble about the same time that Sergeant Reed had his fatal accident—ten days ago; while you were on leave, sir.

WATSON. This is plain stupid. I don't know what he's talking about.

DRUMMOND. Carry on with your questions, Sergeant Vale.

VALE. On the 6th August, Sergeant Major Straw went on leave. Four days later, on August 10th, Sergeant Reed, so the story goes, got blind drunk, split his skull open, and remained unconscious until his death an hour and a half ago. Don't you think it's a pity he didn't live to tell *his* story? [*Clarke remains silent: Vale continues quietly*] I'm appealing to you, Clarke. It's too late for Sergeant Reed. He's dead. Suppose you fill in the picture for me. *This has had its effect. Clarke pauses a bit too long.*

CLARKE. I've told you already, it was nothing to do with me. Nothing happened; ask anyone you like. Go on, ask *them*.

VALE [*angry*] I'm asking you, Clarke. You've got a dead man's story on your conscience. It wasn't an accident. You know damn well it wasn't. For God's sake man, can't you tell the truth?

WATSON [*interrupting quickly*] Mr. Drummond, I really must object. Can't someone tell him the rules of evidence?

DRUMMOND. Sergeant Vale, it's not for you to say it was not an accident. It's for the witness.

VALE. I'm sorry, sir.

DRUMMOND. Have you finished?

VALE. I don't know, sir. No sir. I . . . I . . . I think I have a few more questions.

DRUMMOND. Very well; take your time. Carry on.

Vale has poured himself a glass of water and he now takes a sip.

VALE. Would you say you were more sensitive than most people, Sergeant Clarke?

CLARKE. Yes, I suppose I am. Yes I am.

VALE. More intellectual? [*Clarke doesn't answer*] It's nothing to be ashamed of is it, being intellectual?

CLARKE [*encouraged*] No, no it's not really. Of course it isn't.

VALE. It's just that being more intellectual, more sensitive, makes it harder to get along in the rough and tumble of army life.

CLARKE. I think it does; yes.

VALE. In fact, a fellow like yourself is very easily hurt by someone, shall we say like Bell or O'Mally. What to them is horseplay is real mental suffering for you.

CLARKE. I suppose they enjoy it. You can't expect them to know any better.

VALE. I expect you to know better.

CLARKE. Me?

VALE. You know what it feels like to be hurt. You know with deadly certainty what that boxing championship meant to O'Mally. The one blow he never delivered himself, you delivered for him. The one illusion O'Mally really needed, you took from him; you know that, don't you?

CLARKE. He only got what he deserved. They all deserve it.

VALE. Including Sergeant Reed?

CLARKE. I didn't say that.

VALE. But Bell did—don't you remember? "First it's Reed, now it's O'Mally. Well, we'll just make sure it's the last time, shall we?" But what about a little drink first—— [*He throws the water in Clarke's face*]

CLARKE. You bully—you're all alike; Reed, Bell, the lot of you. He did it, he killed Reed. [*pointing at Bell*] Go on, bully your way out of that.

WATSON. He's mad; you can't believe a lunatic.

DRUMMOND. All right, Sergeant Clarke. Let's have the rest of it.

CLARKE. You see I'd found out about Reed. There must have been about eighty pounds in the mess funds—he was the Treasurer. Well, I'd found out that Reed had spent the money; no-one else in the mess knew about it except me. Well, anyway, things came to a head that night, August 10th. It started with the usual micky-taking—but that wasn't enough for Reed. He said he was going to make a man out of me and started trying to force a bottle of whisky down my throat. Well, I had to do something—so I told them. I said, "What about the Treasurer's Report, honest Joe Reed? Why don't you tell them you've spent their money on that lousy tart in Seoul?" That did it; he started shouting and swearing and throwing bottles. They were all round him trying to hold him, and getting wilder and wilder . . . it was pretty disgusting; then Bell got an arm free and hit him. That was it. [*Long pause*]

WATSON. Well? What are you going to do about it? You know what will happen if you tell the old man about this . . . you know . . .

DRUMMOND. I know very well what will happen. From now on it's up to the C.O. He'll get a full report as soon as possible. This court-martial is over, but I want to make this quite clear. This isn't just Bell's party. We are all in it. I am not exempting myself from blame for what has been going on in this mess. From now on your little games are over. It will be the truth and nothing but the truth. [*They all rise: Drummond goes to the 'phone, watched in a tense silence*] Hallo. Sergeant Major here. Give me the C.O. Hallo, sir. Drummond speaking. I'm sorry to trouble you at this time of night: could I come over and see you? Yes, I'm afraid it is urgent. Very good sir. Rightaway. [*He replaces the receiver and moves centre*] Sergeant Major.

STRAW. Sir.

DRUMMOND. I want everyone to remain in the mess until I get back. That's an order.

STRAW. Yes-sir.

DRUMMOND. Sergeant Vale. [*Vale crosses to face him*]

VALE. Sir.

DRUMMOND. I'd like a word with you. [*They walk out on to the verandah*] That was a pretty dirty job I gave you. You're the only man to come out of it with any credit. I wish I could live it down for you. I'm sorry. That's something you have to do yourself. If it's any help I'll arrange a posting.

VALE. I think I'd rather stay, sir.

DRUMMOND. Well, it's up to you. But don't make a martyr of yourself. Don't put yourself on a pedestal. It won't be easy. Every man in there hates your guts. [*He exits: Vale watches him go, then turns and slowly goes back into the mess*]

   Fade out.

NO FIXED ABODE

by

CLIVE EXTON

CAST

THE GOV'NOR   *Robin Wentworth*

GRANDPA   *Wilfrid Brambell*

LOFTY   *Michael Gwynn*

CORP   *Jack Hedley*

TICH   *Jack Rodney*

DIRECTOR   *James Ormerod*

DESIGNER   *Darrell Lass*

DIRECTOR'S NOTE

When I first read *No Fixed Abode* I was immediately impressed by its outstanding qualities. It was also the kind of play that appealed to me most, relying not on plot and sequences of incidents, but purely on the conflict of character. The remarkable thing about this play was the quality of real experience it conveyed, and the extraordinary accuracy of the dialogue.

Later, when I met its author, Clive Exton, I was fascinated (but not really surprised) to learn that he had got the idea for this play when returning without any money after a disastrous season in a West Country repertory theatre. Together with a colleague he had spent the night in a lodging house in Plymouth. That experience made a deep impression on him—how deep you may judge from reading his play.

JAMES ORMEROD.

A BIOGRAPHY OF CLIVE EXTON

Clive Exton was born in 1930, and was educated at Christ's Hospital and for a brief time at the Central School of Speech and Drama. He has worked in a number of jobs including an advertising agency, a dog biscuit factory, a coffee bar, and as actor and stage manager. He is married to a former actress, Mara Reid, and now lives in Chelsea. His first play on television was *No Fixed Abode* in 1958. Since then he has written several other successful television plays. He now works as a full-time writer and has an ambition to write a good stage play.

ACTION

The action of the play is set in the dormitory of a common lodging house.

TIME

The time is the present.

Act One

The Dormitory of a common lodging house early on a winter's evening. There are five iron beds with folded blankets on them, an iron stove and a door. The floor is of bare boards and the walls have the cream and green paint of all institutions. After a few seconds the door is unlocked from the outside and the Governor enters with Grandpa.

GOVERNOR. Now don't you try this every night, I'm just making an exception.

GRANDPA. I know that, sir, but seeing as I just came out of the 'ospital.

GOVERNOR. But not after tonight, after tonight you come in at the right time like all the others.

GRANDPA. Right-oh, Gov'nor, I know you mustn't . . .

GOVERNOR. Now you'd better get settled in before they get here.

GRANDPA. Thank you, sir. . . . I'll get straight into bed.

GOVERNOR. Go on then and be sharp about it. [*He exits*]

As soon as the door has closed, Grandpa turns to it and makes a two fingered gesture at the man on the other side. He then scuttles as fast as he can to the bed nearest the stove. Without removing his coat he unfolds the blankets and starts to make up the bed. He has unfolded one blanket when a thought occurs to him. He drops the blanket and hurries over to the stove. He gingerly puts a hand on it, it is cold. He shrugs resignedly, goes back to his bed and starts to make it again, then he drops the blanket again and scuttles back to the stove. He lifts the lid and peers inside. There is no trace of a fire. He drops the stove lid on the floor in disgust and goes back to his bed-making. When he has finished it, he stands contemplating it for a moment and blowing on his hands to warm them. Then he starts to unpack the bulging pockets of his overcoat, which contain his entire worldly goods. He unpacks a pair of socks, a knife and spoon, a box of matches, a cake of soap, a razor, a handkerchief and several old newspapers. Eventually he finds what he is looking for, a small paper packet. He unwraps it and takes out a piece of cheese about an inch square. He looks at it with dislike.

GRANDPA. Mice food!

He puts it in his mouth and chews it. Then he puts everything back in his pockets and sits on the bed. He takes off one of his new shoes and holds it up admiringly. This cheers him up slightly. Then

113

*he lowers it and looks dejectedly in front of him. He removes the
other shoe and ties them together by the laces. When he has done
this he tests the knot by trying to pull them apart. The knot holds.*

GRANDPA [*rises*] Food for stinkin' mice!

*He lifts end of bed and puts one shoe under the leg then he pulls
back the top two blankets and clambers into bed, overcoat, bala-
clava helmet and all. He sits there for a moment, thinking. He lies
down with his face to the wall and pulls the blankets over his head.
There are a few moments of silence, broken only by the struggles of
Grandpa to get comfortable. The door opens again and a big man
enters. He wears a short duffle coat and corduroy trousers tucked
into gum boots. An old grey trilby hat is set square above his round
face. He looks briefly round the room, notices the shape of the old
man and moves across to his bed.*

LOFTY. Excuse me, mate. . . . [*There is no reply. He peers over the
blanket at the old man's face*] Sleeping like a baby.

*When he speaks it is with a strong West Country burr—Wiltshire
or Gloucestershire. He goes back to his own bed and starts to make
it. The door opens again and two men come in. The first is a big
man, strong looking but with a gaunt face. He wears a cloth cap
set on the back of his head, a ragged old army greatcoat and old
army boots. Several days' growth of beard adorn his chin. His name
is Corp. Behind him comes Tich, a stringy little man of indeter-
minate age. He has no overcoat but wears the remains of a suit,
a cloth cap and a white silk scarf around his neck. His shoes are
pointed and let water in.*

CORP. You got in a bit sharpish, didn't you?

LOFTY. I can move when I wants to.

TICH. Yeah. [*Pointing to the bed opposite the old man*] That's mine
then. [*He sits on it possessively*]

CORP [*at fire*] [*without emotion*] Get off it.

TICH. What do you mean, get off it?

CORP. Get off it.

TICH. What d'you mean? I was here . . . [*Corp advances on Tich
who hurriedly gets up and moves over to the bed next to Lofty's.
He sits on his new bed and feels the springs*] This one's all right.
Better than that one. [*To Lofty*] It's all right, this one is. [*Pause*]

LOFTY [*looks at both*] That's all right, then.

*Corp goes to the stove and feels it. He looks round at Lofty then
back at the stove. He takes the lid off and looks inside. He turns
back to Lofty who has resumed his bed-making.*

114

CORP. Where's the fire, then?

LOFTY. Don't ask me mate. I'm new here myself.

CORP. You was first in.

TICH. Yeah—you was first in, Lofty.

LOFTY. I'll get the coal in a minute. But I wasn't the first one in here. I'll get the bloody coal. . . .

CORP. Who was then?

LOFTY [pointing to Grandpa's bed] Him. He's asleep.

CORP. He was in before you?

LOFTY. That's right. He's asleep though. I'll get it.

TICH. If he was first in, he gets it, don't he?

CORP. That's it.

LOFTY. No—he's asleep—leave him alone.

TICH. First in gets the coal.

> He moves over to Grandpa.

LOFTY. Leave him be.

CORP. Go on, wake him up. How'd he get in before you, anyhow?

LOFTY. Don't ask me.

CORP. Go on, wake him up.

TICH [shaking Grandpa] Come on, mate. First in gets the coal. Come on, mate. Get moving.

> The old man lifts himself on his elbows and looks around him.

GRANDPA. What's the matter then?

TICH. You was asleep.

GRANDPA. I know.

CORP. You was first in to-night, wasn't you?

GRANDPA. That's right.

TICH. Well, where's the fire then?

LOFTY [gets bucket] Leave him be, Tich. I'm getting it.

TICH [pulling clothes off bed] You stay there. Come on, Grandpa, get out of your pit and start moving.

GRANDPA. Here! What is all this? I'm not well, I'm not. I just come out the hospital.

TICH. What does that make me? A monkey's uncle? First one in gets the coal, don't he?

GRANDPA. Just come out the hospital I have.

TICH. I just come out the nick but I ain't flat on me back, am I?

GRANDPA. Discharged today I was.

LOFTY. Oh, let him alone, now—I'm going to get the coal.

> He picks up the bucket from beside the stove and goes out.

TICH. See what you done now? Someone else's got to do all your work for you.

CORP. These old ones are all alike—dead useless.

TICH. That's right. They are too. All of 'em.

GRANDPA. You got no respect. I only came out the hospital today.

CORP. Give us another tune, Grandpa. We've heard that one already.

TICH. Dead useless they are.

Corp goes back to his bed and removes his hat and coat. He sits on the bed and starts to roll himself a cigarette from a box of dog-ends. Meanwhile Tich stands at the foot of Grandpa's bed and they glare at each other in silence. Eventually Tich moves away back to his own bed.

TICH. Dead useless.

He starts to make his bed. In the middle of this he remembers his previous disagreement with Corp. He feels the mattress approvingly. Grandpa gets ready for sleep again. Corp takes an old newspaper from his pocket and starts to read.

TICH [*sitting up*] Where's he gone with that coal then? Digging it up is he?

CORP. Shouldn't wonder.

TICH. Got a match?

CORP. Use your own.

TICH. What's your name, mate?

CORP. Eh?

TICH. What's your handle?

CORP [*going back to his paper*] They call me Corp.

TICH. Corp?

CORP. Short for Corporal.

TICH. Oh [*Pause*] You in the . . .

CORP. Was.

TICH. Oh. [*Pause*] Regular?

CORP [*still reading*] Shut up.

TICH. Well, no need to get the needle.

CORP. Shut up.

He continues to read his paper. There is a long silence except for the sound of the man singing next door and an occasional shout or door slam.

TICH. What's he doing with that coal? Digging it up? [*He notices Grandpa's new shoes hanging on his bed*] Here, Corp, that's a fair old pair of treads Grandpa's got.

116

There is no response. Tich puts one foot up on to his knee and examines his own shoes.

TICH. Bit better than this lot. [*He takes one shoe off. He has no socks and, removing a wad of paper, sticks a finger through the hole in the sole of his shoe*] Look at that then.

Corp does not look up. Tich puts his shoe back on.

TICH. That's a fair old pair of treads he's got.

CORP [*not looking up*] You leave them be.

TICH [*indignantly*] What do you mean? I only said . . .

CORP. Leave them be.

TICH. Ah get stuffed!

Lofty comes back in, carrying a bucket of coal and a shovel.

TICH. Where have you been—digging it up?

LOFTY. Might as well have—job I had getting it. He said winter hadn't started yet.

TICH. Hadn't started yet?

LOFTY. So I said, "What do we have to do?" I said. "Wait till we've got an icicle hanging off it?"

Lofty starts to build the fire and during the ensuing dialogue is immersed in his task.

TICH. You been in this one before?

LOFTY. Too often. I do the rounds. Here once in ten days.

TICH. In work?

LOFTY. Yes. Building.

TICH. What you come here for then?

LOFTY. Money.

TICH. You're in work though.

LOFTY. Got a wife and four kids in Swindon.

TICH. When do you see 'em?

LOFTY. Once in a blue moon. Have to take work where I can. I'm non-union.

TICH. Oh. [*Pause*] Why?

LOFTY. Principle.

TICH. Oh.

LOFTY. You working?

TICH. No fear. Just out of the nick.

LOFTY. Stupid oaf.

TICH. Stupid getting caught. Still I'm reformed now.

LOFTY. Dam' stove! Oh yes?

TICH. Yeah—not getting caught no more.

LOFTY. This coal's like wet dung.

117

TICH. Well hurry up and get it going. I got some baked murphies here I want to warm up.

LOFTY. You'll have to wait your turn, mate. [*He indicates Grandpa*] He's first—I'm next.

TICH. Him? He didn't light the bleeding fire anyhow.

LOFTY. It won't do you no harm to wait.

TICH. Useless old layabout—that's all he is.

LOFTY [*looking up*] How old are you, mate?

TICH. What's it to you?

LOFTY. One of these days you'll be like that.

TICH. Ah!

LOFTY. You will, mate. You will. You don't believe that, do you?

TICH. When I'm that old, I won't spend me time in a lousy doss house.

LOFTY. Where you going to be then?

TICH. Not in a lousy doss house anyway.

LOFTY. You're going to make money are you?

TICH. That's right.

LOFTY. Live on champagne and cigars, eh?

TICH. That's right.

LOFTY. What's your trade?

TICH. What's it got to do with you?

LOFTY. I'm interested.

TICH [*desperately*] I tell you I'm not going to spend my life in a lousy doss house!

LOFTY [*going back to his work*] You make me tired.

Lofty crosses to Grandpa.

LOFTY [*shakes Grandpa*] Come on, Grandpa. Come on. Wake up.

Grandpa struggles on to his elbows again.

GRANDPA. Gawd stone me! What's the matter now?

LOFTY. I've lit the fire.

Grandpa stares blankly at him, then looks at the other two.

GRANDPA. What's the matter with him?

CORP. He's got the fire going.

GRANDPA. Well, what's he telling *me* for?

TICH. So's you can cook your supper, you lazy old goat.

Grandpa stares at him uncomprehending.

GRANDPA. I haven't got no supper.

LOFTY. You got no supper?

GRANDPA. Course I haven't.

LOFTY. Oh.

CORP. Well you'd better go on back to sleep then.

GRANDPA. That's all very well, that is. I been woke up. I shan't get to sleep again now.

LOFTY. Sorry, Grandpa. You try and get some kip. We'll be as quiet as we can.

CORP. Go on Grandpa—you get off to kip.

GRANDPA. I won't sleep now—I know I won't. I've been ill. Just come out the hospital.

TICH [shouting] For Gawd's sake turn it in, you silly old fool!

There is an embarrassed silence.

GRANDPA. He's a nice one, he is. Very nice. Young layabout.

He lies down and turns his face to the wall. There is a further silence.

CORP. You want to watch that temper of yours, mate.

TICH. Ah—they get on my wick. These old fools. What they done with their lives? End your days in a lousy doss house.

CORP. Ah, knock off. [Tich sits]

Corp goes back to his newspapers. Lofty opens his case and takes out a packet of bacon, half a sliced loaf and a tin mug. He puts two rashers of bacon on the iron top of the stove. Then he goes up to his bed. There is a silence.

TICH. How long you been out the army, Corp?

CORP. Two years.

TICH. What'd you do? Desert or something?

Corp looks up quickly.

TICH. All right then—keep your shirt on!

CORP. No. I didn't desert.

TICH. Well, that's all right then.

Lofty comes to the stove with mug and thermos.

Lofty, kneeling, puts bread on stove.

LOFTY. Smells all right, don't it?

CORP. Yes. Smells good.

Lofty turns the bacon with his fingers, burning them as he does so. He takes four slices of bread and makes two sandwiches with the two rashers of bacon. He stands for a moment with a sandwich in each hand. Corp starts to roll another cigarette.

LOFTY. Think the old man might be hungry?

TICH [despairingly] Oh, Gawd!

CORP. He might.

LOFTY. Don't know if I ought to wake him though.

CORP. He can only swear at you again.

TICH. He will.

LOFTY. He hasn't had no supper.

CORP. Go on, mate—chance it.

While Lofty sits undecided, Tich takes four potatoes from his pockets. He puts them round the ledge of the stove.

TICH. Marvellous these modern electric cookers, ain't they?

CORP. Well don't just sit there. Wake him up if you're going to.

Lofty crosses to Grandpa.

LOFTY. Grandpa. Here Gramp. Wake up a minute.

Grandpa struggles into a sitting position.

GRANDPA. Can't a man get any sleep, without some stupid bas . . .

LOFTY. I just thought you . . .

GRANDPA. What time is it then?

LOFTY. I don't know, mate. Supper time. Here.

Lofty proffers one of the sandwiches. Grandpa looks at it stolidly.

GRANDPA. What's this then?

LOFTY. It's bacon, mate.

GRANDPA. What are you showing it to me for?

LOFTY. It's for you. You haven't had no supper.

GRANDPA. That's my business.

TICH. Ah, let him go hungry.

GRANDPA. You keep out of this. Young layabout.

Tich turns away in disgust and rearranges the potatoes on the stove.

CORP. Look, mate—eat the ruddy stuff!

GRANDPA. I don't have to take charity from the likes of you. I've had a nice bit of cheese.

LOFTY. Look, mate—you eat this bacon or I'll knock your head in!

He puts the sandwich on the bed in front of Grandpa and turns away.

He moves to stool and sits.

He takes a bite from his sandwich then pours coffee from thermos into mug. Tich looks from Grandpa to Lofty and shakes his head.

TICH. Might as well have put it down the 'ole.

LOFTY. Your turn will come, mate—don't worry.

Corp takes a sixpenny tin of beans from his pocket and opens it with the tin opener on his jack knife. Then he takes it and puts it on top of the stove. The three men are now gathered around the stove. Grandpa furtively picks up the sandwich, then looks up at them and puts it down again.

TICH. My guts is fair rumbling.

CORP. And me. How long you been out, Tich?

TICH. Coupla weeks.

CORP. In long?

TICH. Six month. You ever been in, Corp?

CORP. Yes. I been in once.

TICH. How long you get?

CORP. Year.

Grandpa picks up the sandwich again and looks at it as casually as he can. Then with one movement he stuffs the whole thing into his mouth and chews furiously.

TICH [*indicating Grandpa*] I bet he's never been inside. Have you, Grandpa?

GRANDPA. Have I what?

TICH. Been inside?

GRANDPA. No, I haven't. I been in hospital I have. . . .

TICH, No, I mean—never?

GRANDPA. Course I haven't!

TICH. There you see? And look where it's got him.

LOFTY. I had a mate on the building once, *he* went crooked. You know—started going around with the wrong lot. Never did him no good.

TICH. Why not?

LOFTY. He got two years. The others got off, and he carried the can back.

TICH. More fool him.

LOFTY. That's what his wife said too.

CORP. What about his wife?

LOFTY. She went off with another man while he was in prison.

TICH. Ah women!

CORP. What do you know about women?

TICH. They're all the same. Make me sick they do.

LOFTY. You've only met one sort, that's your trouble.

TICH. It's all right for you to talk . . . you're married, ain't you? You're all nicely set up with a wife waiting at home for you. And kids.

LOFTY. I haven't *been* home for four months. Four months! And the kids. You don't know what it's like not seeing them kids for months on end.

GRANDPA. I know.

TICH. You know? What d'you know about it?

GRANDPA. You'd be surprised what I know about it. I've got children. I've got a son in Canada, I have. Making good money.

121

TICH. Why don't you get none then?

GRANDPA. I told you he's in Canada. I got a daughter too. She's married, got a nice house. And a kid too. A boy. He's my grandson.

TICH. He's got it all worked out.

LOFTY. What you doing here then?

GRANDPA. I wouldn't spend the rest of me days scrounging off me family. Besides we didn't always see eye to eye, my daughter and me.

CORP. Why not?

GRANDPA. Oh, I don't know, mate—little things.

TICH. There you are, you see that's women for you.

CORP. Oh, dry up you. I tell you, you know about as much about women as your old man must have done.

TICH. Here you want to watch what you're saying. I don't like that sort of talk.

CORP. You think you know it all, don't you? You think you've got the whole world all sorted out and wrapped up like a box of dates. I tell you one thing for free mate—you haven't learnt to keep your nose clean and your trousers dry! Women are all alike! What the hell do you think you're talking about? Who the hell do you think you are, anyway?

TICH. I'll tell you who I think I am, mate. I'm an old lag same as you.

LOFTY. Here . . .

CORP. No, Lofty—He's all right—let him go on.

TICH. Ah—it's no point talking to you . . .

CORP. No—go on. Go on. What else was you going to say? So I'm a gaol-bird? So what? I met some people inside who should never have been there at all. Intelligent people. And I met some stupid bastards who hadn't got nothing between their ears except the idea that the world owed them a living. I don't know which I was— but I've a good idea which you were. Though I doubt if you have. Have you? Well, have you? Which do you think you are?

TICH. What's that to you then?

CORP. I want to know. For a start-off—what were you in the nick for last time?

TICH. I'm not telling you. What's it to do with you?

CORP. All right, if you won't tell me, I'll have to guess. Petty larceny—or breaking and entering—getting in the back window of an old ladies' sweet shop and pinching a few fags. That's about your mark, I should think. That's about your cup of tea. Isn't it? Well, isn't it?

TICH. Look, mate, you watch it.

CORP. Watch it? What the hell are you talking about? What do you think you're going to do to me?

TICH. You just watch it—that's all. I was inside for something big, I can tell you. Since you're being so clever what was you inside for?

LOFTY. Oh—come off it you two. Give it a rest.

CORP. No—leave him be, Lofty. If he's so interested, I'll tell him. It won't make him any the wiser but I'll tell him. This is going back a few years. I was in the Army then. Been in as long as I could remember. Boys' Service first—the Regular Army. In a good regiment I was. [*Eats*] I liked being an equerry. It was all I knew and I liked it. I didn't do too bad. I kept me nose clean. I went through the war all right. When it was all over I was in Germany. I got married out there. German girl she was. Long fair hair. We was in quarters over there. Well, anyway . . . I don't know—I don't know how it all started. Just sort of happened. I heard that one of our Sergeants had been sniffing around, you know—trying to get off with her. Big fat slob, he was. I didn't think anything about it. I knew she was all right. She was a good girl. Only a little thing, she was . . . only came up to about here. So . . . anyway I thought nothing about it. Eventually the Sergeant left—posted away to Hamburg . . . [*He turns to the stove again. He traces a pattern on its side with the toe of his boot*] Then she told me what had happened. You see her people was all in the Russian Zone. She hadn't seen them in years. This Sergeant had got round her. Told her they'd escaped. You see—he had charge of all the refugees as they come through. Him and a Major. He said he'd send them back where they come from unless . . . well unless she . . . you know . . . did what he wanted. Poor kid didn't know what to . . . didn't dare tell anybody about it. So there you are. Her people hadn't really escaped. So he went off. Anyway . . . she told me. Said she had to tell me. I went raving bloody mad. I went straight out of that house. I saw someone's jeep just along the street and I didn't stop all the way to Hamburg. I found him in a Sergeant's Mess there. I couldn't go in so I sent word there was someone to see him. He came out. Just stood there. I hit him in the belly with one hand then in the face with the other. Then I picked him up and I hit him again. I hit him again and again and again. I couldn't stop hitting him. I felt me arms would drop off. I had blood all over me. I think he must have hit me a couple of times. Then I threw him against the wall . . . That's what did it. [*There is a pause*] He didn't die . . . but he'll never walk again and he only talks like a baby. Has to be fed. Anyway they put me inside for a year. They had to.

He crouches down and warms his hands at the stove, his face hidden. There is a long silence.

LOFTY. So what happened to your wife then, Corp?

Corp does not reply at once and when he does he remains crouched by the fire and talks very softly.

CORP. That's the funny part about it really. I never seen her again after the trial. I'd only been in the prison a couple of weeks when they told me. She was run over. Didn't know a thing about it—killed right out—so they told me. I never even seen where they buried her. That was in Hanover, in Germany like. Course I was in prison over here by then. I'd like to go there just once. Just to see it. Don't suppose I ever will though. She was a good girl. I'd just like to see it. [*There is a pause*] These spuds look like they're about done, Tich.

TICH. Oh—righto mate—thanks.

There is another silence. It is broken at last by Tich getting up to get his potatoes from the stove.

TICH [*embarrassed*] They look all right, then.

He takes the potatoes back to his bed and starts to eat. Lofty takes a final swig from his mug of coffee.

LOFTY. You want to borrow this mug, Tich?

TICH. Thanks.

Tich gets up, takes the proffered mug and goes out of the door, still munching a potato. Corp gets up and stretches, then goes back to his bed and starts to roll a cigarette.

LOFTY. Where you headed for now, Corp?

CORP. Oh—I dunno. I thought of working me way along the South Coast. Down to the West—Cornwall or somewhere. I don't fancy being in the same place too long. I been down there before.

LOFTY. Yes, it's nice by the sea.

CORP. Yeah.

Grandpa heaves himself out of bed and pads towards the door.

LOFTY. Where you off to, Grandpa?

Grandpa looks at him and then goes out.

LOFTY. It's a shame when they get to that age.

CORP. When you going to see your family again, do you think?

LOFTY. Couple of weeks. This job's near done.

CORP. Then what?

LOFTY. I don't know. Same again, I suppose.

CORP. Not much fun.

LOFTY. No.

Tich comes in with a mug of water. He puts it on the stove and stands over it warming his hands.

TICH. Parky out there.

LOFTY. Got some tea, mate, have you?

TICH. Course I have.

LOFTY. That's all right then.

TICH. Where's the old man then?

LOFTY. He didn't leave no message.

CORP. I could do with some kip.

LOFTY. Must be nearly lights out.

Corp and Lofty begin their very simple preparations for bed. Boots off, jackets folded for pillows. Grandpa comes in again.

TICH. Where you been then?

Grandpa looks at him.

He clambers into bed again and gets ready for sleep. Tich remains at the stove—waiting for his tea to boil.

LOFTY. Be lights out in a minute, Tich.

TICH. Who puts the lights out then?

LOFTY. The Governor.

TICH. Well bloody good luck to him. I'm going to have my tea.

Corp and Lofty are now in bed. Corp is smoking his last cigarette. Tich stands at the stove, staring gloomily at Grandpa.

TICH. Look at him. Lying there. No home. No lolly. No brains. All he's got is a new pair of treads someone give him.

Tich takes a packet of tea from his pocket and empties some into the mug. He replaces the packet in his pocket and goes back with his tea to the bed. He sits. From outside a handbell is heard.

LOFTY. Well—that's it then.

TICH. Well, I'm going to wait for my tea.

LOFTY. Ah. Goodnight.

The lights go out. The only light comes from the reflected glow of the street lamps through the high-barred windows. From an adjoining room there comes the sound of a man singing again. There is a chorus of protesting shouts and he stops. His muffled voice can be heard replying then there is silence except for the sounds of the men in the room struggling to get comfortable. Tich sits on the end of his bed, drinking his tea.

Fade out.

Act Two

The same scene. Three hours later. The light of the street lamps is now reinforced by the rising moon, so that there is almost as much light as there was when the electric light was on in the previous scene. Tich is now in bed. Grandpa's shoes no longer hang at his bed end. For a minute nothing happens; then there is a general upheaval from Grandpa's bed and he gets up and totters towards the door. He has just begun to open it when a thought occurs to him and he hurries back to his bed. He looks for his shoes and finds that they have disappeared. He searches frantically under and around the bed. He even looks inside the bed but does not find them.

GRANDPA. Here! [*He stands for a moment, desperately uncertain, then he goes to Corp's bed and timidly shakes him by the shoulder*] Here! Here—wake up mate. Here.

CORP. Hello—what's up? [*He struggles into a sitting position*] What's the matter?

GRANDPA. They've gone.

CORP. What d'you mean? What's gone?

GRANDPA. My shoes. The ones they give me at the . . . my shoes.

CORP. Your shoes? The new ones?

GRANDPA. The ones they give me when I left the hospital.

Corp swings his legs out of bed and starts to pull his boots on.

CORP. You looked?

GRANDPA. Course I looked. They've gone. I ain't got no others. They're the only ones I got.

CORP. All right! All right! Well—we'll have to wake him up.

Corp goes over to Tich's bed and shakes him roughly. Grandpa remains where he is keeping out of trouble.

CORP. Here. Wake up you. Come on.

TICH. Here—what's going on?

CORP. What you done with Grandpa's shoes?

TICH. Shoes? What do you mean? How should I know? I haven't seen them.

CORP. Are you going to give them over? Or do I have to get nasty?

TICH. You just try mate—that's all. That'd be your lot.

CORP. Come on. Hand them over.

TICH. Look mate—I tell you I haven't seen his shoes.

126

During the last couple of lines, Lofty has woken up and struggled into a sitting position.

LOFTY. What's the matter, Corp?

CORP. This little runt pinched the old man's new shoes.

TICH. I never touched them.

CORP. Well, get out of bed and let's have a look then.

LOFTY. That's fair enough. Then if you haven't got them you can go back to sleep again.

TICH. Not likely. Why should I? You got nothing on me. I've had enough of this.

   He lies down again and pulls the bed clothes about his ears. Corp stands irresolute for a moment.

GRANDPA. Here, he can't do that!

   Corp moves to Tich's bed again and rips the bed-clothes back.

CORP. Come on, runt. Get out of there.

TICH [*sitting up*] You lay another finger on me mate and I do you up right.

CORP. Hand over them shoes!

TICH. You know mate—you're getting to be a big laugh. Here— Grandpa—you sure *he* hasn't got 'em? I'm not the only gaol-bird round here you know. He's done his time too.

   Corp grabs the front of Tich's shirt and pulls him bodily out of the bed.

CORP. Now—hand them over—quick!

TICH. Take your dirty hands off me!

   He tries to push Corp away from him.

CORP. Now don't get rough with me sonny. Just hand over the old man's shoes.

LOFTY. For God's sake keep it quiet. You'll have the Governor in here in a minute.

TICH. Right mate.

   Tich brings his knee up sharply into Corp's crutch. Corp staggers away, bent double, towards his bed and collapses on to it. Tich stands, panting, in the centre of the room—the two others watching him.

TICH. He asked for that—he did. Trying to get tough with me. They don't try that twice. Trying to get tough with me. I know a trick or two I can tell you mate. You won't be much good after that for a day or two. You probably never was. That's why your missus got off with another bloke. You probably wasn't much good to her. Trying to get tough with me.

The other men stand appalled. Corp lies quite still. The only sound is Tich's heavy breathing. Lofty moves over to where Corp is lying and bends over him, pushing Tich out of the way.

LOFTY. You all right, mate?

Corp does not reply but slowly and painfully drags himself to his feet. He pushes Lofty aside and moves slowly towards the door. Tich backs away slightly as Corp passes him, not sure what he is going to do. When Corp reaches the door he pauses for a moment before opening it. He stands with the door open, listening. Then he closes the door again and stands facing the room with his back to the door. Tich backs away even more.

GRANDPA. Here. What's going on?

Corp begins to move slowly towards Tich.

TICH. You keep away from me, mate. I don't want to have to really hurt you.

Corp does not reply and gives no sign that he has heard. He continues to move towards Tich.

TICH. Now—I've warned you, mate. Keep away. Go on—keep away.

Corp still gives no sign of hearing. Tich backs away between his bed and Grandpa's.

GRANDPA. Here!

LOFTY. Quiet, Grandpa.

Corp makes a grab at Tich who breaks away and makes a run for the door. Corp catches him, knocks him to the floor and then hurls himself on top of him.

LOFTY. No Corp. He's had enough.

Corp goes to his bed and sits head in hands. Lofty crouches beside Tich and feels his heart.

LOFTY. He'll live.

Lofty lifts Tich up and deposits him on his bed, covering him roughly with a blanket.

LOFTY. Now perhaps we can get some sleep.

GRANDPA. What about my shoes though?

LOFTY. I'd forgotten all about those.

Lofty searches around Tich's bed, he lifts mattress under Tich's head and brings out the shoes.

LOFTY. There you are, Grandpa. He couldn't even hide them properly.

GRANDPA. Young layabout. My new shoes. They give them me at the hospital. Not bad are they? [*He proffers one to Lofty*] Are they?

128

LOFTY. Not bad at all.

GRANDPA. That's the first new pair of shoes I've had in years that is. I don't think they're bad.

LOFTY. They're all right, Granfer. Well I'm going to get some kip. I got to get to work in the morning. Goodnight Corp. Goodnight Granfer. You'd better get to bed.

He gets into bed and rolls over on his side. Grandpa, however, has been woken up by all the excitement and is feeling talkative. His shoes still in his hand, he goes and stands beside Corp. Corp does not move but remains with his head in his hands.

GRANDPA. You all right, mate?

CORP. Yes—I'm all right.

GRANDPA. They ought to get the cat. All them young layabouts like that.

CORP. You'd better get to bed, Grandpa.

GRANDPA. No—I'm all right, mate. Don't you worry about me. I had all the sleep I need in the hospital. Last me for years that will. It was all right in the hospital. You don't have no worries. Well, only whether you're going to die or not. And that ain't a real worry—'cos even if you was to croak—well I mean they're all equipped for it there. They got it all sorted out.

CORP. Yes I suppose they have. You ought to get some kip though.

GRANDPA. No mate. I'm all right. There was one bloke in the next bed to me went off one night. Went out like a light he did. He come in one night with pewmonia . . . Dead the next day he was.

CORP. Tough.

GRANDPA. Oh, I didn't mind. They moved him as soon as they see he was dead. No mate. I didn't mind. I knew. I knew as soon as they brought him in. I knew he was for the high jump. I told him so. When they brought him in I could see. So I leaned over to him and I said, "You don't look so good," I said. He didn't say nothing so I said, "I wouldn't like to be in your shoes, mate," I said. He didn't say nothing. Couldn't, I daresay. They put a screen round him soon after that.

CORP. Yes.

GRANDPA. Look at them shoes then. They're all squashed up. You was quite right doing what you did. I'd give 'em the cat if I had my way. You was quite right. That give him something to think about that did. You ought to have hit him some more. Young layabout. If I was younger I'd have shown him. I'd have . . .

CORP. For God's sake shut up, you old fool!

The old man stares blankly at Corp, who has risen to his feet and is glaring at him. Then the old man turns away from him and moves down to the spare bed beside Corp's. He sits on the edge furthest from Corp. Corp, ashamed of his outburst, stands with head bowed. Then he lifts his head and looks at Grandpa. He takes a pace towards him, thinks better of it and slowly gets into bed. He lies down and covers his head with the bed clothing. There is a long silence. Grandpa does not move. Corp sits up again.

CORP. Why don't you go to bed Grandpa? [*Grandpa does not reply*] You'll catch cold out there, mate. [*There is still no reply. Corp gets to his feet and moves over to beside Grandpa. He stands there looking down at him*] I'm sorry for what I said, Grandpa. I didn't mean it. I'm sorry.

Grandpa averts his face, but does not answer. Corp sits beside him.

GRANDPA. They all think because you're old you don't matter.

CORP. I didn't mean it, Grandpa—honest. You know how it is when you lose your temper. You say things you don't mean. You know.

GRANDPA. They think you ain't got no feelings. Just because you're old I know. Do you think I don't know? Think I don't know I'm useless.

CORP. You're not mate. I didn't mean . . .

GRANDPA. That's why I left my daughter's place. Her husband. He thought I was useless. He said so. Just like you did. He said he was sorry after. But it didn't make no difference. I know he meant it.

CORP. He didn't mean it, Grandpa—no more than what I did.

GRANDPA. I got so now you don't have to say it. I know you think it anyway. I know. I remember *my* Grandpa. He used to come to the sea-side with us on holiday. When I was a nipper. I remember he used to lie on the beach. He used to go to sleep he did and us kids used to play jokes on him. You know how kids do. We used to go on the pier with him and we'd see the Punch and Judy. Used to spend a lot of money on us kids he did. And we used to play jokes on him. Sometimes we'd go and see them pierrots on the beach and he'd always put something in the hat for them. I suppose we thought he was just a silly old fool though.

CORP. Kids are like that.

GRANDPA. There's a life for you now—them pierrots. There's a life. In the sunshine. By the sea. Make quite a tidy sum of money too I daresay.

CORP. You don't see 'em now the way you used to.

GRANDPA. Yeah! You don't, mate, and that's a fact.

CORP. No call for 'em I suppose.

GRANDPA. I suppose not. I suppose there ain't. I suppose there just ain't no call for 'em. I had a mate once—him and me was going in for it. This is going back a few years, mind. Him and me was going in for all that. Not like them pierrots exactly. You know—not the same. More modern like. We got it all worked out. We just thought of it. Like that. We worked it all out together. Just him and me. We got it all worked out.

CORP. What was you going to do then?

GRANDPA. Well—I'll tell you mate. He was a great whistler he was. Always whistling. He could copy all the birds. Any bird you'd like to name he'd copy it for you. Mind you most people don't know one bird from another so it didn't make no odds. But he could do it. Any bird you'd like to name. So what we was going to do was this. First of all he'd do his bird imitations. Then—when we'd got a crowd round—he'd whistle [*whistling*] or some such tune and I'd do me dance to it. I wasn't much of a hand at dancing, but he taught me a few steps and it was all right. Then he'd do some more birds while I took the cap round. We'd got it all worked out.

CORP. So what happened? Did you do it?

GRANDPA. No. No, mate—we never got around to it. He got a job as night-watchman and give the whole thing up.

CORP. Hard luck!

GRANDPA. It's doing something that matters—I suppose. Being good at something. Take that young layabout there. . . .

CORP. Ah—him. . . .

GRANDPA. No—listen. There's nothing he's any good at—that's his trouble. That's what's wrong with him. There's nothing he can do.

GRANDPA. Here, Corp—can you whistle?

CORP. Whistle?

GRANDPA. Yes—you know [*He whistles vaguely*]

CORP. Can I whistle?

GRANDPA. Yes. You see I was just thinking . . .

CORP. What? You mean me and you?

GRANDPA. Yes. You know. Together. You got nowhere to go. No more have I.

CORP. Oh—I couldn't do that sort of thing, Grandpa.

GRANDPA. Why not? We could do it together. Course if you'd sooner not. . . .

CORP. It's not that, Grandpa. You know it's not.

GRANDPA. Well then . . .

CORP. I'm just not cut out for that sort of thing.

GRANDPA. I bet you never even tried. I bet you never even tried it. Have you?

CORP. Well—no . . .

GRANDPA. A whistler can go down very big. Very big he can go down.

CORP. But I'd be no good I tell you, Grandpa.

GRANDPA. Course you would. There's no need to do the birds if you like. Just the song for me to do the dance to. That'd do just as well—if you sung. That might be better. That might be even better.

CORP. Yeah.

GRANDPA. There you are then. You can sing and I'll do the dancing. You can sing while you take round the hat too. Be better than whistling. People don't like being whistled at. Not at close quarters they don't. Especially if your breath's a bit off. How's your breath then?

CORP. Oh—all right . . .

GRANDPA. There you are then you see. Cut out for the job you are. Fine big chap like you. Tell you what—in the winter we can do the smoke—you know all the theatre queues and all that. Then when the weather gets better, we can move down the sea-side. On the beaches.

CORP. Oh—well all right, Grandpa.

GRANDPA. You got to think out all the details. There might be snags. In the morning we'll think the whole thing up proper.

CORP. Yes—in the morning. We'll think about it in the morning.

GRANDPA. We might even get a little sign painted. With our names on it. Then . . .

CORP. Ssh! Wait a minute Grandpa.

GRANDPA. What's up?

CORP. Someone coming.

The door opens and the Governor comes in, carrying a torch.

GOVERNOR. What's going on in here then? Mothers' meeting?

CORP. We were just turning in, Governor.

GOVERNOR. Just turning in? Lights out was four hours ago.

GRANDPA. We couldn't sleep like.

132

GOVERNOR. I don't care whether you sleep or not—when lights out goes you get into your beds and you stay there. Is that clear? If you did a hard day's work for a change—any of you—you'd soon enough sleep.

GRANDPA. I can't do no work yet—I just come out the hospital . . .

GOVERNOR. All the more reason you should be in bed. I know all about you.

GRANDPA. Him and me was just talking over a little business idea we've had.

GOVERNOR. Business?

GRANDPA. Him and me are going in for it together.

CORP. Okay, Grandpa—let's get some sleep.

GRANDPA. Busking. That's what we're going to do.

GOVERNOR. Busking?

GRANDPA. Together, him and me. He's going to do the singing while I do me dance. Then he'll take the hat round to all the people. He'll still be singing while he does that mind. And we might get up a funny bit to do. You know—jokes.

CORP. Let's get to bed, Grandpa.

GOVERNOR. Well it's better than outright begging I suppose.

GRANDPA. What do you mean—begging?

CORP. Come on, Grandpa . . .

GRANDPA. He said it was begging . . .

CORP. No he never, Grandpa. He was just kidding. Wasn't you, Governor?

GOVERNOR. Never you mind about that. You just hop into your beds a bit quick—both of you.

CORP. All right, mate. All right. We're just going.

GOVERNOR. And less of the "mate" if you don't mind. I'm the Governor to your sort.

CORP. All right—no need to get nasty.

GOVERNOR. I'll be judge of that. You just do as you're told.

CORP. Aah.

GOVERNOR. What was that?

CORP [*wearily*] I never said a word.

GOVERNOR. Well all right then. Mind you don't.

Corp and Grandpa get into their beds. They lie down while the Governor watches them.

GOVERNOR. Now no more noise. Right?

The Governor goes out. There is silence. Grandpa gets up on one elbow.

133

GRANDPA [*in a hoarse whisper*] Hey, Corp, Corp. What song will you sing do you think? Corp? What song will you sing? [*After a long silence*]

GRANDPA [*defiantly*] Goodnight!

He lies down.

Fade out.

Act Three

The same scene. Some hours later. The first light of dawn is filtering through the high-barred windows. Grandpa is awake and lying with his hands behind his head, gazing up at the ceiling. During the scene the light gets stronger and stronger until the early morning sun shines brightly into the room. The other men are quite still. After a few moments, a handbell is heard in the distance down the corridor. We also hear the Governor's voice as he goes from room to room, waking the occupants.

GOVERNOR. Come on! Wakey wakey! Come on, you lot—up you get now! [*Exits*]

This last sentence has been accompanied by a banging on the door. The voice fades away down the corridor again. Lofty is the first up. He quickly gets his washing kit from his case and goes out. Grandpa starts to get out of bed, but stops when he sees Tich start to move. As Grandpa watches, Tich painfully swings his legs out of bed. His face is badly bruised and dried blood has run from his nose. He gets to his feet and looks around the room. He sees Grandpa looking at him and goes slowly over to him. He stands menacingly over Grandpa. Grandpa returns his stare—half fearful, half with bravado. Eventually Tich speaks.

TICH. I'll get you, old man.

Grandpa does not move. Tich turns from him and goes to the door. He opens it and turns back.

TICH. You and your mucker.

He closes the door behind him. Grandpa goes to Corp's bed and shakes him.

GRANDPA. Here, Corp! Wake up!

Corp sits up in bed.

CORP. What's up, Grandpa?

GRANDPA. It's him. He's up. He said he was going to get me.

134

CORP. Get you?

GRANDPA. That's right. He come over to me and he just looked. Then he said he was going to get me.

CORP. Ah—you don't want to worry about him, Grandpa.

GRANDPA. He said he was going to get you too!

CORP. Get me, the only thing he'll get me's a cup of char.

GRANDPA [reassured] That's right. [Worried again] I think he's gone to get the Governor.

CORP. He's a lot of hot air. That's all he is—a lot of hot air.
Corp gets out of bed and starts to pull on his boots.

GRANDPA. He didn'arf look a mess.

CORP. I daresay he does. Don't you worry about it, Grandpa—he can't do nothing.

GRANDPA. That's right. [He sits down dejectedly]

CORP. You'd better get a move on, mate. You'd better get a move on if you want to get in the wash-house.

GRANDPA. Don't matter. I ain't too particular about this washing.
He gets up and starts to fold his blankets lethargically.

GRANDPA. Here, Corp.

CORP. What's up?

GRANDPA. You know what you said last night? You know—about the busking?

CORP. What about it?

GRANDPA. It's still on? I mean you did mean it, didn't you?

CORP. Course I did, Grandpa.

GRANDPA. That's all right then.

CORP. Yeah. Well—I'd better get along there. [He picks up his washing kit] Where's Lofty then?

GRANDPA. He's along there already.

Corp goes to the door and exits. When he is gone Grandpa stops folding his blankets and cocks his head on one side, listening. Then he goes to the door, opens it and looks up and down the corridor. Then he closes the door and starts back to his bed. As he passes Tich's bed he stops and glares at it.

GRANDPA. Young tearaway.

He kicks the leg of the bed viciously, then hurries back to his own bed and starts to fold the blankets again. The door opens and Corp returns.

CORP. Queue a mile long. I'll have another go after breakfast.

GRANDPA. We got to get cleared up anyway.

CORP. Yeah. [He starts to fold his blankets]

GRANDPA. Did you see him along there?

CORP. Who?

GRANDPA. That young nark—you know.

CORP. Wasn't in the wash-house.

GRANDPA. There—I told you. He's gone to see the Governor. I told you.

CORP [*turns*] Well, so what?

GRANDPA. He didn'arf look a mess.

CORP. Be an improvement, I should think.

GRANDPA. You didn'arf give him a going over.

CORP. Why don't you relax, Grandpa? Forget it.

GRANDPA. That's all very well, that is. I bet he's gone to stir it up. He would. That's just what he would do.

CORP. Look, Grandpa, there's nothing he can do. Nothing. The Governor brought in the cleaning kit yet?

GRANDPA. Ain't seen him. Ain't seen him since he first came round. Not since that young layabout went out.

CORP. Dunno how he expects us to clean up with no cleaning kit.

GRANDPA [*desperately*] Why don't we go? Why don't we just get out of here?

CORP. What for? What's the matter?

GRANDPA. I tell you he's gone to see the Governor.

CORP. I don't give a monkey's who he's gone to see. What's he going to do to me?

Lofty enters through door carrying washing kit.

LOFTY. What the hell were you two up to last night?

CORP. What d'you mean?

LOFTY. I woke up when the Governor come in.

GRANDPA. Corp and me was talking.

CORP. Lofty don't want to hear about that, Grandpa.

GRANDPA. Yes, he does. Course he wants to hear about it.

Lofty puts away his washing things and begins to make his bed.

LOFTY. How's his Lordship this morning?

GRANDPA. Ain't you seen him?

LOFTY. No, I ain't seen him.

GRANDPA. He's gone to tell the Governor about last night.

LOFTY. I bet he looks a mess, don't he?

CORP. Well, where's all this cleaning kit, then?

LOFTY. Ain't it come yet? I'll be late if it don't come soon.

CORP. What time do you have to clock in?

LOFTY. Seven-thirty.

136

The door opens and Tich enters. He doesn't look at the others but goes straight to his bed and starts to make it. Grandpa watches him. Corp busies himself with cleaning up and pretends not to notice him. Only Lofty is quite unaffected by the atmosphere.

LOFTY [*cheerfully*] You're looking a bit rosy this morning, Tich. [*No reply*] Out on the tiles last night, were you?

GRANDPA [*emboldened by Tich's silence*] He don't look any too bright, do he?

Tich stops work and stares at Grandpa. Grandpa subsides.

LOFTY. Seen the Governor this morning?

TICH. What's that to you?

LOFTY. I got to get off. He ain't brought the cleaning gear round.

TICH. He'll be round. He'll be around, mate.

GRANDPA [*fearfully*] He's been to see him. He's been to see the Governor.

TICH. You keep quiet, you old scarecrow.

CORP. You lay off. We've had enough from you.

TICH. You just wait, that's all.

CORP. Aah—run home and play marbles.

GRANDPA. That's right. [*To Lofty*] He don't frighten me, you know. I met the likes of him before. All hot air, he is. He don't frighten me.

LOFTY. Well, that's all right then.

The door opens and the Governor comes in. Tich continues to fold his blankets, avoiding everyone's eye. Lofty and Grandpa stop work and watch the Governor. Corp works on—apparently unconcerned.

CORP. Where's all the cleaning gear this morning, Governor?

GOVERNOR. Well? What's it all about?

CORP. Can't get cleared up without the gear.

GOVERNOR. Shut up. I'm talking to him. Stop that and listen. What's it all about, eh?

LOFTY. What's all what about, Governor?

GOVERNOR. All this fighting.

LOFTY. Fighting? When was that, then?

GOVERNOR. Don't try to be funny with me. [*Pointing at Tich*] How did his face get like that? Eh? I suppose the fairies did it?

TICH. It wasn't him. He wasn't in it. It was the other two.

GOVERNOR [*to Lofty*] Don't try to be funny, that's all. [*He turns to the other two*] All right, you two, what's been going on?

CORP. What's the matter then, Governor?

TICH. Don't you take any lip from him, Governor.

GOVERNOR. Shut up! Were you fighting last night?

CORP. What if I was?

GOVERNOR. He says you beat him up.

TICH. Yeah—that's right.

GRANDPA. You don't want to take any notice of that young layabout.

TICH. You keep quiet, you bloody old scarecrow!

GOVERNOR. Shut up, all of you. I run a respectable lodging-house here and I'm not going to have hooligans spoiling it all and fighting all over the place. I'm going to get to the bottom of this if it takes me all day.

GRANDPA. I'm not letting him call me names.

GOVERNOR. Shut up! [*To Corp and Grandpa*] You two'd better come along to my room.

GRANDPA. What for? What we got to go to your room for?

CORP. All right, Grandpa, come on. We'll soon get this sorted out.

GRANDPA [*shaking his hand off*] No! I'm not going nowhere. It's nothing to do with me. You did it. You hit him. I told you not to hit him. You did it.

CORP. But, Grandpa . . .

GRANDPA. I'm keeping out of this. I told you to lay off him. I just come out the hospital, I have. . . .

TICH. He egged him on. Don't you believe it, Governor. The old man egged him on.

GOVERNOR. I don't care who did it. You're both coming with me.

CORP. Come on, Grandpa. Nothing's going to happen. You just tell him the truth. . . .

GRANDPA. You leave me out of it. I don't want to be mixed up with your sort. You just leave me out of it. You're all as bad each other. I haven't done nothing. I don't know nothing about it. It was you.

GOVERNOR. *Did* the old man have anything to do with it, or didn't he? That's all I want to know.

CORP [*quietly*] No. It was me. He didn't have nothing to do with it. He was asleep.

TICH. Don't you believe it! It was both of 'em.

GOVERNOR [*going to Tich*] Shut up. I've just about had enough of you. You and your whining. Now wrap it up! [*To Corp*] You come along to my room. [*Corp goes to the door, opens it and goes out. The Governor goes to the door*] The rest of you get on with the cleaning. The stuff's out here.

138

The Governor goes out. Grandpa sits on his bed, his face to the wall. Tich stands looking defiantly at Lofty. Lofty stands silent for a moment, then goes into the corridor and collects the cleaning gear—small shovel, large broom and a bucket for the dirt. He puts the bucket by the stove and starts to sweep the floor.

LOFTY. Clean out the stove, will you, Grandpa?

Grandpa does not reply for a moment, then rises, goes to the stove, gets on his knees and starts to rake the ashes out.

LOFTY [*quietly*] You didn't ought to have said that Grandpa [*There is no reply. Grandpa goes on working*] You only made it worse for Corp. And they couldn't do anything to you anyway. You didn't touch him. It was only that it all started on your account. About them shoes of yourn. If you'd just told 'em that—it'd been all right. You'd no cause to get scared like that.

TICH. Aaah—what you expect? What you expect from a useless old tramp like that?

Grandpa gives no sign that he has heard any of this. But the tears are streaming down his face as he continues cleaning out the stove.

TICH. Dead useless!

Lofty drops his broom, strides over to Tich and catches him up by the lapels.

LOFTY. You just keep your dirty little mouth buttoned! You shut up! I don't often feel like laying someone flat—but one more word out of you and I'll make you wish they'd drowned you at birth, like they should have done. Now—just get away from me, you dirty little whelp!

He pushes Tich away from him and goes slowly back to his broom which he picks up and resumes sweeping.

GRANDPA. Lofty! [*Lofty goes on sweeping angrily*] Lofty, mate!

LOFTY. What you want, Granfer?

GRANDPA. What'll they do to him?

LOFTY. I dunno.

GRANDPA. What'll they do to Corp? They won't put him back in the nick, will they?

LOFTY. I tell you I don't know, Granfer.

GRANDPA. I wouldn't have done that for the world.

LOFTY. I know, Granfer.

GRANDPA. No, you don't. You don't know. We was going in for this business together, Corp and me was.

LOFTY. Business? What sort of business?

139

GRANDPA. We was going to do this busking. Corp and me. We had it all fixed. We was going to do it together.

LOFTY. Oh—well—never mind, Granfer.

GRANDPA. I'm an old man though. I get scared.

LOFTY. I know.

GRANDPA. No, you *don't*. You *don't* know. I tell you I'm an old man. I'm going to die—and nobody won't care. It'll be as if I hadn't lived at all. As if I just hadn't *lived*.

LOFTY. No, it won't. . . .

GRANDPA. That's why I wanted to do this busking. If I'd done this busking—well—there might be somebody. You know—somebody might see me and one day, when I was dead, they might say . . . "What happened to that funny old bloke what used to do that dancing with that other bloke?" . . .

LOFTY. Reckon we're all like that, Granfer.

GRANDPA. But I ain't got nothing. There ain't nothing of me but what there is here.

LOFTY. You got your son.

GRANDPA. He don't know if I'm dead already or not. And he don't care. . . .

He breaks off as the door opens and Corp comes back into the room. He leaves the door open and, rather listlessly, goes to his bed, puts his great-coat on and collects his few belongings. The others watch him in silence.

LOFTY. What'd he say, Corp?

CORP [*half-smiling*] Oh—nothing much. Just not to come here again. I got to get out now. [*He grimaces*] No breakfast.

LOFTY. That all?

CORP. That's all.

The Governor comes in and stands in the doorway.

GOVERNOR. All right now. Out you go.

CORP. Well, all right. Give us a chance.

TICH [*indignantly*] You letting him off like that? What's the matter with you?

GOVERNOR. That's enough out of you.

CORP. Well—cheerio then, Lofty.

LOFTY. Oh—well, cheerio, Corp.

Corp goes to the door. Turns as if he was going to say something, then thinks better of it and goes.

GOVERNOR [*calling after him*] And I don't want to see you here again! [*To the others*] The rest of you want breakfast?

TICH [*gathering up his belongings*] Ah, stuff your breakfast. [*Sarcastically*] You're too bloody hard, you are.

GOVERNOR. Please yourself. You needn't bother to come here again either.

TICH [*indignantly*] What d'you mean? What have I done?

GOVERNOR. Never you mind what you done. I'm telling you. [*Tich goes up to him*]

TICH. You got a nerve!

The Governor and Tich go off still arguing. As their voices die away, Lofty goes back to his bed, puts on his hat and coat and picks up his case.

LOFTY. Well—I'm off now, Grandpa. See you around, mate, eh?

GRANDPA. That's right. [*Not lifting his head*]

LOFTY. Well—cheerio then. I got to get off now, or I'll be late. [*He hesitates, then goes to the door*] Cheerio.

He goes out; after a moment, Grandpa gets up and takes a step towards the door as if to call him back. Then he has a last look around his bed-space for his belongings. He goes slowly to the door and goes out leaving the room empty.

Fade out.

THE MYTH MAKERS

by

WILLIAM BAST

CAST

ANNE SWIFT	*Kate Reid*
PAT SWIFT	*Pat English*
JERRY ROSS	*John Sullivan*
OWEN RUBERG	*Colin Douglas*
MRS. DORIS BRAWLEY	*Doris Nolan*
PHOTOGRAPHER	*Chuck Keyser*
REPORTER	*Nicholas Stuart*
TEENAGE GIRL	*Julie Alexander*
HARRIET SWIFT	*Vera Cook*
MARTIN SWIFT	*Peter Madden*
NEWSCASTER	*Nicholas Stuart*
MISS ALBRIGHT	*Susan Crawford*
MR. JAMESON	*Philip Holles*
HARVEY POTTER	*Nick Brady*
1ST TEENAGER	*Julie Allan*
2ND TEENAGER	*Ann Castaldini*
EMILY RUBERG	*Jill Nyasa*
HOP HEAD	*Kevin Scott*
MIKE	*Orlando Martins*
BOY	*Robin Brown*

DIRECTOR	*Silvio Narizzano*
DESIGNER	*Tom Spaulding*

DIRECTOR'S NOTE

I found this play fascinating to do on two counts. First, because of its social aspect—as a study of group behaviour which has become something of a psychological phenomenon of our time; and secondly because a quick-moving story covering a lot of dramatic ground is one that has interesting problems for the director who has to fit the play into the studio, and yet still create the realistic impression which good television must give if the play is to succeed.

The author, William Bast, has written a biography of James Dean: this play was a fictional extension of some of the more curious habits and customs of our society, which he had come across in the preparation of his book. It illustrates particularly the way in which young people of today crystallize their need for hero-worship in idols of their own making.

SILVIO NARIZZANO.

A BIOGRAPHY OF WILLIAM BAST

He was born in 1931 and was educated at the Universities of Wisconsin and California, where he studied English Literature. He started writing professionally at 21 and spent four years of his career in Hollywood writing comedies for television. For the past four years he has also written for British and American television. In 1957 he wrote a highly successful book, *James Dean—A biography*. A year later, on his first trip to Europe he was commissioned by Granada to write *The Myth Makers*.

ACTION

The action of the play takes place in the following sets:

(1) Railway station—Bull Creek, Kansas
(2) Inside Mrs. Brawley's car
(3) Porch and garden of the Swift house
(4) Living Room
(5) Hallway and stairs
(6) The Den
(7) Pat's room
(8) Mike's Bar
(9) High School stage.

Act One

Station platform. A train has just drawn in and the steam clears to reveal a large sign identifying the stop as "Bull Creek, Kansas." The platform is filled with people—mostly teenagers, reporters and photographers. There is a strange air of excitement mingled with solemnity, evident in the unusually hushed attitude of the the tensed crowd. They whisper to one another and crane their necks to see if anyone has emerged from the coach. A lone figure of a woman slips unnoticed into the foreground near the end of the platform. She stays well out of the crowd and newsmen. Her age is possibly thirty, but dissipation and an unkempt appearance make it hard to estimate exactly. She strains to see what the crowd watches for, but there is no sign yet. Nervously she fumbles in her purse for a cigarette. As she lights it, an excited murmur goes up from the crowd and a barrage of flash bulbs begins to pop off around the exit of the coach. The camera flashes become almost constant as a pretty, if not attractive, young woman steps on to the platform. She is dressed entirely in black and wears a veil over her face. It is apparent that she is confused and somewhat frightened by the mob. She turns for a suggestion of security to the man who follows her from the train. He is plainly forty, confident, sharp with a detectable intelligence and sensitivity just beneath the hard surface. He takes the cue from the woman in black, proceeds through the mob to the exit. The people do not co-operate immediately, although they remain solemn and respectful in their interest. Accidentally someone knocks the woman's hat, revealing her face. Immediately the flashes begin again. Several policemen help to clear a path for the couple. Gradually the crowd separates and the couple move through and out of sight. In the foreground, the lone woman mashes her cigarette out against the building, as the crowd in the background begins to loosen and disperse. Then, just as she is about to leave, the flash bulbs begin to explode with new enthusiasm and a sudden silence hits the crowd. Beyond the crowd something of interest is approaching from the other end of the platform. The crowd quietly separates, allowing passage to two men wheeling a cart down the platform towards the lone woman. On the cart rests a large ornate metal casket. A teenage girl in the crowd bursts into sobs and throws herself on to the casket. A police officer attempts to restrain her, but is finally forced to drag her away. She collapses in his arms. The lone woman's gaze is fixed on the approaching coffin in terrible fascination as though this were an experience she suddenly wished she had not encountered.

Mix to a car travelling fast—inside are four people. In the back seat Patricia Swift, the woman in black from the first scene, and Jerry Ross, the man who followed her from the train. In the front seat Owen Ruberg, an innocent-looking amiable man of fifty; and Mrs. Doris Brawley, ageless—45—beminked and bejewelled, with all the feminine accoutrements for disguising her basic masculine aggressiveness.

JERRY. You all right, Pat?

PAT. No bones broken. Lost: one black hat with veil.

Her nerves are showing. Jerry lights a cigarette and hands it to her.

RUBERG. Can't figure how all them people found out. The Swifts, Mrs. Brawley here, and me was the only ones knew you was coming on the 7.55. We tried to keep it quiet.

JERRY. I'm afraid it was my doing, Mr. Ruberg. I sent out a general press release before we left Hollywood this morning. We were ready for a mob scene.

PAT. More or less.

MRS. BRAWLEY. This must be hell for you, Mrs. Swift.

PAT. I'm becoming immune.

RUBERG. Well that explains it, 'cause we never told nobody you was comin' in tonight. Thought you'd prefer it that way. You newspaper people sure move fast.

MRS. BRAWLEY. I thought you were in charge of publicity for the studio, Mr. Ross.

JERRY. That's right.

RUBERG. My mistake.

JERRY. Forget it.

RUBERG. Been so damn busy with all these preparations for the funeral tomorrow. [*He remembers Pat with a furtive glance*] Well, we can go over that later.

MRS. BRAWLEY. The Swifts are waiting at the house. You haven't met them yet, have you, Mrs. Swift?

PAT. No.

RUBERG. Martin and Harriet's wonderful folks. Known 'em all my life. Sure made me sick to see this happen to such good people.

MRS. BRAWLEY. You'll love them. They're darlings. Of course this whole business has been too much for them. That's why we thought it best for them not to meet you at the station tonight. Tell me, Mrs. Swift—may I call you Pat?

PAT. Please.

MRS. BRAWLEY. It seems odd you've never met your in-laws.

PAT [*uncomfortably*] Well, my husband . . . Alan was . . .

JERRY [*covering for her*] Alan was always too busy to get away for a visit to Bull Creek.

PAT. He wanted to though.

RUBERG. Too bad you gotta see the town like this for the first time. You'd of liked it. It's small, quiet and friendly. Population 2,245— unless Martha Dawson dropped her fifth to-day. That'd make it 2,246. [*He forces a chuckle at his little joke*]

PAT. You're not from Bull Creek, are you Mrs. . . . Sorry.

MRS. BRAWLEY. Brawley. Doris Brawley. Never mind, honey. After what you've been through these past few days, I'm surprised you can remember your own name. No, I'm from Chicago. My husband owned some canning factories in this area. He had a mental breakdown last year, and I've taken over the business since. I'm in and out of Bull Creek constantly.

JERRY. Say, Mr. Ruberg, they were supposed to put in a special telephone—a direct line between the Swift house and the studio in Hollywood.

RUBERG. Yep. They rigged it up this afternoon.

JERRY. Good. Any word from the reporter from Epic Magazine, Albright?

RUBERG. She's comin' by the Swift house tonight. Wants to talk to you, Mrs. Swift.

PAT [*to Jerry*] Not tonight?

JERRY. I'll cut it short. She's from Epic.

PAT. I don't think I can take much more, Jerry.

JERRY. Hang on, honey. Just a little longer.

The Swift house at night. It is old and in the American Victorian style. There is a porch which runs around the entire house.

There is a light from the living-room windows. A woman's face peers into the night, searching for a sign of someone expected. The drone of a television newscaster's voice can be heard coming from within the house. At the edge of the driveway farthest from the house are two newspaper photographers smoking and talking in muffled tones. Two or three teenage girls stand nearby, autograph books poised for action.

1ST PHOTOGRAPHER. What's the word?

REPORTER. They should be here any minute. I left the station just before they did.

149

One of the girls steps up cautiously.

GIRL. Are they coming yet, Mister?

REPORTER. Yeah, kid, they're coming. Don't wet your pants.

1ST PHOTOGRAPHER. Hey, take it easy, Bob.

REPORTER. Aw, the little creeps. Why aren't they out somewhere necking?

We go inside to the living-room which is large, warm and friendly. The furniture is old and well-worn, but neat and clean. Most of the pieces are bulky with antimacassars sprinkled generously about for protection. There is an old grand piano in one corner. Hanging prominently over the sofa is a large portrait of a handsome young man, a byronian beauty of sorts. It is badly painted and bordered in black crêpe. There is a small photograph of another young man on the piano. He is less handsome than the one in the portrait and wears an army uniform.

Harriet Swift keeps vigil at the window. She is a small woman, frail and slightly timid. Her husband, Martin, is at the other side of the room trying to talk on the telephone, while the television set blares out the voice of the newscaster. Martin is in his late fifties, slow but strong and direct in his manner. They are both rather attractive people, simple and homely.

MARTIN [*into phone*] . . . I can't hear you, operator . . . Who?

NEWSCASTER. . . . said Mr. Dulles in his report on the current Middle East problem. There has been no reaction from the Kremlin as yet. National interest is still focused . . .

MARTIN [*into phone*] Mr. Ross? No he hasn't come yet. . . . I don't know. . . . What? . . . Well, they're expected any time now. . . . What's that . . .

NEWSCASTER. . . . on the tragic death three days ago of movie idol Alan Swift. [*Harriet turns to watch set eagerly*] Swift's bride of seven months, Patricia, left Hollywood this morning on the sad journey to Bull Creek, Kansas, where the body of the famous actor will be laid to rest in the family burial plot. Mobs of teenagers and fans flocked to Union Station in Los Angeles to bid a final farewell to their hero . . .

MARTIN [*into phone*] No, no. I say they're comin' in on the 7.55 . . . Yep, that's it . . . They should be here any time now . . . No this is Martin Swift . . . no, Swift . . .

NEWSCASTER. . . . Just over a year ago Swift sky-rocketed to fame as star of his first film. Overnight he became the hero of millions of moviegoers from New York to Tokyo. The rebellious young man with the moody face and flaring temper seemed to symbolize the fears and torments of the so-called "beat generation". The first sign of happiness in the brooding young actor's life came seven months ago when he married pretty Patricia Alexander, a secretary at Falcon pictures in Hollywood where Swift was filming. With an Academy Award for his first film role and a lovely bride at his side, there was new hope for the Lost One, as he became known. He began his second picture. His popularity in Hollywood was unprecedented. His studio claimed that Swift received ten times the fan mail of any other star. Then, riding the crest of this wave of success and popularity, Swift was struck by unexpected tragedy. Three days ago, just a few weeks after completing work on his last film, he was burned to death in a raging blaze that swept his Malibu Beach home. Swift was reported to have been trapped in the house, while trying to rescue his wife who escaped the blaze unharmed . . .

MARTIN [*into phone*] No, no . . . I say, they haven't arrived yet . . . what? [*Unable to tolerate the noise any longer, he turns and shouts at Harriet*] Harriet, turn that damn thing off!

HARRIET. But he's talking about Alan, dear.

MARTIN. I don't care. I can't hear myself think. Turn it off!

NEWSCASTER. . . . thus ended one of the most sensational careers in the annals of film history. Not since Valentino has there been such a public display of affection for a movie idol. Within forty-eight hours of the accident, Hollywood, Swift's studio, his wife, and the columnists were deluged with wires and phone calls, expressing the grief of . . .

Delaying slightly to snatch the last few words, Harriet finally switches the machine off.

MARTIN [*into phone*] Now, what was it you was saying? . . . Hello? . . . Operator. [*He hangs up in disgust*] Now see! I've lost the connection. I dunno, Harriet, sometimes I think you must be deaf the way you blast that thing.

HARRIET. If it was important, they'll call back.

Martin goes to the window and checks his vest pocket watch for the time.

HARRIET. I can't imagine what's keeping 'em. They shoulda been here by now.

MARTIN. There's always the unexpected. You should know that by now.

HARRIET. Yes.

MARTIN. Why don't you go lay down a while?

HARRIET. I'm not tired. Not really. Would you like me to fix you some coffee?

MARTIN. Not now.

HARRIET. It's too quiet. I don't like the house when it's so quiet.

MARTIN. Where's Anne?

HARRIET [*uncomfortably—lying*] I . . . I think she went to the library to do some readin'.

MARTIN. Now, Harriet, why lie for the girl? You know as well as I do she's most likely out at Mike's Bar. The minute she puts little Bobby into bed, she's outa this house. I don't like it. Tonight of all nights. She's got no responsibility. Somethin's gotta be done about that girl. She's gone from bad to worse.

HARRIET. I do wish they'd get here.

MARTIN. And at a time like this! You'd think she'd have the decency to pull herself together—at least while all them strangers are here. What kind of an example . . .

The sound of a car pulling into the driveway is heard. Harriet flits to the window.

HARRIET. They're here, Martin. They've come.

Harriet rushes to the front door and through the screen door on to the front porch. Martin follows her.

Mrs. Brawley's Cadillac has stopped in the driveway near the house. Pat is out of the car and talking to Mrs. Brawley who still sits behind the wheel. Owen Ruberg and Jerry are taking the luggage from the boot and setting it on the lawn. The photographers have rushed over and are taking shots of the arrival.

PAT. Thank you so much, Mrs. Brawley.

MRS. BRAWLEY [*corrects her*] Doris, honey.

PAT. Thanks for the lift, Doris.

1ST PHOTOGRAPHER. Over here, Mrs. Swift.

Pat turns obligingly to look into his camera. As she does, Mrs. Brawley takes Pat's hand in hers and quickly assumes an expression of grief and compassion. The picture is taken.

1ST REPORTER. Thanks.

MRS. BRAWLEY. Now listen, you let me know if there's anything I can do to help.

POLICE [*from porch*] Need a hand, Mr. Ruberg?

RUBERG. No thanks, Jim. We'll manage.

Ruberg and Jerry are lifting a heavy wooden crate from the trunk and having a bit of difficulty with it.

PAT [*to Mrs. Brawley*] You're kind.
One of the teenage girls approaches Pat.
GIRL. Excuse me, Mrs. Swift. Can I have your autograph?
Pat smiles wanly and obliges.
JERRY [*to Ruberg*] A little higher on your side.
RUBERG. What ya got in here—a cor . . . lead bricks?
GIRL. Thanks, Mrs. Swift.
She runs off to her friends and shows them the autograph. Pat turns and spots the Swifts who are now coming down the porch steps. She approaches them.
PAT. Mother Swift?
HARRIET. Oh, my dear child!
They embrace one another. Harriet begins weeping. Owen and Jerry bring the luggage and wooden crate to the porch and set it down. The second photographer gets a shot of the two women embracing. Jerry turns to them.
JERRY. Okay, boys, that's enough. These people would like to be alone.
Snatching that one last shot, the newsmen move off away from the house.
PAT. Hello, Father Swift.
MARTIN. It's mighty nice to meet you at last, Pat.
MRS. BRAWLEY [*from her car*] Well, I'm off. Goodnight.
There are general "goodnights" and she backs the car slowly out of sight down the drive.
PAT. This is Jerry Ross, Alan's publicity man and our closest friend.
They shake hands and exchange greetings.
HARRIET. Pat here's written about you in her letters.
MARTIN. Say, Mr. Ross, there was a call for you came in on our phone, not the special one. I was cut off before I could get the name.
JERRY. Thanks. Don't worry about it. They'll call again.
JERRY. I think we'd better open this out here, Pat.
HARRIET. Oh, can't it wait? Whatever is it?
PAT. It's for you. One of the few things I was able to salvage from the fire.
Jerry begins prying the lid off with a pen knife.
JERRY. I'm going to need a crowbar or a hammer.
MARTIN. Hold on. I'll fetch one.
Martin exits quickly into the house.

HARRIET. That awful fire. I had such a terrible dream about it last night.

PAT. I know.

HARRIET. Was he . . . I mean . . he was always such a beautiful child. It's so ugly to go like that.

Martin returns from the house with a crowbar and hands it to Jerry.

MARTIN. This should do it.

Harriet composes herself quickly. Jerry begins to prise the lid off the crate. Owen Ruberg helps him.

MARTIN. I was so disappointed when Alan didn't bring you home after you got married. Last time we saw him must've been three years ago—same time's Robert was home.

HARRIET. We didn't hear much after that—just what we read in the newspapers. And the letters from you.

PAT. He talked about you all the time—and Bull Creek. He loved you both very much. That's why I felt this was something you people should have.

JERRY. There we are.

Jerry lifts a well-sculpted bust from the crate and sets it on the porch. The face is the same as the one on the picture above the sofa, but somehow this face is more sorrowful, more doleful. It looks as though it were done with a touch of self pity behind the hand that moulded it.

PAT. Alan sculpted it himself. If you only knew how important it was to him. He used to say it was the only thing he ever created honestly.

MARTIN. Looks like a pretty good likeness. That's one thing I gotta say—the boy was always good with his hands.

HARRIET. It's a beautiful thing—but so sad.

PAT. He called it his Gold Star.

HARRIET. His Gold Star. D'you hear, Martin? Martin used to give the boys gold stars for their good deeds. Of course, that was way back when they was just little ones. Remember, Martin? They'd paste the stars on their calendars, one for every day they did something to deserve it. Alan didn't get very many—but he tried so hard.

MARTIN. Don't know how to thank you, Pat. It's a fine gift.

PAT. It's not a gift. It was never really mine.

RUBERG. What say we go inside? Gettin' a mite damp out here.

HARRIET. I know just where we'll put it. Would you carry it in, Mr. Ross?

Jerry carries the bust into the house following Harriet. Ruberg and Martin follow Pat in with the luggage. They leave the luggage at the front of the stairs in the hall and go into the living-room.

HARRIET. Right here on the piano. [*She moves the photo of the other boy to make room for the bust. Jerry places the bust in its place*] That's it. Oh, it's perfect there. Don't you think, Martin?

MARTIN. It's all right.

RUBERG. Mighty fine piece of work. People should get a look at it. Say, speakin' of people, you folks shoulda seen the mob down to station tonight. And along the streets. It's somethin' to see, I tell ya.

MARTIN [*to Pat and Jerry*] This has been goin' on ever since the accident. People pouring into Bull Creek on every train and bus for the funeral.

HARRIET. I never seen anything like it—except maybe the State Canners' Convention in Topeka two years ago. That's the year Martin was elected to represent the canning factories in our county.

MARTIN. There ain't but one hotel and two boarding houses in Bull Creek, ya know.

HARRIET. Our friends and neighbours have been takin' in visitors and puttin' 'em up wherever there's room to sleep.

RUBERG. That's Bull Creek hospitality for ya.

HARRIET. It gives you such a wonderful feelin'. Why, I can't go anywhere in the town without someone just walkin' right up to me and sayin' the nicest things about Alan. Complete strangers, too, all so kind and lovin'. I just can't get over it. It's all so unlike dear Robert's funeral. He was our other boy, you know. Alan's older brother. [*She takes photo from piano and hands it to Pat*] This is him in his uniform. Not so handsome like Alan, but a real good boy. He was taken from us in the war, way off in Korea—four years ago come Spring. But there was no big commotion when they brought him home. They gave him a medal.

MARTIN. The Distinguished Service Cross.

HARRIET. I got it framed. Hangs right over our bed. Seems so odd, they're both gone now. Wasn't it just yesterday they was only little boys gettin' under foot? Seems so far away now. I guess I never dreamed . . . my boys . . . [*She begins to weep*]

MARTIN. Now, now, Harriet. Mebbe you oughta go lay down. Grief's a private thing.

PAT. You're not among strangers.

155

HARRIET. It's all right, Martin. I'm all right now. [*She struggles to control herself before the tears are spent*] Really I am. See?

A car door is heard slamming shut outside.

MARTIN. Now, I wonder who that could be.

RUBERG. Prob'ly that Albright woman. She's a reporter from Epic Magazine.

JERRY. Sorry, Mr. and Mrs. Swift. I know this isn't the time, but these things can't be helped. I'm afraid it'll go on until after the funeral. But if you don't feel up to it now, I'll send her away.

HARRIET. No, don't be silly. We're all right. Anyway it wouldn't be hospitable to send her off without her story, now would it ?

The sound of Miss Albright's footsteps coming up the porch stairs can be heard. Then a knock at the front door. Jerry opens the door for her. She is a newspaper woman through and through.

JERRY. Come in, Miss Albright.

ALBRIGHT. Hope I'm not too late. Had a devil of a time getting a ride out here. You're?

JERRY. Jerry Ross. This is Mrs. Swift, Mr. Swift, Pat, and Owen Ruberg.

General greetings.

JERRY. Look, we couldn't have planned this at a worse time. Can you hold off on the personal stuff until tomorrow, if I guarantee you ample time?

ALBRIGHT. Sure, sure. But I'd like the dope on the funeral arrangements for tomorrow. I've gotta get it in tonight. The town's crawling with people. What're the plans?

MARTIN. Owen here's the president of our Chamber of Commerce. He's been handling most everything.

ALBRIGHT. Okay, Owen, what's the bit?

RUBERG. Well, I gotta say it took some plannin'. It all happened so quick, ya know. But I think we got everything under control now.

ALBRIGHT [*taking notes*] What about the services?

RUBERG. Well, you know, the church is just too small to get all them people in. I figure there must be somewheres around three thousand in town by now. Every one of 'em will want to be there. That's what they come for. So, we just had to restrict the inside seating to the family and friends . . . and the newspaper people, of course.

ALBRIGHT. Good.

During the above, the lone woman in the background at the station in the opening scene, enters the foyer from the rear of the house. She stands unnoticed, near the staircase, listening to Ruberg.

156

RUBERG. Now, I figured we gotta give all them folks somethin'. After all, they was nice enough to come out here for the funeral. Can't just forget 'em. It wouldn't speak well of Bull Creek. Not when Bull Creek's got a native son she's mighty proud of.

HARRIET. Bless you, Owen.

RUBERG. Well, Harriet, it's true. And the whole town wants you to know it. That boy meant a lot to us. Our loss is great.

MARTIN. Don't think we ain't grateful for the way our friends and neighbours have shared our sorrow.

RUBERG. Your sorrow is theirs. Anyway, we got the combined Methodist and Presbyterian Choirs to do the singin'. Fred Rook got up a fine sermon, and we're gonna see to it that everybody gets a chance to hear it. I got the manager of the Creek Theatre to let us use their public address system. We'll hook it up outside the church so's everybody can hear what Fred's got to say about Alan. The high school and the Legion Hall kicked in with a total of eight hundred foldin' chairs. We'll have 'em set up out on the front lawn. That way at least some of 'em can sit down during the services. The rest'll have to stand, I guess. There just ain't enough foldin' chairs in Bull Creek to set all them people.

ANNE [*from the hall*] Who gets the popcorn concession?

Every eye in the room turns sharply to her. She is obviously, but not sloppily tight. No one speaks.

ANNE. It was just a bad joke.

MARTIN [*with subdued anger and embarrassment*] This is our other daughter-in-law, Anne.

HARRIET [*nervously*] Anne, dear, this is Pat—Alan's wife. And this is Mr. Ross from the studio. And this lady's . . .

ANNE. I know—a female reporter.

PAT. You're Robert's wife.

ANNE. Widow, honey. Widow. Just like you. Well, not quite. You're the widow of the famous one—but we do have one thing in common. We're sisters in mourning. Hello there, Owen. I just heard you fillin' everybody in on the plans for the Big Celebration.

MARTIN [*snaps*] Anne!

ANNE. Sorry. No real offence intended. But that's what it looks like —a big celebration.

HARRIET. Maybe you better go up to bed, dear. You're not yourself.

ANNE [*ignoring her*] Have you seen our town? Have you walked down Main Street? Now, what do you suppose all those people are doing in a stinking little hick town like this? Biggest thing

157

that's ever happened here. You'd think it was for something important. You know, he should be here to see it. If he weren't dead already, he'd laugh himself to death.

MARTIN. I think that's enough, Anne!

ANNE. I say something wrong again? You'll have to pardon me. I've got a reputation around here for doing the wrong thing. I'm sorry sister Widow. I guess I was a little rough. But it wasn't meant for you. So, don't worry your pretty little head. You *are* pretty. Prettier than your pictures, at any rate. Where's my baby, Mother Swift? Where's Bobby?

HARRIET. Why, he's asleep long ago, dear. Upstairs in your room.

MARTIN. Go up to bed, Anne.

ANNE. Go up to bed, Anne. Sure. Sure. It's safer there. Well, if you'll excuse me now—and I know you will—I'll peek in on my son. He's getting so big sometimes he crawls out of his crib and sleeps on the cupboard floor with my furry slippers. I wonder if that means he'll grow up to be a pervert. Well, goodnight all.

She turns and mounts the stairs in the hallway. There is complete silence until she's out of sight.

MARTIN. Sorry about that. I can't abide to see a woman drunk. There's no excuse for it.

HARRIET. You see, Robert's death hit her mighty hard. In all this time she never rightly got over it. All this—well, it's the upset over Alan now. I hope you understand.

PAT. She must have loved Robert very much.

ALBRIGHT. Well, look, I've got most of what I need. I'll get the rest in the morning.

JERRY. You need a lift back to the hotel?

ALBRIGHT. No, I've got my little man waiting outside. Well, thanks to you all. . . . I'll see you tomorrow sometime.

JERRY. I'll walk you to the car.

Jerry and Miss Albright exeunt.

RUBERG. Guess I better be gettin' back, too. Emily's bound to be waitin' up for me. I'll pick you up in the morning, Martin.

MARTIN. I'll be ready at eight.

RUBERG. There's just some last-minute details at the church and cemetery. Well, goodnight Harriet . . . Mrs. Swift.

PAT. Goodnight, Mr. Ruberg. And thank you for all your trouble.

RUBERG. No trouble 't all.

Martin sees him to the door and out.

HARRIET. Can I fix you something? Coffee, maybe?

PAT. Oh, please don't bother. All I need is some rest.

HARRIET. Well, I'll show you to your room soon's Martin comes in. I put you in Alan's old room. It's just the way he left it.

Jerry enters followed by Martin.

JERRY [*to Pat*] That was rough, but I think I smoothed it over. For a minute there I thought we'd be reading every word of that in Epic next month. [*To Martin*] You've got to stay on your guard with these reporters.

MARTIN. Hear what he says, Harriet?

HARRIET. What do you mean?

MARTIN. You know what I'm talking about. What you told that reporter feller that came around this afternoon—it was shameful.

HARRIET. Oh, Martin, please don't start all that again.

MARTIN. All that nonsense about Alan being a hero in town. What're folks around here gonna think when they read a story like that? If you're gonna tell 'em anything, you shoulda told the whole story.

HARRIET. I didn't think there was any good of bringin' all that up now, Martin. Anyway, that's what Mr. Ross is talkin' about now. You got to keep things like that quiet.

MARTIN. Ain't no use talkin' to you.

HARRIET. You always did make too much of a fuss over little things, anyway. After all, what difference does it make now?

MARTIN. Now don't go makin' it sound like I'm pickin' on the boy— rest his soul. I just don't want you tellin' half truths so's people around here can get a laugh at my expense. You know how folks are. You know, Pat, from what we been readin' in all those magazines and newspapers about Alan, always puttin' on a act and behavin' wild like that, seems like people got the idea he was pretty clever. Well, they might think it was clever, but we didn't. Like the time Harriet here was talkin' about. Sure, he won the championship for the high school football team. The whole town went wild. But then, he went right off and got himself kicked out of school for drinkin' in the locker rooms. It was always somethin' like that. Now, Robert wasn't half the trouble that boy was. He took his schoolin' serious and never got into trouble, but Alan wouldn't listen to me. I never could get through to him noways.

HARRIET. He was a good boy. Maybe not the way Robert was. But he had his own kind of goodness. I often said you'd of seen that, Martin, if you'd taken the time. That day when they expelled him from school—he was a big boy then, but he cried hard. I mean, he put his head in my lap and cried and told me how sorry he was. When I asked why he did such things he said he just didn't know. Then, he promised me someday he'd do somethin' to make us proud of him. And he did that, Martin. Oh, not just because he became a famous movie star. But the way he died. That's the proof. It took a good heart to run into that fire after Pat. And I'm proud, Martin. Very proud. [*She loses control completely and begins to weep*] Excuse me. Martin can show you to your rooms.

She runs off and up the stairs. Martin is slightly upset and embarrassed.

MARTIN. It's the strain. She'll be all right.

PAT. Maybe I can help her.

MARTIN. No. I better tend to her. Just make yourselves to home. If you want to use that special telephone, it's through there [*indicates doorway opposite the living-room*] in the den. [*He follows Harriet up the stairs*]

JERRY [*when Martin is gone*] Well, just another happy, wholesome, human zoo.

PAT. I feel sick.

JERRY. Come with me. [*He takes her by the hand*] I've got to call Cooper. You going to be all right? [*She nods*]

He crosses to the den door and goes through; Pat follows him. It is a small room, sombre in décor. There is a large desk, leather sofa, bookcases, etc. It is obviously Martin's room. Jerry enters and switches on the lights. He reacts to the room.

JERRY. Um. Cheery nest.

He crosses to the telephone on the desk, towing Pat behind him.

PAT. Can't you make the call later?

JERRY [*picking up phone*] He's expecting me to call about now. [*Cynically*] Wants to know if we got good coverages at the station. [*Looks puzzled at phone*] It's dead. Damn. Well, it's an excuse not to call.

PAT. Good.

JERRY. Getting an idea why Alan turned out the way he did?

PAT. I can't help feeling sorry for that poor girl.

JERRY. Look, don't start letting yourself get involved in all this. These people don't mean anything to you. To-morrow night you'll be on your way out of here—and it's all over. You're free.

PAT. I suppose you're right. But I wish we hadn't come. I don't like the whole business.

JERRY. Honey, I don't like it any more than you do. But I'm stuck with it. This is my job—it's the last one I'll ever have to do for Alan. I just want to do it and get out. All we've got to do is hold on another twenty-four hours. Then we'll go away somewhere for a few weeks—until the fuss lets up.

PAT. I've got a feeling it's not going to be that easy.

JERRY. Sure it is. After a respectable time, we'll go to Mexico and get married.

PAT. Sounds so simple. You're forgetting I'm the widow of the Alan Swift.

JERRY. People forget.

PAT. Do they?

JERRY. They think what they're told to think. You know that. Why do they think he was the big hero type for trying to save your life? 'Cause I fed them that little tale. If we'd have told them the truth—that he was trapped because he passed out on the living-room floor dead drunk—they'd believe that, instead. . . . But this way he is a nice guy, and nobody gets hurt. He gets a hero's tribute; you become a saint; and Falcon Pictures gets some sensational publicity for their stinkin' film. Everybody's happy. No harm done. In a few weeks, a month, there won't be any need to cram Alan's name down their throats. They'll forget all right—when we give them something else to think about.

PAT. You paint such pretty pictures.

JERRY. I didn't order the world. If people need fairy tales, let them have them.

PAT. Just one short year ago, I didn't know how beautifully obscure I was. How did I get here?

JERRY. I'm not asking any questions. Why tempt fate?

PAT. Jerry, I'm not good at all these games. I just want to stand up— and tell the truth. Just one time—I want to shout it out. Listen to me everybody! I was in love with Alan Swift when I married him, but I couldn't give him the kind of love he needed. We weren't happy. I'm not the poor grieving widow. I'm the wife who was ready to sue for divorce. I'm in love with another man.

JERRY [taking her to him] Pat, baby.

PAT. It's all right, Jerry. They didn't hear me. Even if they could, they'd never understand. They'd label me, Wicked Woman Number One—or they'd blame poor, weak Alan. Damn them! They've always got to have everything black or white. There's no in-between.

JERRY. Baby, you don't owe them any explanations. Listen to me. What they think—it's not important. You and me—that's what's important. Try to hang on to that.

PAT. I don't know what's wrong with me. Everything is slipping away so fast. I can't keep up with it, Jerry. I don't know how to act. I don't know what to be. I wish to God someone would tell me, so I could stop guessing.

Jerry holds her close and tries to kiss her, but she turns away.

JERRY. What's the matter?

PAT [*avoiding his eyes*] Not here, Jerry. Not now. He isn't even buried yet.

Jerry stands back in disbelief. The cold fear of what is to come passes through him.

MARTIN. I'll take you to your rooms now.

And we see Martin standing in the doorway. A recriminating frown shrouds his austere face.

Fade out.

Act Two

Pat's bedroom. The following morning. This was Alan Swift's room when he was still living in Bull Creek and growing up. There is a large comfortable bed above which hangs a model airplane suspended from the ceiling. College and State pennants decorate the walls. There are several paintings and sketches done by a moody adolescent. A high school diploma and a football are prominently on display. The room is cheerful in its wholesomeness. Pat has just finished dressing. The bed is unmade and rumpled indicating a restless night. As she combs her hair before a mirror, she notices the diploma. She stops to read it. Momentarily tenderness sweeps over her, brought on by the fonder memories of her marriage. There is a knock at the door.

PAT. Come in.

Anne Swift enters. She is quite sober now and looks fresher than the previous night. She smiles and enters.

ANNE. Good morning. Mind some company?

PAT. Please.

ANNE. You were sleeping so soundly they decided not to wake you.

PAT. I was exhausted.

ANNE. I can imagine. Mr. Ross asked me to tell you he'd be back around noon. He went into town with Father Swift and Owen Ruberg this morning.

PAT. I guess I slept through everything.

ANNE. Mother Swift went along to buy a dress. Feel like some breakfast?

PAT. Not really—but I suppose I'd better.

Anne starts out the door. Pat follows (Just outside the door is the upstairs hall, staircase to the downstairs, and several bedroom doors).

ANNE. I was hoping you'd wake up before I put Bobby down for his nap. I wanted you to see him.

PAT. Oh, yes—I wanted to see him. Do you suppose I could take a peek now?

ANNE. Sure. He's in there. [*Indicates door*]

Anne opens the door for Pat. Pat peeks in. After a bit, she closes the door and turns smiling to Anne.

PAT. He looks so sweet. You're lucky.

ANNE. I think so. Ordinarily he doesn't nap in the mornings any more—he's getting too big for that now. But Mrs. Jenkins—a neighbour—she's taking him home with her this afternoon to keep him out of the way. I know he'll never get a nap over there. Not with her three kids running wild. C'mon downstairs. There's some coffee brewing.

They start down the stairs.

Mr. Jameson, the postman, is mounting the steps of the front porch. He carries an impressive sack of mail. Setting it down, he rings the doorbell as Pat and Anne enter the room.

ANNE. It's the postman.

She crosses to the front door.

ANNE. Mornin', Mr. Jameson.

JAMESON. Mornin', Anne. Got another load for ya.

Anne opens the door and Mr. Jameson enters, setting the sack down on the living-room floor.

ANNE. All this for us?

JAMESON. Yep. And there'll be more later.

ANNE. If there's anything important in there, we won't find it for months. Oh, Mr. Jameson, this is Alan's wife, Pat.

JAMESON. How d'ya do, Mam.

PAT. Hello, Mr. Jameson.

JAMESON. Can I say, Mam, folks around here's mighty sorry about your husband. You got every bit o' their sympathy—and that goes for me too.

PAT. Thank you.

JAMESON. Well, I gotta shove off. I'm way behind in my deliveries this mornin'. Nice to meet you, Missus Swift. G'day to you Anne.

ANNE. Bye, Mr. Jameson.

He exits. Pat reaches into the mailbag and withdraws a few of the letters.

PAT. Here's one addressed to Alan.

ANNE. That's enough to make your skin crawl. I mean, addressing a letter to someone who's dead. Weird.

PAT [*she opens one of the letters and reads*] ". . . I haven't the slightest fear that his memory will ever dim. His films convinced me that shining through the human frame was a monumental burning sincerity that touched me so deeply that, it is true, I am writing this now in tears. . . ." [*She opens a second letter*] "I guess you'd probably laugh or think what I am going to tell you is stupid. But I have a picture of Alan right above my bed, and every night before I turn the lights off I bid him goodnight. And sometimes I can feel that he's right in this room, standing next to my bed".

Pat is obviously distressed by the letter and puts it aside.

ANNE. Maybe you'd better leave them for later. C'mon, have some coffee. Why not sit on the porch? I'll bring it out to you.

PAT. Thanks.

Anne leads her to the den door and indicates the way.

ANNE. Through there. Anything to eat? Eggs?

PAT. I don't think so. Thanks.

Pat goes through and on to the porch. She sits in a wicker lounge chair and lights a cigarette. She rises and steps to the porch railing to scan the view. Anne enters with a tray and sets it on a small table between two chairs.

ANNE. There we are. [*hands Pat coffee and sits in the chair beside hers*] I want to apologize for last night.

PAT [*sincerely*] Oh, please, don't. I think I understand. . . .

ANNE [*interrupting*] No, don't tell me you understand. I'd say I don't know what got into me—but I do. I drink a little too much. And when I drink I sometimes say nasty things. Oh, it's nothing new, the drinking. It started just after Bobby was born. Only it wasn't serious at first. Nobody even noticed. I went right on teaching school. But last year it started to show. Then, everyone knew. You can't keep a thing like that a secret for long. That was the end of my teaching career. Oh, they were nice enough about it. That's what made it worse—everybody understood. Poor thing, losing her husband with a child on the way. You can't really blame her. Well, if they couldn't blame me, I couldn't blame myself. So, I went right on drinking—and being "understood". I'm not just a common drunk. I'm one of those special people who drinks mostly alone. Once in a while I go out to Mike's Bar—that's a road house tavern just outside town. I can't go to just any bar here in town. It embarrasses the respectable folks who come in for a bit of social drinking. So, I go out to Mike's Bar where it isn't so respectable. That's not very often though. Father Swift doesn't approve—and when he doesn't approve of something, you just don't do it. When I'm not drinking, I stay with my son. It isn't much of a life, but it's all mine. I rather enjoyed it, though, until all this started. Things have changed a lot around here since your husband died. You've no idea. But I didn't mean to upset you last night. It was pretty rotten, after what you must've been through.

An old Ford drives up the driveway in front of the porch and stops just before the two women. Harriet Swift is in the passenger's seat. The driver is a young farm hand, Harvey Potter. He is thirty, animal in his virility.

HARRIET [*from car*] Mornin'!

PAT. Good morning, Mother Swift.

Harriet gets out of the car with some bundles in her hands. Harvey gets out and takes some more packages from the back seat.

HARRIET. I'm sorry I wasn't here when you got up, Pat, but I had to go into town to fetch some things. Lucky for me Harvey here was around to drive me back—else I would've had to wait for Martin.

She mounts the stairs to the porch.

HARVEY. Mornin', Anne.

ANNE [*acridly*] Good mornin'.

HARRIET. Just take 'em in and dump 'em on the dining-room table, will you Harvey?

Harvey glances at Anne, but she avoids his stare. He smiles and enters the house.

HARRIET. Oh, my! I'm about run out. [*She sits in Anne's chair*] Martin insisted I go buy me a new black dress. He thought I best have somethin' nice for today—what with photographers and all.

ANNE. I wish you wouldn't bring him here.

HARRIET. Well, dear, he was the only person around. I didn't want to wait for Martin—they was havin' some sort of a meeting with Mrs. Brawley. Run into Harvey in the store.

ANNE. I just don't like him hangin' around—you know that.

HARRIET. Well, now, I don't think he's all that bad. What'd you want me to do—walk home?

Harvey returns to the porch.

HARRIET. Thanks, Harvey. Woulda been lost without you.

HARVEY. It's okay, Mrs. Swift.

HARRIET. Oh, Harvey, this is Alan's wife, Pat.

HARVEY. Howdy, Mam.

PAT. Hello, Harvey.

HARRIET. Will you have some coffee?

HARVEY [*aware of Anne's attitude*] Naw, I gotta be gettin' back to work. Thanks anyway. So long Anne.

He steps down from the porch and gets into his car.

HARVEY [*from car*] What's the matter, Anne? Can't you say goodbye?

ANNE. Sure. I just didn't see anybody leavin'.

Harvey runs his motor and backs out of the driveway. Harriet rises and goes to the front of the house along the porch, watching Harvey back out.

HARRIET. Careful there, Harvey! My goodness! He almost took my rose bushes with him. [*She notices something out front*] Now what's that?

Harriet rounds the corner to the front porch and sees two teenage girls on the front lawn. One of the girls is snapping pictures of the house with a box camera. The other is crouched on the lawn, collecting something into a small envelope.

HARRIET [*from porch*] Here now! What're you girls up to?

Harriet's voice attracts a policeman's attention. Startled, the girls turn to leave.

HARRIET [*coming down from porch*] No, don't go runnin' off. I just asked you what you was doin'. No need to be afraid.

1ST TEENAGER. I hope you don't mind, but I took a little grass from your lawn. Not much. See?

Pat and Anne have come around to the front and approach. The girl produces the envelope.

HARRIET. Grass? Whatever for?

2ND TEENAGER. Because it's from HIS lawn.

1ST TEENAGER. We took some pictures of your house, too. The girls at school will just die when they see them.

2ND TEENAGER. They'll absolutely flip when they see the grass! [*Recognizing Pat*] Oh, gee! It's her! I mean, gosh—Mrs. Swift!

PAT. Are you girls fans of Alan's?

1ST TEENAGER. Sure. Anybody who knows anything thinks he's the most. I mean, he *was*. No, I don't either. He still is the most. There'll never be another Alan Swift.

2ND TEENAGER. Gosh, Mrs. Swift, we never expected to meet you— not in a million years.

PAT. That's a long time.

2ND TEENAGER. We want you to know we know how you feel. We felt terrible about—you know. When we heard the news on television, a lot of us got together and cried. We did. We just sat around my house and cried all one night.

1ST TEENAGER. I still cry when I think about it. Oh, Mrs. Swift, you were so lucky to be his wife. I think almost anybody would just die to be in your place.

POLICEMAN. O.K. kids—let's go.

2ND TEENAGER. Sure. We understand. We're going over to the church to get our seats early. We'll be praying right along with you, Mrs. Swift.

1ST TEENAGER. Bye.

The girls go off, staring until the last moment at Pat. Harriet turns to go back to the house. Pat remains, troubled.

ANNE [*touching Pat's arm*] They're just kids. It doesn't mean anything.

PAT. I wonder.

HARRIET. Feature that! Grass—tearing grass outa the lawn. Who'd ever of thought. . . .

They all go back into the living-room.

PAT. Where does it all come from? I mean, what makes them like that?

HARRIET. I've asked myself the same thing, dear. But I guess it's a case of not being able to see the forest for the trees. Maybe we were just too close to see what they all see.

A car is heard pulling into the driveway. The sound of several car doors slamming shut.

HARRIET. I hope that's Martin. It's near time to be gettin' ready.

Jerry Ross enters first. Something is disturbing him. Martin and Owen follow.

JERRY [*to Pat*] Hi. How are you feeling?

PAT. I'll make it. [*Puzzled by his mood*] What's wrong?

RUBERG [*to Martin as they enter*] It was Emily's idea. She'll be here in a while. . . .

HARRIET. What's that you're sayin' about Emily?

RUBERG. Oh, I was just tellin' Martin—Emily got a bright idea. She got the ladies of the Church Guild to serve a buffet supper after the services. She figured a lot of them folks are going to be mighty hungry afterwards, and there ain't a restaurant in town can handle that many. I hear there's almost four thousand here now. People been pourin' into town all night.

JERRY. Yeah. It's like a real boom town.

RUBERG [*uncomfortably*] Got a request from the State Highway Patrol to mark the route to Bull Creek better so's they wouldn't get so many calls from lost out-of-staters. Dave Lundi got up some nice big signs pointing the way here. We put 'em up on Highway 51 and the county trunk roads around town. They're big enough. Nobody'll miss 'em.

JERRY [*annoyed with Ruberg's stalling*] Mr. Ruberg has something he wants to discuss with you Pat. I think you'd better listen carefully.

RUBERG. Well, yeah—you see, Mrs. Swift, a lot of folks around here got things they'd like to say about Alan. The mayor for one. The boys on the City Council and myself, well, we figured we got to provide these visitors with something special.

MARTIN. What Owen's trying to say is, they're going to hold a sort of Memorial Ceremony at the high school auditorium . . . tomorrow afternoon.

PAT. I don't see anything wrong with that. What's the problem?

RUBERG [*uncomfortably*] Well, it ain't exactly a problem. We had a meetin' last night—kinda late—and it was unanimously agreed that the town should do somethin', you know, somethin' permanent in Alan's memory. Now, we got one of the finest libraries in these parts right here in Bull Creek. But we never had anything to put out in front—in the square. Just that plaque to the war dead. But we always needed somethin' impressive out there. So, what we want to do is put up a lastin' memorial to Alan—right there where everybody can see it.

MARTIN. They want to use the statue, Pat. I told them it was more up to you. As far as Harriet and me is concerned, I guess we feel the boy woulda been proud to have it there. Doesn't seem right to keep it ourselves. If the town wants a memorial to Alan, then I think that statue's about the finest we can give 'em.

PAT. Well, I gave it to you. It's yours to do with as you think best. Personally it sounds all right to me.

HARRIET. Imagine that! Alan, right up there in the centre of Library Square. Right where everybody can see him and where everybody can see him and remember—even strangers passin' through. Oh, Martin I'm so proud....

   She begins to cry.

MARTIN. Harriet, it's near time to leave for church. Why don't you get into your dress?

   Harriet exits.

JERRY. The Council didn't stop with the bust, Pat. There's more.

PAT. Well, what is it? What's all the intrigue?

MARTIN. Ain't no intrigue—'cept what Mr. Ross here's whippin' up in his mind.

RUBERG. This is the way it stands. And I want you to know, Mrs. Swift, it's entirely up to you. This thing come to us from the outside. It was Mrs. Brawley who suggested it—and we think it's a fine idea. It's an Alan Swift Memorial Fund—a sort of scholarship fund in your husband's name. If the truth was to be known, we been thinkin' about doin' somethin' like that right here for our own school. But Mrs. Brawley thinks it should be national. Now, she's willin' to donate a hunk of money to start the ball rollin'. And she said she'd stay right here for a time and help organize the project for us. She's willin' to be Director of the whole business. She's a good business woman, as any man in Bull Creek can tell you. And she says she's done this sort of thing before. To her way of thinkin', what with Alan's popularity and all of his fans, there won't be much trouble gettin' donations. Sounds like this could be a mighty big thing.

JERRY. Well, that's certainly skirting the issue. He's just leaving out the finer points, Pat. Nothing important. Like, this woman wants you to dedicate the fund tomorrow afternoon at the Memorial Ceremonies. They plan to have the whole thing broadcast and filmed for television. It'll be a nation-wide appeal direct from grieving widow. They haven't missed a bet.

PAT. I don't understand. Why do you need me?

JERRY. Don't you see? You make the whole thing official. You lend it the proper authority. People are suspicious of fund raising campaigns, but if the wife of Alan Swift says it's all right, it must be on the up-and-up.

MARTIN. Well, that stands to reason.

JERRY. That's right. And here's something else that stands to reason. If you don't give your support, that nice rich lady from Chicago doesn't want anything to do with it. And if the nice rich lady from Chicago loses interest in her social work, she also loses interest in building a nice new food freezing plant right here in Bull Creek. And if she loses interest in building that food freezing plant, Bull Creek is going to lose a lot of money. And if Bull Creek loses a lot of money, the boys on the City Council and Chamber of Commerce aren't going to be very happy. Does that make it plain enough?

RUBERG. Now, hold on, Ross. You're jumpin' to conclusions. This ain't got nothin' to do with that food freezin' plant. I don't know how you found out about that anyways.

JERRY. I've got big ears.

MARTIN. I think Mr. Ross has got another axe to grind. Maybe he's got personal reasons for objecting.

JERRY. You hit pretty low, don't you?

RUBERG. Well, what is your reason? After all, you're here in the studio's interest, ain't you? Well, you couldn't ask for more publicity than you'll get outa this.

JERRY. Oh, no. You can stop right there. You're not dragging me into this thing too. Not on your life. Let me set you straight on something. I'm not out here because it's my idea. Falcon Pictures sent me out here to do a job—one job. To get some coverage on the funeral. And that job ends to-day. I didn't come here—and neither did Pat—to underwrite a new industry for Bull Creek under the guise of a charity in the name of Alan Swift. No thanks. I'm getting out of here to-morrow—and so is Pat. This thing stinks of bad breath.

MARTIN. I'd say you take a lot for granted, Mr. Ross. You Pat's legal adviser too? Or just what is your trouble?

Harriet enters and stands in the doorway for a moment. She has changed into her black dress.

RUBERG. Yeah, Ross. What're you so up in arms about? If there's any stink around here, I'd say it came with you and your damn newspaper people.

HARRIET [*shouting for the first time*] Stop all this shouting. D'you hear? Just stop all this shoutin' and carryin' on! For shame, Martin! And you're the one who talks about respect. Where's your respect now? Did you forget what we're doin' to-day? Look at me, Martin! I've got on my new black dress—the one you had me buy special. Mournin' black. Remember? We're going to bury our second son this afternoon, Martin. This is my house, too— and I say I won't have any shoutin' here to-day.

The men stand, ashamed and embarrassed by Harriet's censure. No one speaks. Then, footsteps can be heard on the front porch. The screen door opens and Emily Ruberg enters. Emily is Owen's sister, a spinster in her late forties, with a highly intense spiritual nature. Immediately she mistakes the mood for one of great sorrow and reverence.

EMILY. I hope I didn't keep you waitin'.

RUBERG [*uncomfortably*] This is my sister, Emily. Emily—Mrs. Swift and Mr. Ross. [*Jerry nods*]

PAT. How do you do.

EMILY [*crossing to Pat*] My poor dear. This is a dark day for us all, and your sorrow must be the blackest. He was a great man, my dear—one of the greatest. If we had only known how great he was! If there had just been a sign. But we didn't know—any more than they knew that day at Calvary.

RUBERG. I think we better be goin'.

EMILY [*persists*] When I saw his first movie, I knew. I saw his eyes and I knew. There was somethin' about him that seemed to cry out for attention. He was like every mother's son. I wanted to reach right out and hold him in my arms—to protect him from the loneliness that haunted his spirit. You were the one chosen. And even though your grief will follow you the rest of your days, you will find happiness just knowin' that you were the one to give him the love we all had for him. He was more than we'll ever know or understand. He was Alan Swift, my dear—and you were his wife.

And she bends reverently to kiss the hand of the wife of Alan Swift. The silence that follows is jarred by the uncontrollable laughter that escapes Anne. Her face hidden in her hands, she shakes with growing hysteria. Harriet reaches out to comfort her.

ANNE [*shouting hysterically*] Don't touch me! Don't anybody touch me! Keep your saintly hands to yourself. Well, what're you waitin' for? Why don't you go? Go bury him! No! No! Plant him! That's it. Plant him, so he can grow into a great crawlin' thing—and we'll never be able to get away from it!

Completely out of control, she rushes to the front door and out of the house. Martin runs to the door after her. We hear the sound of a car door slamming shut and a motor starting.

MARTIN. Anne! Anne! Come back here!

HARRIET [*quietly*] Let her go, Martin. Let her go.

The sound of the car speeding off can be heard.

EMILY. Now, whatever got into her?

MARTIN. It's time we left.

JERRY. Yeah. Wouldn't want to miss this funeral.

PAT. Oh, my God. My God.

Funeral music.

We mix to outside the Swift House just after the funeral. A funeral dirge is played throughout the following sequence.

A large crowd of people have preceded the Swift family to the house from the cemetery and are lined up along the barricade in front of the house, waiting for the family to return. Police make a path through the people to allow the family car to pass into the driveway. The family gets out of the car and goes to the porch and into the house. Martin assists Harriet who is in a state of collapse. Several of the teenagers in the crowd duck under the barricade and rush Pat with requests for autographs, or to give her flowers, or cherished mementos. Jerry frees Pat from them and conducts her to the house. The scene is one of unreality, almost dreamlike in atmosphere.

We mix to the living-room at dusk.

MARTIN. I think she'll be all right now. I got her into bed and gave her them sleepin' pills the doctor ordered.

JERRY. You look like you could use some rest too.

MARTIN. I'll be all right. If I could just stop thinkin' about that funeral. All them people—cryin' over him. The way they reached out and tried to touch us when we passed. It just don't make sense.

JERRY. I know. Try not to think about it. Get some sleep.

MARTIN. I want to find out if there's been any word about Anne. Had the Highway Patrol lookin' out for her car. Maybe they've found her.

JERRY. Have you seen Pat?

MARTIN. Think she went in the den.

Martin's footsteps retreat up the stairs. Jerry goes to the door of the den, pokes his head into the dark room. He strains to see if Pat is there.

JERRY. Pat?

Pat doesn't respond.

JERRY. Pat? You in here?

He swings the door full open so that the light illuminates the

172

*room. He spots Pat sitting in the chair. Without switching on the
lights, he crosses to her and stoops before the chair.*

JERRY [*almost whispering*] Honey? Pat honey, this is no good. Don't
dwell on it. It's over now.

PAT. Did you see their faces? I'll never forget those faces.

JERRY. Come on. You're going to bed.

PAT. No, Jerry. Let me stay here a while.

JERRY. So you can brood like this. Not on your life. [*He switches on
the desk lamp*] There. No boogieman. See? Now, come on—up
to bed.

PAT. I couldn't sleep if I tried.

JERRY. A couple of sleeping pills can remedy that. Look, honey, the
best thing for you right now is rest. And there's no need to worry
about getting up in the morning. Our train doesn't leave till
afternoon.

PAT. I can't leave to-morrow.

JERRY. Why?

PAT. They expect me to be there.

JERRY. What're you talking about?

PAT. The Memorial Ceremonies. No, I can't leave.

JERRY. You're kidding. What has that got to do with you?

PAT. I said I'd be there.

JERRY. I don't get it. Last night you were all for shouting the truth
from the rooftops.

PAT. That was last night.

JERRY. Well, I've got news for you—nothing's changed since then.

PAT. But it has. This afternoon—the funeral—convinced me.

JERRY. This is crazy.

PAT. I don't know. All I know is those people believe in Alan
Swift—and I can't take that away from them.

JERRY. Take what away from them? Oh, I'm sorry, but this is too
much. You're actually falling for all this hokum.

PAT. Look, Jerry, all this is happening. Don't try to tell me it's a
figment of my imagination. You were there. You saw. Those
people—thousands of them—they came here because they were
drawn by a man they believe was great.

JERRY. They came to see the side-show.

PAT. They love him. They respect him. They worship him. That's
real. I saw it, in their faces. You can't deny it's there.

JERRY. They're just feeding on the lies we gave them. They worship
a god that never existed. Look, maybe they need some phoney

idol to believe in because they haven't got enough within themselves to hold on to—but you, Pat, I can't let this happen to you.

PAT. Let what happen?

JERRY. Let you be swallowed up by this myth. Let you revel in this souped-up glory.

PAT. This is something you had a hand in. Remember? You blew your trumpet so loud the whole world turned around to look at your side-show. Well, now you've got your audience—and you've got no complaints coming.

JERRY. Do you think I'm proud of my part in this?

PAT. Then why don't you get off the bandwagon?

JERRY. Look at me—I'm trying! I did my job—full promotion and coverage of the last dramatic scene by Alan Swift. That's all they asked me to do, and I'm through.

PAT. Very noble. When the fire got out of control, the arsonist washed his hands of it. Well, I don't see you running for water.

JERRY. All right. I'm afraid. Is that what you wanted to hear? Look Pat I could find some way to break up this little party, but I'd have to destroy my secure little world to do it. *Our* secure little world. Well, maybe I'm not the hero type. Maybe I don't want to lose the only thing that's important to me. But at least I won't add any more kindling to the fire, Pat. And that's just what you'll be doing. If you lend your name to this Memorial Fund, you'll feed this thing just what it needs to become a craze for fanatics. Every fad-happy kid and infatuated old maid will buzz with new excitement. Another pep-pill for their dull lives. After the funeral I heard one woman telling a reporter that she'd communicated with Alan through a medium. She swore she talked to him. He told her he was coming back. The Messiah! But you can stop it all, Pat. If you refuse to be a party to this farce, they probably won't go through with it. There won't be any national memorial funds and food-freezing plants. All those nice gullible people out there will go home where they belong. And within a couple of weeks, Alan Swift will be quietly remembered as the wonderful actor he was. He won't be a spook, visiting every crackpot who has an over-active imagination. He won't be a distorted idol for all those teenagers . . . filling their nights with jazzed-up sex dreams. And if he's lucky he'll take his place in theatrical history as a remarkable actor and an unusual man . . . which is as it should be. That's sane. But you're the only one who can stop it now, Pat. You've got to.

174

PAT. Jerry! Jerry! You helped put me up here on this pedestal. Now you want me to throw myself off. You don't expect much, do you?

Pat gets up and goes out of the room. As she starts up the stairs Jerry walks slowly into the hall and looks after her.

We mix to the den. Moonlight peeks through the shuttered windows illuminating the face of the clock. It strikes 11. There is the distant sound of a motorcycle approaching down the road outside in the night. Then, the motor cuts off and there is silence.

Outside the house we see a dark figure wheeling a motorcyle up the driveway. It is a young man, possibly 22, wearing a black leather jacket, jeans and motorcycle boots. Quietly he wheels the bike up to the porch and parks it in the bushes. He moves to the french doors and finds one open. Careful not to be heard or observed, he slides the door quietly open and slips inside the room. He fumbles in his pocket for a match and strikes it. In the light his face appears intense, with a look of wildness about the eyes. They could be the eyes of a dope addict. He moves toward the door.

We cut to Pat's bedroom and see her lying on the bed in her nightgown. Her gaze is fixed blankly on the ceiling, where the tangled web of her emotional existence is spinning and respinning itself. There is a knock at the door. She rises and goes to the door. But does not open it. We see Pat on one side of the door and Jerry on the other. He is in his dressing gown.

JERRY [*whispering*] Pat? [*Raps again*] Pat, are you awake?

PAT [*at door*] What do you want?

JERRY. I want to talk to you.

PAT. Not now, Jerry. Go back to bed.

JERRY. Please. I've got to talk to you.

PAT. I'm undressed—in bed.

JERRY. Are you all right?

PAT. I'm fine.

JERRY. Can I get you anything?

PAT. No, honestly, Jerry, I'm all right. I'm just going down for a glass of warm milk. Now, please go back to bed before you wake somebody.

Jerry turns and moves away to another door on the landing. Pat listens for him. He hesitates, shakes his head in puzzlement, and exits into his room. Pat leaves the door and puts on her dressing gown.

Inside the living-room the young-man is striking a match to get a closer look at the bust of Alan Swift.

HOP HEAD [*patting the cheek of the bust—full voice*] Hi, Daddy-o!
[*Catching himself—whispering now*] Shhh. [*He giggles*]

*The match burns his fingers, but he merely watches it burn,
giggling at it. When it goes out, he strikes another one to survey the
room. He spots the portrait of Swift over the sofa and moves closer
to it. The sound of Pat's footsteps on the stairs startles him. He
flicks the match out quickly. He flattens himself against the wall
withdrawing a switch blade knife from his pocket and snapping it
open so that the gleaming blade can be seen. He remains motionless,
waiting. As Pat reaches the bottom of the stairs, she begins looking
for a light switch. Not finding one, she moves into the living-room,
passing the Hop Head in the shadows. As she is about to switch on a
lamp, he grabs her from behind, clamping his hand over her mouth,
thus muffling her startled cry. He holds the knife blade to her throat.
She struggles but he is strong.*

HOP HEAD [*whispering*] You shut up, or I'll fix it so's you can't
scream.

Pat stops struggling.

HOP HEAD. Now, you be a cool head and I'll let you off the leash.
You dig?

Pat nods.

HOP HEAD. One peep outa you . . . chickie, and. . . .

He slides the point of the knife along her throat.

He releases her carefully. She rubs her mouth and faces him.

HOP HEAD. Ain't no cause to be scared. Nothin' gonna happen to
you, if you play it cool.

PAT. What . . . what do you want?

HOP HEAD. Nothin', mam. Just sight-seein'.

PAT. Who are you?

HOP HEAD [*giggles*] I dig—we're playin' Twenty Questions.

PAT. Look, you can get into a lot of trouble like this.

HOP HEAD. Yeah. [*Giggles*]

PAT. What're you doing here?

HOP HEAD. They tell me this pad's where Alan Swift did the school
days bit. Just come to give it the nod.

PAT. Well, I hope it meets with your approval.

HOP HEAD. Say now—this one's a real sassy lassie.

PAT. You're drunk.

HOP HEAD. Drunk? [*Giggles*] Yeah, that's it—drunk. Man, what a
cube. This I gotta dig.

He strikes another match and holds it to Pat's face.

176

HOP HEAD. Well, flip me! The frau, herself.

PAT. Look, you get out of here, or I'm going to call for help.

HOP HEAD [*shows knife and giggles*] Now, that wouldn't be playin' it cool. Anyway—what am I doin'? Just wanna talk to you, that's all. See, all my buddies think I'm just like your Daddy-o. [*Indicates bust*] I figure you should know.

He holds a match to his face and giggles. Pat stares at his face and eyes, terrified.

HOP HEAD. C'mon. Give. Do I pass?

PAT [*humouring him*] Yes—there's a—a strong resemblance. It's—it's amazing.

HOP HEAD [*giggles*] Oh, that's cool—real cool. See, what they say . . . [*The match burns his fingers. Pat watches it go out*] I'm just like Daddy-o. Look like him, talk like him, just like him.

PAT. Oh, you are you are. Very much like him.

HOP HEAD. Yeah, that's the action. [*Giggles delightedly*] I'm gonna be just like him. Gonna do what he did and everything [*He strikes another match*] 'cause I think he was the most. Yeah, I dig everything like Daddy-o. [*He looks her up and down*]—Everything.

He blows out the match quickly. He moves toward Pat.

PAT. No. [*Backing away*] No, don't.

With a violent movement he snatches Pat to him and kisses her savagely. Pat loses her balance and they back into a table, knocking it to the floor. Pat struggles wildly to free herself.

PAT. Stop! Help! Jerry!

She gets away from him and runs to the stairway in the hall.

PAT. J-E-R-R-Y!

He runs after her and tackles her on the stairs. Jerry appears at the head of the stairs. The Hop Head scrambles to his feet and rushes into the den. Jerry runs after him. The sound of a motor-cycle motor revving and starting can be heard. The motorcycle takes off at high speed. Martin comes to the head of the stairs in his dressing gown. Pat collapses on the stairs hysterical.

MARTIN. What's the trouble? What's goin' on?

Jerry comes back from the den.

JERRY. He got away.

MARTIN. Who?

JERRY. Some kid. I don't know. [*Sits beside Pat on the stairs and takes her in his arms*] Pat, honey. It's all right, baby. Shhh. It's all right. He's gone. Shhh.

PAT. Oh, Jerry. He had a knife . . . he was crazy . . . he tried to . . .

JERRY. Shhhh. It's all right.

MARTIN. I'll call the police.

JERRY [to Martin] Forget it. Call a doctor.

Martin goes to the phone.

PAT. He thought he was Alan. He was crazy. He thought he was Alan.

JERRY. Shhh. I know, baby. I know. [*Almost to himself*] Now it starts.

MARTIN [*into phone*] Hello, Doc. This is Martin Swift . . . there's been some trouble. You better come right over.

Fade out.

Act Three

The next morning in the den. Jerry Ross is talking on the direct line phone to Hollywood. He is furious.

JERRY [*into phone*] Look, Cooper, I don't care what kind of a build-up you think we can give it, I'm not touching it . . . yeah, you heard me right . . . Aw cut it out, Alex. You can't bully me into this . . . I don't give a damn what my contract says . . . So, sue me . . . look, you can take the damn thing and shove it! [*He slams the phone down in a rage*] Of all the back-handed, dirty. . . .

He crosses to the den door and exits into the living-room. Harriet and Martin are going through some of the mail. Stacks of letters are piled on the coffee table before them. Jerry enters and confronts Martin.

JERRY. That's the lowest punch of all, Mr. Swift. What kind of a man are you anyway?

MARTIN. What you talkin' about?

JERRY. I'm talking about the sneak who called the studio and tipped them off about this Memorial Ceremony. Pretty clever. You figured they'd snatch at the publicity. Well, you were right. I just got my instructions. Only there's one thing you didn't count on—I'm not co-operating. They'll have to get someone else to do their dirty work.

MARTIN. Now, hold on. Seems to me you're getting pretty riled up over something that's kinda natural. If Alan's fans and his neighbours want to do somethin' in his memory, I'd say there was nothin' wrong in it. You'd think Alan's studio'd be only too happy to lend a hand.

JERRY. Then, you're the one who called Cooper?

MARTIN. I don't know anything about that phone call.

JERRY. I'll bet you don't. I'll bet it never occurred to you or your friend, Ruberg, to fix it so as I'd have to drag Pat into this freak show of yours. What a bunch of frauds—behind that home-spun exterior there lies the cunning of a real S.O.B.

HARRIET. I think you've said just about enough around here, Mr. Ross. If my husband says he doesn't know anything about this, then that's what you'll have to take for the truth. I'll thank you to leave us alone now. Ain't we got enough these past few days? The funeral—and worried sick about Anne disappearing. Take your complainin' somewhere else. We ain't interested.

JERRY. Okay. Okay. But I've gone this far and I'm not going to stop until I get Pat out of here. [*He starts for the door*] When she gets up, tell her I'll be back for her in an hour.

MARTIN. Where should we tell her you went?

JERRY. Just tell her I went to look under a few rocks.

He slams out the front door and almost knocks Owen Ruberg off his feet as Owen is about to enter the house.

RUBERG [*looking after Jerry*] Hey! Watch where you're goin'.

Owen enters the living-room.

RUBERG. What's his rush?

MARTIN. Somethin' to do with a phone call from his studio. He's mighty burned up about it. You wouldn't happen to know anything about it, would you, Owen?

RUBERG. Now, don't go pointin' fingers at me, Martin. If it's anybody's doin's, it's Mrs. Brawley's. I just told her about the row yesterday. She sorta said somethin' about knowin' a way to keep Ross quiet.

MARTIN. I don't think I like this kinda thing. Seems to me she coulda asked us first.

Pat comes down the stairs.

RUBERG. Oh, mornin', Mrs. Swift.

Harriet goes to Pat immediately.

PAT. Good morning.

HARRIET. How do you feel, my dear?

PAT. Much better, thank you.

MARTIN. Police report they ain't had a sign of no motorcycle riders in . . .

HARRIET. Hush, Martin. Let's not talk about it. We'll be best to forget it.

PAT. Where's Jerry?

MARTIN. He got a call from his studio and went rushin' outa here on business. Said to tell you he'll be back. . . .

RUBERG. He's sure to be back in time. I don't mean to rush you, Mam, but we should be gettin' down to the high school auditorium soon. The television people want to have a rehearsal before the Ceremonies. [*He hands Pat several pieces of paper*] Hope you don't mind, but Mrs. Brawley and me just wrote out some notes on what you might care to say.

PAT [*indecisively*] Well . . . I hadn't planned on making a speech. As a matter of fact, I'm not really sure I should go through with this.

RUBERG. Oh, now Mrs. Swift, you wouldn't want to let us down like that. Why, everything's been announced. The newspapers carried the story this mornin' and the television 'cause they heard you was gonna make a special announcement. It'd look mighty funny if you didn't show up.

PAT. But I didn't really expect to make a speech.

RUBERG. Ain't but a few minutes of talkin' there.

Pat looks at the speech and begins to read it.

We mix to the backstage of the high school auditorium which is being prepared for the ceremony.

MRS. BRAWLEY. I know you can do it for me, Mr. Shelley. I need that backcloth on this stage by 3 o'clock. Now don't fail me— Miss Clarke, send a telegram to the television people that I guarantee Mrs. Alan Swift will speak tonight. [*To Jerry*] All right boys, let that go now and arrange the loudspeakers at the front of the school steps. [*She sits next to Jerry*] I'm sorry for the interruption but I don't think you understand, Mr. Ross. I'm quite sincere about this project. Soda?

JERRY. Fine.

MRS. BRAWLEY. This is something the country has needed for a long time—a National Scholarship Fund for the theatre. [*Hands him a drink*] With Alan Swift's name and Mrs. Swift's support, we can't miss. [*Toasts*] Cheers.

JERRY. All right, Mrs. Brawley, I'm going to level with you. You're a wealthy woman. This thing is just a toy for you. I mean, it doesn't really make any difference in your life. I think there's more behind this than some social activity and business advantage. Something, shall we say, a bit more personal.

MRS. BRAWLEY. How astute of you, Mr. Ross. You've discovered my deep dark secret. Yes, you might say I'm a terribly enthusiastic fan of Alan Swift's. I think he was magnificent.

JERRY. So much so, you used to write him fan letters?

He's dropped the bomb. She tries to cover her shocked senses by preserving her cool exterior but Jerry has caught it. He simply smiles.

JERRY. Alan read me a couple of the letters. It never would have occurred to me. Then I remembered, the "rich dame from Chicago" mentioned in one of her letters that she sometimes visited Bull Creek on business. As I recall, they made for some good—laughs.

MRS. BRAWLEY. I don't know what you're talking about.

JERRY. I think you do. Those letters would look very funny in print. But I don't think they'll be printed. I'm not asking you to give this up completely. Just make it a local project—and leave Mrs. Swift out of it.

MRS. BRAWLEY. You know, it's beginning to sound like you're trying to intimidate me, Mr. Ross. Well, forget it. I found out a long time ago I've got nothing left to lose. You want to print— you print.

JERRY. You turn my stomach. You're just as sick as those drooling kids and mooning old maids—sicker. You're as bad off as that hopped-up kid who broke into the house last night. You're out to identify yourself with Alan Swift, because, Lady, you're hot for him. And all this jazz about a Memorial Fund is nothing but a front.

MRS. BRAWLEY. Why, Mr. Ross, I'm shocked. You talk just like my husband's psychiatrist. Next thing you'll be quoting from the Bible. You know, I think you're the sweetest, most naive man I've ever met. Now, I don't think we have anything more to discuss. So, if you'll excuse me, I must get dressed. They're expecting me at the high school for rehearsals.

We mix to Mike's bar. This is a small bar, partitioned into two rooms. The entrance and bar on one side; a small area with tables on the other. There is a curtained exit beside the bar and a telephone just inside the curtain. The bar is deserted except for Mike, the bartender, who stands behind the bar polishing glasses. Mike stops his work to put a coin in the juke box. A rock 'n' roll record starts to play, as he goes back to work. Anne Swift enters. She is wearing the same clothes she was wearing the day before. She looks tired and very tight. She walks to the bar.

ANNE. Hiya, Mike.

MIKE. Where you been?

ANNE. Give me a drink. Why, they been lookin' for me?

Mike nods. Pours her a drink and leaves the bottle on the counter.

ANNE. Topeka.

MIKE. You drive all the way to Topeka?

ANNE. Um-hum. You ever been to the Crystal Hotel in Topeka, Mike? [*Mike shakes his head*] You oughta try it sometime. It's a dream—a real nightmare. Cockroaches get bigger every year. [*Drinks*] Old Man Swift been in here after me? [*Pours herself another*]

MIKE. State Police.

ANNE. My, my. Looks like my prestige rating is goin' right up. [*Laughs*] Call out the Marines!

MIKE. Why don't you go home, kid?

She takes the whisky bottle from the bar before he can snatch it from her.

ANNE. In a while, Mike. In a while.

She goes to a table in the corner.

Harvey Porter enters and strides up to the bar. He is hot and sweaty from work.

HARVEY. Howdy, Mike. Man I'll sure be glad when I get this job done.

MIKE. What'll it be?

HARVEY. Beer . . . and make it cold. Where's your customers?

MIKE. They knew you was comin' in.

He puts an open beer bottle before Harvey who immediately takes a long drink. Then, catching Harvey's eye, he makes a head motion to Anne off in the corner. Harvey takes his bottle and strolls over to Anne's table. Anne doesn't look up from her brooding until Harvey is standing right over her.

ANNE [*looking up*] I didn't hear anybody invite you.

HARVEY. Now, whata you got against me? Every time I see you, you treat me like somethin' dirty. I just wanna get friendly, Annie—that's all.

ANNE. Do I have to call Mike over here?

Harvey shrugs and turns to leave, but Anne has a turn of mind and grabs his sleeve. She indicates the chair next to her. Harvey sits and slips the chair as close as possible.

HARVEY. That's better. [*Indicates whisky bottle*] Ain't you startin' a little early to-day?

Mike leaves the bar and disappears through the curtains to the back room.

182

ANNE. You know, Harvey, I've had you all wrong.

HARVEY. That's the way to talk.

ANNE. All wrong. Everybody in this town's a fool—'cept you. You don't feel sorry for me, do you, Harvey? [*Harvey shakes his head*] Good! That makes you the only one who knows what's what. Well, not really—but you're no fool. You want to know why they're all fools? I'll tell you why. 'Cause they understand. They make me sick. [*She downs another drink*] Why aren't you in town payin' homage to my brother-in-law? Don't you know that's the place to be? We should all be right there, tellin' her how lucky she was. [*She pours a drink*] You know the last time I saw Alan Swift? He came back here on his way out to Hollywood. Oh, it was a real magnanimous gesture he made. Robert—dear sweet Robert. I married Robert in Witchita, and he brought me here to live with his family while he went off to Korea. [*Sings*] When Johnny comes marching home again, tra-la, tra-la. Only my Johnny never came home again tra-la. They brought him home in a coffin. But brother Alan wasn't around that time. He was too busy makin' movies. [*Drinks*] But he did come home to say goodbye to Robert when he was on leave that time. Just before Robert was shipped out. Alan Swift just dropped out of the sky one day—the day after Robert and I got back from our honeymoon in Topeka. Alan laughed when Robert told him. He thought it was real funny—a honeymoon at the Crystal Hotel in Topeka. Yes, sir—there he was —dropped right out of the sky. For five whole days he took over everything. Hour after hour, sat there tellin' us what a big man he was going to be in Hollywood. He was going out there to let them know how good he was. I was so impressed! I couldn't get enough. He wasn't like the rest of the people around here. He didn't feel sorry for me either. He didn't feel sorry for anyone. He just dropped out of the sky one day and there he was, big as life—and beautiful. [*Drinks*] They're all a bunch of fools. They wouldn't be so full of pity not if they knew. But, you know, don't you, Harvey? That's why you don't pity me. I don't know how you know, but I always felt you must. Well, let me tell you what they don't know and you do. [*Leans in confidentially*] They don't know the day after I kissed sweet Robert goodbye and sent him off to Korea, the beautiful Alan Swift made a very successful pass at me. That's what they don't know. The fools! But you do, don't you? You could smell it, couldn't you, Harvey? That's why you always come sniffin' around, isn't it?

Harvey leans in to take her invitation. He grabs her and starts to kiss her. She tries to free herself, but can't. She reaches for Harvey's beer bottle on the table and smashes it over his head. Harvey staggers, stunned. Horrified and disgusted, Anne rushes out of the bar.

We go back to the high school auditorium. The stage is now set for the memorial ceremony. At stage left there is a platform for the choir. Downstage centre is a speaker's rostrum. Just to the right of it is a four foot pedestal on which rests the bust of Alan Swift. A large sign is hanging over the stage—"Alan Swift—In Memoriam". The scene is one of common backstage confusion and chaos. Television technicians add to the mayhem as they set up microphones and check camera angles for the proceedings. A choir director is arranging the combined Methodist and Presbyterian choir.

Martin and Harriet Swift are seated in their chairs being interviewed by Miss Albright and some of the Press people. Mrs. Brawley and Owen Ruberg seem to have taken things over. Owen moves quickly from one group to another, trying to co-ordinate things. Pat and Mrs. Brawley stand at the speaker's rostrum going over Pat's speech.

PAT. But I don't like the idea of making a direct appeal for money. I think it should come from you.

MRS. BRAWLEY. Yes, I understand—but it won't have as much punch that way.

RUBERG [*shouting*] Get them kids organized, Emily. Time's runnin' short. [*He crosses to Pat and Mrs. Brawley*] We're way behind schedule. The audience is waitin' out there—and the television people want to get started. Can't keep 'em waitin' much longer.

MRS. BRAWLEY. All right. [*To Pat*] Okay, we'll leave it like that. [*Turns to people on stage*] Attention everybody! May I have your attention, please!

No one heeds her call.

MRS. BRAWLEY. Listen, everybody! [*To Ruberg*] Maybe you can make yourself heard.

RUBERG. Quiet, everybody!

A young boy comes running up to Owen.

BOY. Mr. Ruberg! Mr. Ruberg. That guy, Ross—he's here. I can't keep him out.

PAT. Jerry? Well, let him in.

BOY. But, Mr. Ruberg said . . .

RUBERG. Just never mind what I said. Do like Mrs. Swift tells you.

BOY [*puzzled*] Sure.

The boy turns to exit, but Jerry has come on to the stage already.
Two policemen can be seen behind him in the wings. Jerry crosses
directly to Pat. He is determined.

PAT. Jerry. Where have you been?

JERRY. C'mon. We're getting out of here.

PAT. I can't leave.

RUBERG. Now, hold on, Ross.

JERRY [*to Pat*] I got back to the house after you left, so I came right
over here. They tried to keep me out. Now, come on—we're
leaving.

MRS. BRAWLEY. Just a minute, Mr. Ross. Who do you think you are,
breaking in here and dragging people off like this? You're not
running this thing. We are. Now, if you don't quiet down and
leave Mrs. Swift alone, we'll have to ask you to get out.

JERRY [*grits his teeth and ignores her—to Pat*] Let's go.

PAT. But, Jerry, I can't just walk out.

MRS. BRAWLEY. There's a way to handle this.

She nods to Ruberg who gives a signal off-stage to the two police-
men.

RUBERG. All right boys!

The two policemen enter and move to take Jerry.

PAT. What do you think you're doing?

BOY'S VOICE. Hey lady, you can't go in there!

JERRY. You're asking for trouble, Ruberg.

ANNE'S VOICE [*off camera—shouts*] Hey, everybody! Look what I've
got!

Everyone's attention turns towards the wings from which Anne
emerges carrying a large highway road-marker. It has obviously
been broken off. She carries it as a banner high over her head and
waves it triumphantly. It reads: "This way to Bull Creek—Home of
Alan Swift".

ANNE. This way to Bull Creek, the home of Alan Swift! Isn't it
pretty? I found it beside the road outside our fair city. Thought
you might like to get a look at it. The home of Alan Swift!
[*Laughs*] Nobody else ever lived here.

MRS. BRAWLEY. Get out of here.

The policemen release Jerry and start for Anne.

PAT. Don't touch her.

ANNE. Thanks, Sister Widow. [*Crosses toward Pat*] How's the
lovely lucky little wife? You see? [*Indicates sign*] I came to help
you glorify your husband. Aren't you glad?

MRS. BRAWLEY. Get everybody out. Do you want everyone to hear? Everybody off the stage.

Owen, the TV director, and the cops start clearing the people off the stage quietly, but quickly.

ANNE. Praise be to Alan Swift! Gloria in excelsis to the prodigal son! Hail the misfit! That's what he was—or didn't they tell you? You'd never guess they hated his guts, would you? The whole town's here and half the country it looks like. All here to sing the praises of the great Alan Swift. The hypocrites! That's what they are. Liars! The whole damn town is living a lie! There was a time when they didn't even care he existed. But then, I forgot—death cures a lot of things. Or does it? Robert's dead over three years now, and they've just about forgotten him. [*Turns to Martin Swift*] You remember Robert Swift. You must. His name was in all the papers. Dear, sweet, trusting Robert. But why shouldn't they forget him? He wasn't much of a hero. Not really. Just a tiny one. He doesn't deserve a monument. No, let's forget him. But Alan Swift! Now there's a horse of a different manure. What'd he do? I'll tell you what he did. He died and put Bull Creek on the map! Yes, sir, right there on the map where the town fathers could see it—real big and proper. [*Stands before Pat*] That's what your important husband did, Sister Widow. And you're helping him. Sure—you rushed right in and gave the whole thing a nice shot in the arm. Why not? The glorified widow of the glorified god!

PAT [*with compassion*] Anne. Please, don't.

ANNE [*feels it—afraid she might falter, but regains her spite*] I wish he'd come back. Just so I could watch you all crawl in your holes. Sister Widow, I'm going to tell you something you don't know. Do you have any idea why poor Robert is dead?

PAT [*crying*] Please. Please.

ANNE. Because I killed him, that's why. I sent him off to the war and wished he'd get killed. I got my wish, didn't I? You know why I wanted him dead? Because I was in love with your husband. That's right. I loved Alan Swift so much I killed my own husband. But I didn't get Alan, did I? Nope. You got him, Sister Widow. And after all the trouble I went through. You got him and you got everything that goes with him. Well, you can keep it. You can keep your glory. You can keep your tender memories! You can keep your memorial funds and monuments! As a matter of fact, you can keep Alan Swift! And I'll tell you why—if you go over to the Swift house and go upstairs to my room, you'll find his son! But you can't keep him. He's something you'll never have! Because he's mine. Pretty little baby Bobby . . . [*She begins to break down*] . . . Can't take my baby . . . my little boy . . .

She turns away crying and starts to leave. She stops at the sight of the bust of Alan Swift on the pedestal. She gazes at it through the tears. Then, with a sudden burst of hate built on years of guilt, she moves to throw the bust from its place of prominence onto the floor. But she stops, unable to destroy so obvious a symbol of her guilt-filled love. Defeated she turns and stumbles off stage and crumples in a corner of the wings. There isn't a sound on the stage. Harriet and Martin are drained of their senses. Jerry steps to Pat and puts his arm about her to brace her. Mrs. Brawley finally moves to her and breaks the silence.

MRS. BRAWLEY. Never mind. I don't think anybody heard.

Pat ignores her. Only raising her eyes to smile weakly at Jerry.

PAT. I didn't understand.

She takes Jerry's hand and begins walking off stage with him.

MRS. BRAWLEY. You can't leave now.

PAT [*turns bitterly*] Why don't you have the police stop me too?

As she turns back to leave with Jerry, she gazes helplessly at Harriet and Martin Swift. Then without a word, she and Jerry walk off into wings.

Just before they reach the stage door Pat sees Anne Swift crumpled in the corner weeping. She hesitates a moment then starts towards her, but Jerry stops her, simply shaking his head.

The sound of rhythmic clapping and the stamping of feet has started in the audience beyond the front curtain. It becomes increasingly louder throughout the preceding.

RUBERG [*to Mrs. Brawley*] Well, I guess that's that. [*Indicating the audience*] Listen to the damn fools.

MRS. BRAWLEY [*ignoring him and stepping to the left side of the stage —to the people off stage*] All right everybody. Let's get back into our places. Come on. Places everybody! We're ready to begin. Hurry it up!

The people shuffle back on to the stage quickly and resume their places. During this:

RUBERG. You gonna go ahead with it?

MRS. BRAWLEY [*not really answering Ruberg*] Why not? [*To the people*] Hurry, everybody! We're very late! Is that little man ready to pull the curtain? [*Looks off stage and gets a nod from the man who is ready*] Good. All right, now, start the singing!

Emily Ruberg, the choir director, has just gathered her group on the platform once more, but stands dumbfounded by all the confusion.

RUBERG [*to Emily*] Well, don't just stand there, Emily. Do what she says.

Emily shakes herself and turns to the choir. Mrs. Brawley crosses to her seat next to Harriet and Martin Swift and takes her place beside them.

HARRIET. I think we'd better leave, Martin.

MRS. BRAWLEY. Don't you think that would start people asking too many questions?

Grasping the significance of her threat, Martin simply nods his head, dazed and trapped.

The curtain goes up and the combined Methodist and Presbyterian choir begins to sing "The Lord's Prayer".

At the stage door Pat has been putting on her coat with Jerry's aid. They hear the hymn, and look back to the stage. The voices of the choir are gradually fortified by the voices of the audience which has ceased the stamping and joined in the praising. The voices build to a crescendo. Pat and Jerry turn and walk out of the stage door. Fade out.

A BIT OF HAPPINESS

by

ALEXANDER BARON

CAST

ROSE HANBURY	*Isabel Dean*
TONY ROBERTS	*Kevin Stoney*
LEONARD HANBURY	*Nicholas Meredith*
MRS. FITCH	*Arnold Bell*
MRS. GREEN	*Sheila Robins*
MR. GREEN	*Alan Wilson*
GRAHAM HANBURY	*Peter Hempson*

DIRECTOR	*Herbert Wise*
DESIGNER	*William Brodie*

DIRECTOR'S NOTE

In many ways *A Bit of Happiness* is remarkable. On first reading it did not strike me as a first play, for it was written with great economy. The author, Alexander Baron, had managed to achieve a style of deliberate understatement which suited the story perfectly, and yet which sacrificed none of those qualities of acute and sensitive perception which reflect the author's own sympathetic, but unsentimental, interest in his characters.

Here was a concise, instantly recognizable evocation of life in middle-class suburbia, showing people in prisons of their own making desperately searching for a way out and feeling, because of their own human inadequacy, unable to match up to life's demands. Of its type and within its own limits it is to my mind a masterly short play and I am continually struck by the fact that people remember it in detail.

HERBERT WISE.

A BIOGRAPHY OF ALEXANDER BARON

Alexander Baron was born in 1917 and was educated at a London Secondary School. Before becoming a television playwright he was already the author of eight novels—among them *There's no Home*, *The Human Kind*, and *From City, from Plough*—of which nearly two million copies have been sold in England and several editions have been translated into other languages. Before the war he worked as a clerk in various departments of the London County Council. After six years in the Army he became editor of the *New Theatre Magazine* and from 1946–49 was Chairman of the Unity Theatre Club. He had not tried his hand at writing plays until he wrote *A Bit of Happiness* in 1958 and sent it to Granada.

ACTION

The action of the play takes place in the following sets:

(1) A park bench
(2) The lounge of a small, quiet, sea-side hotel
(3) A double bedroom in the same hotel
(4) A small stretch of beach with deck-chairs.
(5) The hall, living-room, kitchen and back door of the Hanburys' semi-detached house in a London suburb
(6) Tony's bed-sitting room in Earl's Court.

TIME

The time is the present.

Act One

A park: it is a grey day with rain in the offing. A couple are sitting on a bench. They both wear raincoats. The man is turned towards the woman, who is not looking at him.

ROSE. Why do we go on? You get on my nerves, but I can't keep away from you. Love! You get used to someone and you can't let go of them. You and Leonard and me . . . and none of us will let go. And you haven't even got time to take me shopping.

TONY. But I told you. . . .

ROSE. You told me enough.

TONY. What do you mean by that?

ROSE. What do you mean, what do I mean by that?

TONY. I mean just what I say. What did you mean when you said that?

ROSE. I meant exactly what I said. . . .

THE MAN. Oh, did you?

THE WOMAN. Yes, I did. Any objections?

THE MAN. No.

THE WOMAN. Well?

THE MAN. Well what?

THE WOMAN. What do you mean, well what?

THE MAN. Oh, don't be silly.

A brief silence.

THE WOMAN. So that's what it's come to? You call me a fool to my face.

THE MAN. I didn't say that you were silly. I merely told you not to be silly.

THE WOMAN. Oh, I see. Very subtle.

THE MAN. Look—all I said was—I can't pick you up in town to-morrow.

THE WOMAN. And what about my shopping? All the bags I'll be carrying?

THE MAN. There are taxis, aren't there?

THE WOMAN. Thank you very much. My husband works hard for his money.

THE MAN. You're very considerate to your husband all of a sudden.

THE WOMAN. Why shouldn't I be? He's considerate to me. That's more than you are . . . my lover.

193

THE MAN. Look . . . I just won't have time.

THE WOMAN. If I was coming to your room you'd have time. Or would you?

THE MAN. Look—you can nag your husband. But don't nag me. [*From now on the woman's face is in close-up. Her expression is different: as if she is now looking at something beyond this quarrel. The man's voice continuing off*] I don't have to put up with it. I'm not your husband. You know what we said at the beginning. You're free. I'm free. No strings. A bit of happiness on the side. D'you call this happiness . . .? [*His voice fades into a background grumble*] I don't. I know what I call it. I call it downright misery. You start off by saying you won't make any demands on a man. Then you act as if you own him lock, stock and barrel; and if he doesn't play, you do a great big deserted tragic heroine act. What d'you think it's like for me? You've got a home. All I've got is a rotten little back bedroom. I've never meant you any harm, Rose. I've only wanted to make life bearable for you. And what do I get in return? Scenes, scenes and more scenes. . . . [*The woman has ceased to listen to him. Her thoughts are going their own way, and we hear them, spoken in her voice, but a voice more appealing, more musical than the one we heard raised in anger*]

WOMAN'S VOICE [*over the background murmur of the man's*] Happiness . . . A bit of happiness . . . Hark at us, snarling at each other. Like . . . I sit here and I listen to the awful stupid things I'm saying, and I can't stop myself saying them. It isn't me speaking, it's the pain.

We mix into shot of a deserted sea-side promenade: the front of a house with a board outside "High Cliff Hotel". Move into the bay window, down which rain streams. Inside we see the woman. Over this, her voice.

WOMAN'S VOICE. I can't believe all this is happening to me. Me! Rose Hanbury. Respectable Rose Hanbury. I must have been mad when I . . . Why did we ever go to that place? How can a woman change the way I have? For the last year I've felt as if some complete stranger had taken my place. Someone who was saying and doing things that . . . horrified me. And my old self was watching all the time . . . helpless . . . A year . . . Is that all it is? God, it seems a lifetime!

Inside the room: the woman is still alone in the picture, sitting in the bay window, gazing out, dreaming. From off camera, but close at hand, a man speaks.

194

MAN'S VOICE. Well, I thought, I'm not mean. But if I paid for the deckchairs the least he could do was pay for the bus.

ROSE [*abstractedly*] Yes dear.

MAN'S VOICE. I know these people on holiday. They're bosom pals, but you don't catch 'em paying.

ROSE. Yes.

MAN'S VOICE. If there's one thing I won't have, it's being taken advantage of. So, when the conductor came, I just looked out of the window, and old Fitch had to pay up.

ROSE. Yes.

MAN'S VOICE. After all, sixpence a head for four people . . . that's how your money slips away . . . Rose, are you listening?

We are in the room with them: Leonard Hanbury is near his wife in the bay window. He is three years older than his wife. Between them is a table with the remains of "afternoon tea".

ROSE. I heard every word you said.

LEONARD. They want watching, those Fitches.

ROSE. Wouldn't it be easier to avoid them?

LEONARD. Well, she does talk as if she thinks she was Lady Luverduck, and he's a bit of an old sponger. But they are company.

ROSE. This damned rain. I don't think it'll ever stop.

LEONARD. Yes it will. The day we go home. It always does. Anyway, it's a change for you. I'm glad of that.

ROSE. Yes . . . It's a change for you, too. You do work hard.

LEONARD. Oh, I don't know. Do you miss Graham?

ROSE. I suppose so . . . No. No, I don't. I've got to be truthful. It's such a relief not to have to feed him and get him off to school; and I'm sure he's happy with your Mum and Dad.

LEONARD. He's a King of the Castle with them. You know how they spoil him . . . If only the weather'll clear up before you take him down to his Aunty's. He loves that farm.

ROSE. At least he'll have his cousins to play with.

LEONARD. Anyway, we were right not to bring him down here. He'd have been bored stiff in this weather. You can't go on the beach. And I did want you to.

The door opens and an elderly couple come in. The Fitches.

MR. FITCH. Here we are then. Oh, there are those nice people the Hanburys.

The Fitches come toward them. In the foreground is the man in the armchair, who lowers his newspaper and watches discreetly, as if just to break the monotony. He is the man who was on the park bench.

195

MRS. FITCH. Hallo there Mr. Hanbury. Hallo, Mrs. Hanbury.

LEONARD. Come along and sit down.

MRS. FITCH. Thank you. [*Leonard has bustled to provide chairs for them*] Well, I thought you'd be out braving the rain.

ROSE. What, with that wind?

MR. FITCH. You youngsters are mollycoddled. Eh, Mother?

MRS. FITCH. You leave them alone. [*To Rose*] Have you heard from your little boy, dear?

ROSE. Yes. We had a nice letter from him.

MRS. FITCH. He must be such a nice little boy . . . Isn't he upset, not coming with you?

LEONARD. Oh, the wife'll take him away later. Let's hope the weather'll be better.

MRS. FITCH. It was much better this time last year.

MR. FITCH. And the year before we didn't have one rainy day; not one.

MRS. FITCH. Years ago it never used to rain for the holidays. I don't know what's happening. Don't you often wonder, dear.

ROSE [*not really with them*] Oh . . . yes. Yes, I often wonder.

LEONARD. I always say you can't trust the weather.

MR. FITCH. Still, two holidays for the wife. You certainly do your family proud.

LEONARD. Yes, that's the best of a good steady job. I've kept the books for Grimshaws now for thirteen years. They've been very good to me. I'm sure I've got nothing to fear for the future.

MRS. FITCH. You can't ask for more than that, can you? A safe job and a nice little boy and a good wife.

LEONARD. I've got a good wife all right. Do you know, we've never had a quarrel or a day apart in twelve years?

MR. FITCH. Ha! Wait till you've had forty-six years.

MRS. FITCH. Yes, I often say to myself, every day for forty-six years George and I have been together. And not gadding about, either. When George was working he'd come home every night, we'd sit by the fire; a nice quiet life.

LEONARD. Same as us. We never go out. I like my armchair. And Rose here . . . you know, she's a quiet one. She can sit for hours, just with her thoughts. Hours on end, honestly. I wonder where she is sometimes. [*Rose's expression has undergone a change. She is not dreaming but listening, to them and to the rain, with growing despair*] No sense in spending money out when you can enjoy your own home, is there?

MR. FITCH. You've got your head screwed on the right way, young man. If I was asked to advise a young couple, I'd give 'em one word . . . save. There's the key to a good life. You save, and you'll get the benefit when you're old.

MRS. FITCH. Yes, when you're old. That's when you get the benefit.

MR. FITCH. Look at us. We've got everything we want. Everything. Two years retired. Well provided for. A little walk . . .

MRS. FITCH. . . . A nice garden . . .

MR. FITCH. A sit by the fire in the evening; early to bed. Isn't that something to look forward to?

LEONARD. It certainly is.

MR. FITCH. Yes . . . life begins at sixty-five. You take it from me.

LEONARD. That's the way I look at it, Mr. Fitch. We haven't done too bad, you know. We've had our home for nine years. Mortgage'll be paid up in another eleven. We've got all *we* want.

MR. FITCH. What more can you say than that?

MRS. FITCH. What more *can* you say?

Rose stands up abruptly, almost confused, as if the instinctive movement has taken her by surprise.

ROSE. I think I'll lie down. I've got such a headache.

LEONARD. Rose, dear . . .

Simultaneously.

ROSE. No, please. I'll just go upstairs.

She smiles an excuse. As she goes out of the room she passes Tony and from his chair he watches her walk to the door. The talk of the group follows her as she goes out.

MRS. FITCH'S VOICE. Oh, I am sorry. Shall I go up with her?

LEONARD'S VOICE. She'll be all right, Mrs. Fitch. She gets these turns at home sometimes.

MR. FITCH'S VOICE. Migraine, eh?

LEONARD'S VOICE. Oh, no, she always tells me, it's not serious. She just goes up on her own for a bit, and lies down. . . .

We cut to a small hotel bedroom. Two single beds. Rose comes in and shuts the door. Rain drums on the window. She lifts the curtain (the view is on to an interior yard) then drops it wearily. She turns on the tap and bathes her face in silence except for the loud rush of the tap.

When she has wiped her face she studies herself in the mirror. She smooths the skin of her face back with her hands and smiles. She is reassured by the attractive face that confronts her from the mirror.

197

Her expression changes. She pinches a fold of loose flesh under her chin. She looks at the mirror in dismay.

She goes across to the bed, lies down with her hands behind her head and kicks her shoes off.

ROSE [*rather mimicking*] "Wait till you've had forty-six years of it" . . . [*then herself*] Oh, God—what *for*?

Crash of rain on the window. She rolls over and lies face downwards, head in her arms.

We are in the lounge. It is evening now and the lights are on. Mr. and Mrs. Fitch are sitting at a table. Mrs. Fitch is sorting a pack of cards.

MRS. FITCH. This used to be a very select resort. Quite as good as Bournemouth. It was a pleasure to walk on the promenade when we were young. One only saw the best class of people . . . clubs, yes. . . . Really, now, we have to put up with all sorts. . . . Father, count these diamonds [*Pushing cards across the table*] . . . I saw a man drunk the other night. Drunk! And people undressing on the beach . . . [*More business with the cards absorbs her*] . . . It's the electric railway. They never used to come before these electric trains were put on. . . . And all these high wages. And football pools.

We see a couple at a small table by the wall nearby. They are nicely dressed but subtly distinguishable as working class as opposed to the suburbanism of the others. The wife is knitting. The husband is doing his pools. On Mrs. Fitch's words he furtively moves the blotting paper over his coupon.

MRS. FITCH. There . . . [*shuffling expertly*] . . . It's a full pack. Now for some whist. Mr. Hanbury? You mustn't go to sleep after that *nice* dinner . . . What about some whist?

LEONARD. Oh, yes, thank you. Very kind. Rose? . . .

ROSE [*remains seated*] No. Please excuse me, Mrs. Fitch.

MRS. FITCH. What about the new gentleman? Mr. . . . ah . . .?

Tony rises from his chair. He comes so that he is standing by Rose's chair.

TONY. Roberts. [*He indicates the working-class couple by the wall. The wife has put down her knitting and is smiling eagerly*] I think this lady would like a game.

MR. GREEN. Go on, Maud.

MRS. GREEN. I'll have a basinful.

MRS. FITCH [*a shade unhappily*] Oh . . . yes . . . of course . . . come and sit down, Mrs. Green.

The game is made up.

A BIT OF HAPPINESS

Tony [*to Rose, indicating Leonard's vacant chair*] May I?

Rose. Please.

Tony [*sits down*] Mrs. Hanbury, isn't it? I couldn't help catching the name.

Rose. Yes . . . You came down this morning?

Tony. Just for the week. How long have you been down?

Rose. A week. And one more to go. Awful weather, isn't it?

Tony. Awful. Don't you care for cards?

Rose. No, I lose interest.

Tony. Me, too. I'm more for active games. Squash. Golf. Mr. Hanbury go in for sports?

Rose. He doesn't have the time.

Tony. Pity. I'm lucky. Time's my own, more or less. I tootle around boosting domestic appliances. [*A pause. He takes out a cigarette case*] Cigarette?

Rose. No, thank you.

Tony. Sorry I can't offer you a drink. These small hotels!

Rose. Oh, it's no hardship to me. It never even occurs to me—except at weddings and funerals. [*Silence at card table*]

Tony [*leans a little to her, confidentially*] This is a bit of a funeral, isn't it?

Rose [*laughing a little*] That's unkind.

Tony. It's true. And I bet you feel as if you're the one that's being buried.

Rose. I see you don't know what it's like to be a housewife. Just to do nothing and be waited on is enough for me.

Tony. I shouldn't have thought so.

Rose. Why not?

Tony. I've been watching you.

Rose. Have you? Excuse me.

She moves to rise but he checks her with a touch of his hand and a smile of appeal.

Tony. Please. . . . Let me apologise. . . . But first you must tell me what for. . . . Because I said I'd been watching you? I've been watching everybody. Not much else to do here. Is there? [*He leans close and mimics Mrs. Fitch softly but with startling accuracy*] "You mustn't all go to sleep after that *nice* dinner". [*A comic grimace and a "Brrr" of disgust*] [*Rose smiles*] Do you know, they must pay an engineer to cut that beef. Accurate to one five-thousandth of an inch.

Rose, laughing, breaks in.

ROSE. And the cabbage. It tastes like boiled cardboard. [*They both laugh*] I don't know what I'm laughing at. I cook like that myself.

TONY. Impossible.

ROSE. Really.

TONY. No. Casseroled cardboard, perhaps. But not boiled . . . Look, you could be a good cook. You're the type. I know. All you need is tuition. And appreciation . . . Do you go for Italian food? I love it. Pasta. Scallopini.

Rose can only answer with an ambiguous move.

You should eat out more. That's the way to learn about good food.

ROSE. Out . . . We don't like going out.

TONY. Don't you? *You*, I mean . . . Have you ever been abroad?

Rose shakes her head.

TONY. Pity. You'd love Monte.

ROSE. Monte?

TONY. Monte Carlo. It's got what you need. Not just putting your feet up. Sunshine. Blue sea. Dancing. Life.

ROSE. Life . . . Have *you* ever been to Monte?

He is about to answer then checks himself and laughs.

TONY. No. Abroad, yes. Monte, no.

ROSE. Well at least you tell the truth.

TONY. And it's such a relief. I was just going to do a great big act. You know, some excuse why I was staying at a small place like this. Why I didn't happen to be going abroad this year. And then I just couldn't. Compliment to you, I suppose.

ROSE. Thank you, kind sir.

TONY. Mustn't blame me, you know. Funny—in a place like this everyone tries to make out they're a bit more than what they are.

ROSE. Yes, I know. I suppose I've done it as much as anyone else.

TONY. So no hard feelings?

ROSE. Oh, no . . . It's not often I hear anyone talk frankly.

TONY. It's not often I can talk to someone frankly. Takes a rather special kind of person. But I feel damn good when I do.

ROSE. Yes.

A pause.

TONY. It's stopped raining. I wonder if you'd care for a run in the old car . . . [*He catches her suspicious glance*] . . . You and Mr. Hanbury, of course. She's an old job, but she's fast.

ROSE. Really fast?

TONY. She'll go.

ROSE. Well—— [*Then her eagerness overcomes her doubts*]—Let's
ask him. . . . Leonard. . . .

*A winding road at night; the headlamps of a distant car move at
high speed. Over this we hear Rose's laughter. Peal after peal of
joyful laughter.*

*Rose is still laughing. We see her with Leonard and Tony sprawling
in deckchairs on the beach. It is a typical grey day. Rose and
Leonard wear raincoats. Tony has his blazer draped dashingly over
his shoulder.*

ROSE [*gasping with laughter*] Oh, Tony, I don't think I've stopped
laughing since that night you came.

LEONARD. And she's not one for laughing, Tony, I can tell you that.
She's a serious one. We certainly owe you a lot, old man. [*Tony
makes a dismissive gesture*] Taking us out in your car. And the
Hippodrome. And that dance. And all your funny stories. We
shall miss you.

TONY. Why? We'll get together in town.

LEONARD. Oh, yes, we must. You must come to dinner with us.

TONY. I'm only sorry I can't entertain at my place. Only a bachelor
flatlet, you know.

LEONARD. But Knightsbridge! That's up in the world!

TONY. Well, you must come out with me. To my little Italian
restaurant. And we must do a show.

LEONARD. Well——

TONY. As my guests, of course. And I shall be your guest at home.

ROSE. Leonard—be a dear. Go and get us some orangcades.

The two men rise.

TONY. Let me——

ROSE. No, you go, Leonard. We let Tony do too much.

LEONARD [*looking off*] There's an awful crowd at the kiosk. People
won't queue.

ROSE. Well, you just go and push in. [*He goes off. Rose and Tony
loll back in a brief silence*] Tony . . . Why did you stick around with
a dreary couple like us all the week? You could have found no end
of pretty girls here.

TONY. I told you when we were dancing the other night. I've found
one.

ROSE. Oh, you and your sweet nothings. [*A silence*] Tony . . . why
are you a bachelor?

TONY. Oh, I'm a rolling stone. Rather wait for the right woman.

ROSE. You must be hard to please.

Lolling back, they have turned their heads so that they are looking at each other.

TONY. I am. But I'm pleased now.

Rose turns her head away.

ROSE. Oh! [*It is a laugh, mildly scornful yet pleased*] I'm a dreary, weary housewife of thirty-four, with a boy of ten. You see, you've taught me to speak the truth. And it feels so good. I've not been able to talk to anyone like this before.

TONY. Your husband?

Rose rolls her head against the canvas of the chair and utters an "uh-uh" of negation in her throat.

ROSE. And it's so good to be made to laugh. [*She turns her head and gestures off*] He lets everyone push in front of him.

TONY. Shall I go?

ROSE [*shakes her head*] You'd get to the front in no time. Wouldn't you?

Silence.

TONY. This is the first time we've been together. Just the two of us. Except when we danced. . . . [*Rose does not speak*] Rose—I do hope we'll see each other in town.

ROSE. Of course.

TONY. No—just you and me. . . . Don't misunderstand me, Rose. I know you're not the sort . . . well . . . don't think I want anything that's not right . . . but we do like to talk to each other. Don't we?

ROSE [*after a silence*] Tony—in twelve years I've never been alone with any man except Leonard.

TONY. But there's nothing wrong in it. You're a woman of the world.

ROSE. Am I? . . .

TONY. Aren't you?

ROSE. We're supposed to be telling the truth.

TONY. We are. . . . You could be, even if you're not. If you gave yourself a chance. Mixed with people more.

ROSE. People!—We don't know anyone—*anyone*. We see Leonard's family. And my family. And "good morning" to the neighbours. That's all.

TONY. That's not good for you.

ROSE. It's a life. Millions of people live it.

TONY. *You* shouldn't. [*A pause*] Why don't we meet now and again? Just for a cup of tea? And—our kind of talk. I could drop in—any afternoon.

202

ROSE. You don't know my neighbours. I can just see them peeping when your car stops at the gate.

TONY [*after a pause*] Well, I expect you go into town sometimes. To look at the shops.

ROSE. Yes, I do.

TONY. Well?

They both laugh.

ROSE. Would I tell Leonard?

TONY. Why not?

They laugh again.

ROSE. Here he comes. The conquering hero. No, Tony. . . . No.

The hall of the Hanburys' small house. Empty. From a rear door (the kitchen) voices are heard.

LEONARD'S VOICE. Hurry up, Graham.

SMALL BOY'S VOICE. Plenty of time, Dad.

LEONARD'S VOICE. Clean those shoes, my lad. You're not at your Grand-dad's now. The holiday's over.

Leonard comes out of the kitchen. He is dressed for the office. He pauses.

LEONARD. Don't forget to pay the gas bill. And try to pop in to my Mother's.

ROSE'S VOICE [*through the open door*] I will.

As Leonard goes out we see her through the door slipping Graham's navy blue raincoat on to him. She is not dressed yet but she looks neat in a flowered housecoat.

ROSE. Be careful how you cross the road, dear. [*She gives him a small fibre attaché case*] Here are your ham sandwiches. Don't give them all away to your friends.

GRAHAM. No, Mum.

ROSE [*as he starts into the hall*] And come here. And don't bang the door.

She kisses him.

GRAHAM. Ta-ta, Mum. [*Bang*]

She watches him to the street door. She goes back into the kitchen, takes the plastic bucket of waste and steps out into the garden. She is emptying into the big bin when she hears a voice off camera.

WOMAN'S VOICE. Morning, Mrs. Hanbury. I see you've changed your upstairs curtains.

ROSE. Morning. You don't miss much do you, Mrs. Shaw?

Back in the kitchen she grimaces her distaste and sits down for a few moments with her shopping list, lips moving. Her glance travels

203

over the kitchen. The pile of washing-up that waits. The dirty laundry. She goes into the hall and starts to hoover.

The 'phone bell shrills into her consciousness. She picks up the receiver.

ROSE. Hallo. . . . Tony! . . . Why? Can't you come? . . . Oh! [*A slight laugh*] You had me scared. . . . No. . . . No. . . . Oh, *shut* up! . . . We're *both* looking forward to seeing you. . . . Wednesday night, then. Seven? . . . And the cabbage *won't* taste like cardboard. . . . 'Bye.

She goes back to the hoover. As she works it her eyes are bright. We mix to the Hanburys' living-room. Rose is not there. The three-piece suite is drawn up to the fire.

LEONARD. The evening has gone quickly. Let's have another drink, eh? Just the two of us.

TONY. Love one. It'll have to be for the road, though.

LEONARD. I'll pour one for Rose while I'm about it. I think she liked it before. Mind you, she's not used to it . . . Mustn't give her too much . . . *She* made me buy this. For to-night, specially. Hope it's the right stuff.

TONY. It's the right stuff, all right.

LEONARD [*crossing with glasses*] I'll put Rose's down here. [*On the coffee table in front of the settee, among the used cups*]

TONY [*raises his glass*] Bash on, the infantry.

LEONARD. Bash on. [*A pause*] Must you go so soon? You've got the car.

TONY. Long day to-morrow, old boy.

ROSE [*off*] Just another five minutes. [*She enters*] I am sorry, Tony. Graham'd keep his light on all night if I didn't go up.

She plumps down on the settee, sighs with pleasure and takes up her glass.

ROSE. Mmmm. Devils, aren't we? Cheers.

LEONARD. Cheers!

TONY [*he raises his glass and looks straight at her*] To you.

Rose looks away. Tony leans back with his glass.

TONY. Cosy . . . I shall have to go, but I don't feel like it. You've fed me too well. [*To Rose*] You see, you are a good cook.

LEONARD. She really went in for the fancy stuff tonight, didn't she? Shall I tell him the secret, Rose?—She bought a book.

TONY. Good for you. [*To Leonard*] Now you know what to do when you want a good meal—ask me round.

The other two laugh.

LEONARD. You're a real tonic. Specially for her. She's been properly down in the dumps lately.

He goes on talking and we see Rose's and Tony's hands dangling over the edges of their chairs out of Leonard's sight.

And tonight, well, you'd think she was on holiday again.

TONY'S VOICE [*as his hand moves closer to hers so that the little fingers just touch*] Is that true?

ROSE [*she places her hands in her lap*] Oh, Leonard exaggerates.

TONY. I expect it's lonely in the house all day.

LEONARD. Lonely? These women don't know how lucky they are. Staying at home all day.

TONY. It's not such fun being a woman, Leonard. It can be hell stuck indoors every day with the same old grind. You do meet people at the office. She's got no-one.

LEONARD. She can always go round to Mother's, for a chat. [*During this Rose is watching the two men. Not only their general appearances but their attitudes contrast sharply*]

TONY. You've got to make it up to a woman, Leonard. Understand her, give her a bit of help.

LEONARD. Oh, my Rose is happy enough. Aren't you, dear?

ROSE. Yes. Yes, of course.

Idly she moves her arm so that it dangles again over the arm of the settee.

TONY. Well, I want to see you both getting out more. I'll be down in Surrey this week-end. Looking up my old C.O. Rather a grand place he's got . . .

Again we see the two hands between the settee and chair. Tony's moves closer to Rose's.

TONY'S VOICE. . . . but perhaps the week-end after we'll all go for a drive together. Like we used to.

ROSE'S VOICE. We'd love that.

The little fingers of the two hands just touch. Rose does not remove hers.

TONY'S VOICE. That's a date then . . . [*His fingers pry tentatively between Rose's*] . . . You've got to learn how to enjoy life, old boy. And I want Rose to enjoy herself, too. [*The two hands clasp together, tightening on the following words*] It's time you both got a bit out of life. High time.

TONY [*rising*] Hmm, look at the time. I really must run along.

LEONARD. It's not all that late.

ROSE. We mustn't keep him. Get his coat, dear.

LEONARD. Just one more drink.

TONY. No, no, old boy, that's it.

ROSE. You know what you're like in the morning if you stay up late. I will say that for my Leonard. He loves his shuteye. Snores the moment his head touches the pillow. Every night.

LEONARD. I don't mind. . . .

ROSE. Get his coat, dear. [*Leonard goes out. Rose stands turned away from Tony. Silence: growing tension: at last she turns to him*] Tony, I shall be in town tomorrow. Shopping.

Tony's bed-sitting room in Earl's Court: footsteps and voices on the stairs. Rose enters followed by Tony. Tony closes the door and moves into the room, but Rose stands by the door, looking keyed up, almost hostile.

TONY. Welcome to my palatial home.

ROSE. So this is the bachelor flatlet? [*Tony laughs uneasily*]

TONY. Complete with kitchen . . . [*opens cupboard to reveal a built-in wash basin*] and bathroom. Come in. Don't let the butler frighten you; he's been with us for years. Let me take your coat. [*Rose is still and silent*] Look, I know what we need. Let's start off with a drink. [*He moves to table*]

ROSE [*harsh*] I don't need that. I had two double whiskies before I met you.

Tony is close to her. She is tense, almost quivering.

TONY. Rose?——

She puts her arms round him and clamps herself to him. He embraces her, but in their long, silent kiss, it is she who is clasping, devouring him.

Fade out.

Act Two

Tony's room. Later. Rose stands in front of the mirror doing her hair. Tony is in shirtsleeves, stooping over the gas ring.

ROSE. Just think. If . . . If we hadn't gone away when we did . . . If we'd stayed somewhere else . . . we'd never have met. [*Tony brings a cup of tea and puts it on the chest of drawers next to her. She looks at him, then laughs*] Just like my husband.

Tony lays a hand rather timidly on her shoulder.

TONY. Rose? . . . Happy?

ROSE. Happy? [*A little laugh*] I suppose all men are the same.

He holds her in a way that seems apologetic. And her embrace seems consoling.

ROSE. I noticed something before. You're getting thin on top. Just like Leonard . . . Oh [*A reaction to him*] . . . I'm sorry, darling. Yes, I am happy. [*She moves away and sips her tea*] Not in the way I'd imagined. I suppose it's these books give you the idea there's some sort of thrill to be had. [*She laughs*] . . . I've always felt lonely. Even with people. Even with my husband. . . . I don't feel lonely with you. I suppose you don't know what it is to be lonely? [*Tony does not answer*] Have you had lots of other women?—I don't mind.

TONY. I've lived my life.

ROSE [*she is moving about picking up things . . . the rugger ball . . . the photo of Tony in uniform . . . the cricket cap . . .*] Sorry, I'm being nosey.

TONY. Why did you marry a chap like Leonard?

ROSE. A chap like Leonard? . . . He's all right. I'm a bit sorry for him. He has tried . . . Because he was more or less the boy next door, and I didn't know any others. I was a well brought-up girl. . . . Will your—market boosting, or whatever you call it, take you from me a lot?

TONY. No, I only do the London region.

ROSE. Oh, good. You've never said exactly what it is you boost.

TONY [*after a brief pause*] Lavatory brushes.

ROSE. Lav——. [*She bursts out laughing*]

TONY [*doggedly*] I get orders for them from shopkeepers.

ROSE. Oh, darling, why not? You're not cross with me for laughing? That's what I like you for. You make me laugh. You must always make me laugh. Tony, I'm babbling on, and I haven't asked *you* —you can tell me the truth—do you want us to go on meeting?

TONY. Terribly.

ROSE. Me, too. Who cares about thrills? It's laughing, and having someone you can talk to. It makes me feel so good, just talking my heart out . . . And I don't know, I do feel a sort of thrill, because I've broken out, I've escaped. Any time I like I can come to this room and be myself . . . Darling, I won't be a nuisance. We're both free. But why shouldn't I have a little happiness on the side? Oh, Tony, you get old so quickly . . .

We mix to a scene of murderous gunplay in a Wild West setting and draw back to reveal that it is on a TV screen. We are in the

Hanburys' lounge. The lights are on and an electric fire, designed to look like a coal fire, is burning. Graham, in pyjamas, is perched on the arm of a chair tremendously absorbed. In the other chair, equally absorbed, is his father.

LEONARD [*not taking his eyes off the TV*] You really *ought* to be in bed, son.

GRAHAM. It's nearly finished.

The Western is ending in a spatter of shots and music.

LEONARD. You shouldn't have stayed up in the first place. Anyway, I don't know that you ought to see all this violence.

GRAHAM. You never miss it, Dad. [*The Western ends in a spatter of gunshots and a commercial begins*] Although it is a bit far-fetched. I mean, he's a Marshal, that's like a policeman, and what's the use of policemen going round shooting people?

Rose enters, a rubber hot water bottle in her hands.

ROSE. Graham!

GRAHAM. Just another half-hour, Mum. It's the half-hour of magic, Mum. Only a half-hour.

Rose switches off the set, thrusts the water bottle in the boy's hands and propels him not unkindly by the shoulders to the door.

ROSE. No! Up you go. And don't come down again without your dressing-gown. It's winter. And you know what you are for colds. Say goodnight to your Dad.

At the door.

GRAHAM. Good-night, Dad. Good-night, Mum.

She closes the door after him.

ROSE. And be a good boy and turn your light out in half an hour. [*To Leonard*] And why you didn't do that, I can't imagine.

LEONARD. He was only seeing the end of the programme.

He gets up and approaches the set.

ROSE. Oh, leave it alone.

LEONARD. It's the half-hour of magic, Rose.

ROSE [*sitting down tiredly*] Aren't you capable of anything except gaping at that?

LEONARD [*returning to his chair*] Well, what else can we do?

ROSE. Nothing. Just sit here every evening like a couple of corpses.

LEONARD. But you've always liked it.

ROSE. Yes, I've always liked it. [*Pause*]

LEONARD. Wilkins came late to the office again this morning.

ROSE. Did he?

LEONARD. I didn't say anything, but I gave him a look.

ROSE. Did you?

LEONARD. Yes, I could see he didn't miss it. I said to Miss Hawkes, I wasn't going to stand for it much more. He comes late and we do the work.

ROSE [*she has started on some knitting*] Did you? And what did she say?

LEONARD. She said I was right. She said everyone was fed up with Wilkins. And I said, someone ought to talk to him straight. And I said——

ROSE. And you said and she said. . . .

Leonard stares at her.

LEONARD. I don't know what's come over you lately. I always tell you about the day at the office.

ROSE [*knitting grimly*] You do.

Leonard sighs, gives up and opens his newspaper.

LEONARD [*over the newspaper*] I reckon you miss going out. [*Rose knits on*] We had some nice evenings with that Tony. [*Rose knits on*] Ages since we've seen him. Must be—what?—two months. No, I'm a liar, it's over two. Holiday friends!

ROSE. Oh, I don't know.

LEONARD. Well, he was a nice chap.

ROSE. Was he?

LEONARD. You seemed to think so. Didn't you?

ROSE. These people drop you as quickly as they take you up. I haven't thought about him for ages.

Leonard gives up and disappears behind the newspaper.

From now on the silence is broken only by sounds of activity. Rose, impassive, knits like a machine. Leonard busies himself with turning pages and folding his newspaper. The rustle is tormentingly loud. Her eyes go up over her knitting and watch him struggling with the pages.

He puts the paper down and stretches himself absurdly, with a grunting sigh.

He takes an apple from a bowl and starts to eat. We hear the loud bites, the wet crunching in his mouth. He contorts his face to suck bits of skin from between his teeth.

Rose knits.

Leonard glances up. Sees her. Comes over to her.

LEONARD [*putting an arm around her*] You are in the dumps, old girl. Here, cheer up.

He tries clumsily to kiss her cheek. She turns her face away.

LEONARD [*trying to turn her by the shoulders*] Ah, come on, love. We haven't had a kiss for——
She shakes her head. He goes on trying to embrace her.

ROSE. No . . . please . . . no . . .

LEONARD. Rose . . .

ROSE. Leave me alone . . . [*She stands up abruptly and furiously*] Leave me alone!
She is almost trembling with nausea. Leonard stares at her.

LEONARD. Rose, are you all right?
She cannot answer.

LEONARD. Rose——

ROSE. I'm tired. That's all . . . Here . . . [*She switches on the TV*] Look at your half-hour of magic. I'm going upstairs.

LEONARD. I'll make you a cup of tea. You sit down. I'll——

ROSE. I'm all right. I'll be down in a few minutes. There's a play at nine o'clock. I want to see it. . . .
As the set warms up she turns the sound up quite loud and forces a small smile.

ROSE. No, you sit down. . . . I'm all right. I won't be long.
Hesitantly he goes back to his chair: then she goes out.

In the hall Rose stands quite still by the lounge door. Over all that follows comes the sound of the TV. Then swiftly and silently she goes to the telephone. She watches the closed lounge door all the time. She dials.

ROSE [*very quietly*] Tony? . . . Oh, God, oh, thank God you're there. . . . [*She is watching the door all the time*] . . . Look, I can't talk. I must see you tomorrow . . . Yes, I know I saw you yesterday, I know we have a date for next week. But I must see you to-morrow. . . . Not now. I can't explain . . . All right . . . yes . . . yes . . . 'Bye, my sweet.
Her lips shape a kiss. She puts the 'phone down. She is still watching the closed door.

We mix to Tony's room the next day. He is checking through his order book when he hears light quick footsteps on the stairs. He rises as Rose lets herself in with a Yale key.

TONY. Angel.

ROSE. Hallo. Didn't give you a scare, did I? 'Phoning like that?
They kiss.

TONY. Honey, what was wrong?

ROSE [*a slight laugh*] Nothing. [*She kisses him again then turns away*] I put your hankies in here. [*She indicates a drawer of the chest of drawers*] They're all ironed. I forgot to tell you yesterday. How did you get on with United Stores? Did they give you an order?

TONY [*pouring drinks*] Only for samples. Three dozen. [*Gives her a glass*] Cheers.

ROSE. Cheers, darling. Oh, they are swine. After all their promises. [*She has sat down rather tensely*] Did you go out with the boys last night?

TONY. Usual pub-crawl.

ROSE. Hangover?

TONY [*shakes his head*] Didn't drink much.

ROSE. The tube was packed, coming here. There are so many people looking at shop windows, I always wonder who does the work.

Tony has sat on the divan to face her. He leans across and puts a hand on hers.

TONY. Come on, old girl. There's something on your mind. [*She looks away*] Why the 'phone call? You sounded awful.

ROSE. Just a panic. . .

TONY. Come on . . . take a deep breath . . . out with it.

She pauses for a long time. Then.

ROSE. Tony, I'm leaving him.

He does not answer.

ROSE. I'm leaving Leonard. Darling, I've got to.

He is still silent.

ROSE. I know it's mad bursting in on you like this. But I couldn't wait. I just couldn't bottle it up till next week . . . I suppose I ought to go and walk round the block or something while you take it in. . . . Tony, I want to marry you. I've come to ask if you want to marry me.

He is stroking her hand.

TONY. Of course. You know I do. . . . But you *did* come in like a bombshell. . . . Honey, what made you blow up like this?

ROSE. I don't know. I don't know at all. In one second it just came to me last night. Another day of him and I'd go mad.

TONY. Yes, dear, yes.

He comes and sits on the arm of her chair, his arm round her shoulder.

ROSE. He tried to kiss me. [*She laughs*] That was a change. . . . And . . . I couldn't . . . I couldn't let him touch me. . . .

TONY. I'll get you another drink. Eh? [*She shakes her head quickly and impatiently*] We'll make you better. Trust your old Tony to make you feel better. Eh, dear?

ROSE. I'm all right. Tony, I did ask you something very important.

TONY. I know. That's why I want you to relax. We've got to think about this. Carefully.

He stands up, gets himself another drink and downs it with evident relief. She looks round at him.

ROSE. There isn't really so much to think about. You've had as much time as I have—all these months—to find out how you feel.

A pause.

ROSE. Well?

TONY. How come you've never said this before?

ROSE. You never guessed? After all that's happened? And the way I've looked after you?

TONY. I know . . . you've been wonderful. And I've been grateful . . . I knew you were bored at home. But we had our good times. And I've cheered you up. I have, now. Haven't I?

ROSE. Yes, darling, you have.

TONY. Then what's happened?

ROSE. I wish I knew. I never meant it to get like this . . . You don't feel the same as me. Do you?

TONY. Rose, you're the only woman in the world.

ROSE. No . . . You don't . . . It's not as if I worshipped the ground you walked on, or anything. I haven't got any illusions about you. I never had. It's just that . . . because of you, I can't stand *him* any more. I can't stand him or that house.

A pause.

TONY. And Graham?

ROSE [*rapidly*] Oh, I'd bring him. I couldn't leave him . . . He wouldn't be any trouble. You'll like him, I know you will. You'd get on fine. Tony, I thought it all out last night. We'll get furnished rooms. I'll work . . . I won't be a burden. Darling, you'll have a proper home. You won't have to go on living like this any more. I'll look after you. And we'll save, and later on we'll get an unfurnished flat . . . [*She breaks off*] Tony, you haven't answered my question yet.

TONY [*slowly*] I don't think you've thought out all the implications of this, Rose. It's a big decision. I want you to know just what you're doing.

ROSE. I know.

TONY. I don't think you do. What I'm going to say now is for your sake. Don't think I'm . . . hesitating or anything. But before you decide——

ROSE. I have decided——

TONY. I want you to know just what's involved. First of all, you might lose the boy.

ROSE. No, I'm sure I wouldn't.

TONY. Leonard could claim custody of the child. He could say you weren't a fit mother.

A pause.

ROSE. Oh, no . . . No. . . . They wouldn't dare take a child away from his mother. Don't be silly, Tony, he's mad on sport. He'd worship you. Really he would . . . And don't think I care what people will say. I know what Leonard's family will call me; and my own. They'll all be on his side. It'll hurt me if my own flesh and blood turn their backs on me. But that wouldn't stop me.

TONY. Rosie . . . this is a big thing. We've got to be patient . . . give it a little time——

ROSE. Time! Have I got to tell you any more what it's like for me? I've got so that everything he does hurts me. Poor devil. His breathing. And his eating. And coughing in the mornings. Things I never noticed before make me sick.

TONY. I know——

ROSE [*standing up angrily*] You know—and you still won't answer me.

TONY. Be reasonable. He could sue me. He could ruin me with the firm.

ROSE. Oh, God! You stand there and talk about jobs and money. What you mean is, you don't want me.

TONY. You're twisting it all round——

ROSE. What you mean is, you thought it was nice and safe with a married woman. But you'd never bargained for this.

TONY. Rose—give me time. . . .

ROSE. Time for what? Time to think of more excuses? Don't you know if you want me or not? Please . . . explain to me carefully why you need time before you can say yes . . .

TONY. Rose—do we have to quarrel. . . .

ROSE. Yes, we do. What do you expect from me? If you want me, here I am. If you don't . . . Don't touch me! What do you think I am? A little bit of fluff? If that's what you want, you can go out and find it.

TONY. Rose . . .

ROSE. It's one thing or the other. God! To come here like this and be turned down [*He tries to embrace her*] . . . No!

He stands, sheepish and silent, as she turns to the door.

ROSE. If I walk out of here, you'll never see me again. [*Silence: she moves to the door*] Well? [*She opens the door and steps into the hall*] Well?

    He stands there without speaking and she slowly goes.

    Fade out.

Act Three

    Rose is working in the kitchen. Her back is turned to Leonard who, dressed for work, stands in the doorway.

LEONARD. You think he'll get his scholarship, then?

ROSE. Why not? He's an intelligent boy.

    As she speaks a postman's knock sounds from the hall. Leonard goes out and returns with a letter.

LEONARD. Another letter from your girl [*Rose takes it*]. It's postmarked in London again. If she comes up to town all that often, why can't she come and see you?

ROSE. She's shy. Afraid of meeting you, I suppose. [*She drops the letter into her apron pocket*]

LEONARD. Aren't you going to see what she says?

ROSE. It can wait. You'll miss your train.

LEONARD. 'Bye. . . .

    He goes.

    The 'phone goes in the hall and Rose picks it up.

ROSE. . . . Tony . . . Tony, you've got to stop it . . . No, I don't want to listen. And I won't meet you. And stop hanging about in the street. . . . No. . . . No, I don't want to know. It's over. Don't you understand that? Finished.

    She hangs up. She has just gone into the kitchen when the 'phone bell rings again. She returns, picks up the 'phone, listens, then puts it down (not on the hook).

    Evening. The Hanburys' lounge. The lights are not on but the fire is burning. The radio is playing soft dance music. We hear the street door open. There is an odd scuffle of footsteps. Then the door of the room opens. Leonard comes in, switches on the lights and shuts the door behind him. Although the room is empty he still conceals something behind his back. In the lines that follow there is an odd boisterousness in his voice and manner.

LEONARD. Rose . . . Rose . . .

214

Rose comes in from the kitchen.

ROSE. Leonard—what are you doing in here?

LEONARD. Good evening, my dear. For the Queen of my heart.

ROSE. You're half an hour late. What? . . . Flowers! . . .

He produces a bunch of chrysanthemums from behind his back and presents them with a clumsy bow.

ROSE. I wouldn't be surprised if the supper was dried up. Oh . . What on earth are these in aid of? . . . What kept you? . . . They are nice. . . .

LEONARD. Not from me, my dear. Guess who from?

ROSE. I'll put the supper out.

LEONARD. Guess. Guess.

ROSE. I haven't the faintest idea.

LEONARD. Big surprise. The prodigal returns to the fold.

He flings open the door. Tony stands in the hall. Rose and Tony stand and look at each other.

LEONARD. Tony's flowers. Tony wants to say he's sorry for not seeing us all these months. Come in—come in, old man.

Rose moves as if she is in a trance. She switches off the radio. Tony is in the room.

TONY. Hallo, Rose.

ROSE. Hallo, Tony.

TONY. Nice to see you.

ROSE. Yes.

LEONARD. Rose—is that the way to greet an old friend? Shake hands with him. Make him feel at home.

ROSE. You've been drinking.

LEONARD. Not drinking. Just having a drink. Reunion celebration . . . Rose, he 'phoned me at the office. In the middle of the day, the checky fellow.

ROSE. I see.

She and Tony are looking at each other throughout all this.

LEONARD. He 'phoned to say he was sorry for neglecting us. Business. That's what it is. And he wanted to know when he could come round. And I said—tonight.

ROSE. Couldn't you have 'phoned me. . . . Supper. . . . I——

TONY. I've eaten. You two just go ahead, and give me a drink. I'll be all right.

LEONARD. Here, my dear. You're standing there as if you were waiting to have your picture taken. [*He takes the flowers*] Let me put them in water.

Throughout the next passage while he is out of the room we hear him in the kitchen. The other two just stand and look at each other. Leonard whistling. A tap runs. Glass clinks as he fills a vase.

LEONARD'S VOICE. Give him a glass of port wine, dear. Have one yourself. This is an occasion.

Rose starts to move. Tony shakes his head slightly. She stops. Leonard comes in with a vase of flowers and puts it carefully on a mat on the sideboard.

LEONARD. You sit down, Tony.

ROSE. There isn't any port.

LEONARD. Give him a glass of stout, Rose? . . . Oh, dear, we haven't any. And I walked past the off-licence like a fool.

TONY. It doesn't matter. You just go and eat.

LEONARD. No. No. Absolutely no, sir. The guest comes first. Rose, dear, I'm going to the off-licence. I shan't be more than ten minutes. Talk to Tony.

He goes out.

Tony and Rose stand there while the door closes. They hear his footsteps cross the hall. Then the sound of the street door closing.

Another moment then.

TONY. I'm sorry. This was the only way.

Rose stands face to face with him. From her expression you would think she hated him. Suddenly she utters a cry and flings herself upon him. They stand embracing. Rose can only gasp, "Oh, Oh——"

TONY. Why wouldn't you see me?

ROSE. Because I was afraid of this, you fool . . . [*She senses his nervousness*] Darling, don't worry. He'll be gone ages. And Graham's at the boys' club. Hold me again—please. . . . You've got a nerve. Making *him* bring you home. . . . You devil . . . What's it been like, dear? Has it been too awful?

TONY. Awful.

ROSE. I know. . . .

ROSE. Dearest, what do we do now? Do you really want me? And Graham?

There is the faintest hesitation before

TONY. Yes—yes.

Rose laughs and holds him closer.

ROSE. It's no use. I heard. That little second you hesitated. You do want me, don't you? And you want to do the right thing. But you're terrified, all the same.

TONY. No.

ROSE. Yes, you are. And you only really want to go on being one of the boys.

TONY. No. I hate the bloody life.

ROSE. Yes ... But could you live any other? ... All right, darling. I shan't park myself on you. All I want is to see you. We'll go back to just the way it was before.

LEONARD'S VOICE [*quietly*] Will you?

The door is open. He is in the room. Silence.

TONY. Look, old boy, we were just——

ROSE [*impatiently*] Don't you realise? He's been listening. Haven't you?

LEONARD. Yes.

ROSE. You didn't go out.

LEONARD. No.

ROSE. I suppose this is what they call a trap.

LEONARD. I suppose it is.

ROSE. I never knew you had the brains.

LEONARD. No. I was the mug. Running out for the beer.

ROSE. How did you find out? Detectives or something?

LEONARD. Detectives? On my salary? ... You must be as daft as you seemed to think I was. ... In a road like this you don't need detectives. ... There's an amateur one watching behind every front curtain. ... I had a 'phone call. At the office. [*He mimics as best as he can, a woman's voice, savagely, as if more bitter against it than against Rose and Tony*] "This is a friend, Mister Hanbury ... I thought you ought to know ... There's a man hanging round your house. He's the gentleman that used to come and visit you. I thought he might be annoying your wife. I thought you ought to know." A friend. If our dear neighbour Mrs. Shaw thinks I don't know her voice, she's as big a fool as you two. ... And I didn't need her. ... A few weeks ago I found a key in your handbag. A Yale key. It was an accident. But I couldn't forget it. I kept asking myself, what's my Rose doing with a Yale key that isn't for this house? ...

ROSE. I see.

LEONARD. And those letters. From your old school chum who was too shy to visit us. That was a poor effort. Do you think I gave you all the letters that came? Ask him how many he sent. Go on. Ask him. [*He pulls out his wallet*] I've got a couple of 'em here. ... And then *he* 'phones to-day. ...

ROSE. So that's that. ...

217

TONY. Look, Leonard, you don't understand. We had a bit of an innocent flirtation. We shouldn't have, I know, but it was quite harmless. And it's all over.

LEONARD [to Rose] You didn't pick a very bright one, did you? You call these letters innocent? And what I saw just now—and heard.

TONY. There's no need to get worked up.

LEONARD. No, I've just got to go on working. For her. While you two get up to your old tricks, and have a good laugh at the funny man. . . .

TONY. There's no need to get worked up. . . .

ROSE. This is impossible. I'll get my coat. Tony, you can see me to a hotel.

TONY. Rose, don't you get excited, too.

Leonard laughs hysterically.

LEONARD. Do you hear that, Rose? Do you hear your passionate lover speaking? He's afraid if you walk out, he'll be landed with you, and he doesn't want that.

TONY. I'll look after you, Rose.

LEONARD. Yes, he'll take you—like a dose of medicine. I heard what you said to him—you know he doesn't really want to. Well go on, grab him by the arm, and march out with him, and see he doesn't get away. And when Graham comes in, I'll tell him what his mother is . . .

ROSE. Graham!

LEONARD. Yes, your son. Forgotten him, hadn't you? Too busy with Mr. Romeo Roberts here, with his blazers and his knife-edge crease and his la-de-da talk. A twopenny-farthing commercial traveller. I bet he hasn't got twenty quid to bless his name.

ROSE. Must we go on hurting each other?

LEONARD. You've been hurting me, haven't you? It's been hell these past few weeks . . . And you [to Tony] . . . The good old back-slapping friend. To be able to *do* a thing like that. And smile. That's what got me . . . Haven't you got *any* decency? Do you have to run after other men's wives? Why don't you get one of your own? [To Rose] There's your Romeo, for you? Look at him. Better man than me, eh? Can't even get himself a woman. Except you——

ROSE. Leonard——

LEONARD. And you—why d'you think he picked on you? Not because you were such a catch. Look at yourself. Look at yourself in the mirror. You've got crows' feet. The wrinkles are coming. That's why he knew you'd be easy. Because no-one else'd bother.

Rose sits down wearily.

TONY [*to her*] Let me take you somewhere.

ROSE [*looking up*] Somewhere? . . .

TONY. I won't let you down.

ROSE [*a faint tired smile*] That's big of you.

TONY. Rose——

ROSE. You'd better go.

Leonard is looking from one of them to the other.

TONY. Rose, listen——

Rose shakes her head.

ROSE. Please go.

TONY. But Rose . . .

LEONARD. She told you to go. [*Tony still hesitates*] And I'm telling you to go. [*Tony moves to the door*] Go on, clear out. This is *my* house, and I'm ordering you out. The funny man's giving you an order.

TONY [*at the door*] Rose——

Rose does not even raise her head. Tony goes out. Leonard watches in silence. The street door closes. He closes the lounge door. He moves toward the seated Rose. He stands in front of her, fists clenched. Rose looks up.

ROSE. What now? Divorce?

Silence. Then Leonard falls on his knees and puts his head in her lap.

LEONARD [*sobbing*] Don't leave me. Rose, don't leave me. Please. [*He looks up*] Rose, he's no good. He let you down. Didn't he?

ROSE. Yes.

LEONARD. You can't want to see him any more . . . [*Then eagerly*] You had tried to put him behind you. Hadn't you? I do know that. And just seeing him, you lost control.

ROSE. Yes.

LEONARD. It won't happen again. I'm sure it won't. You won't see him any more. Will you? [*Rose is silent*] Rose . . . please . . . I wouldn't have let you down like he did.

Rose puts a hand absently on his head.

ROSE. No. . . . You wouldn't.

LEONARD. We've got a good home, and our boy, and our families.

Rose nods.

LEONARD. It hasn't been all bad, our twelve years, has it?

ROSE. No, Leonard.

LEONARD. Graham would be so unhappy.

ROSE. I know.

LEONARD. You mean you won't see him again?

ROSE. I won't leave you.

LEONARD. Oh, Rose—if you only knew how frightened I was. I don't know what I'd do without you. The world's such a terrible place, it would be too much for me without you.

She strokes his head. On the mantelpiece among the photos, stands a calendar in a frilly silver frame. The date is January the eleventh.

We mix to the mantelpiece of the lounge. The frilly silver calendar indicates June the second. It is evening but still daylight. The curtains are open. Graham has been reading a comic. He rises and puts it down as he hears someone coming in at the street door.

Leonard comes into the room. He is dressed as from work, with a briefcase under his arm.

GRAHAM. Hallo, Dad.

LEONARD [*with deep pleasure*] Graham! [*Nearing his son he hesitates rather shyly and puts a hand on his shoulder*] I'm very pleased. Your Mum 'phoned. I hear we've got to go and see your Headmaster.

GRAHAM. Saturday morning.

LEONARD. Where's your Mother?

GRAHAM. She's getting ready to go out. Dad, can I have a bike, now?

LEONARD. We'll get you a nice leather attache case to start your new school with.

GRAHAM. You promised me a present if I passed my eleven plus.

LEONARD. Not a bike. I won't have your Mother worried sick.

GRAHAM. But, Dad. . . .

LEONARD. When you're sixteen, son. That *is* a promise. [*He opens his briefcase and starts spreading account books, etc. on the table*] Now, you go up and do your homework, while I do mine, and I'll call you when your supper's ready.

GRAHAM. I'm ever such a good bike rider. . . .

LEONARD. That's enough. Up!

Graham goes out as Rose enters, ready to go out.

ROSE. Now be a good boy. [*She kisses him*]

LEONARD. He's a good boy. I always knew he'd win that scholarship.

ROSE. It never worried me a minute. Down to work already?

LEONARD. Off to the pictures already?

ROSE. The last programme starts early.

LEONARD. Our boy at a Grammar School. It makes it all worth while, somehow.

He settles to his books.

ROSE. You don't mind me running off to the pictures?

LEONARD. No, you enjoy yourself. I've got a good three hours' overtime here. Mustn't keep you shut up in the house all the time must we?

ROSE. Oh, it's not so bad.

LEONARD. Look who's talking! No, I reckon we've got things worked out nicely now. After all, I am getting extra money for this. And it does mean a holiday abroad. That'll make a difference, too. . . . Rose—things are better now—aren't they?

ROSE. Of course . . . What about you?

LEONARD. We're together. That's all that counts.

Rose goes to the door. He watches her.

ROSE. You'll take your supper from the fridge when you want it?

LEONARD. Yes.

ROSE [*fumbling in handbag*] Oh, damn. Where's my purse?

LEONARD [*looking at his books*] You'd better hurry. You'll keep him waiting.

ROSE. Oh, here it is. [*Pause*] What did you say?

LEONARD. Nothing. I said you'd better hurry.

Rose stares at him, but he does not look up.

ROSE. Don't let Graham work too late.

LEONARD. I'll give him his supper in an hour's time.

Rose hesitates then goes out.

We mix slowly to the park bench as at the beginning of the play.

TONY'S VOICE. . . . a bit of happiness. That's what we said. Do you call this happiness? I don't. I call it downright misery. You start off by saying you won't make any demands on a man. Then you act as if you own him, lock, stock and barrel. And if he doesn't play, you do a great big deserted, tragic heroine act.

ROSE. Why do we go on? When we *do* meet, you get on my nerves—and yet I can't keep away from you. I've told myself again and again I'd put an end to it . . .

TONY. So have I. . . .

ROSE. I suppose we shall get over this. In time. Maybe that's what Leonard clings to. That doesn't alter the fact that you can no longer find time to take me shopping.

TONY. But I told you. . . .

ROSE. You told me enough.

TONY. What do you mean by that?

ROSE. What do you mean, what do I mean by that?

TONY. I mean just what I say. What did you mean when you said that?

ROSE. I meant exactly what I said . . .

TONY. Oh did you?

ROSE. Yes, I did. Any objections?

TONY. No.

ROSE. Well?

TONY. Well, what?

ROSE. What do you mean, well what?

TONY. Oh, don't be silly. [*A brief silence*]

ROSE. So that's what it's come to? You call me a fool to my face.

TONY. I didn't say that you were a fool. I merely told you not to be silly.

ROSE. Oh, I see. Very subtle.

TONY. Look—all I said was—I can't pick you up in town to-morrow.

ROSE. And what about my shopping? All the bags I'll be carrying . . .
Fade out.